American Women Report World War I

American Women Report World War I

An Anthology of Their Journalism

Edited by Chris Dubbs

University of North Texas Press
Denton, Texas

10 9 8 7 6 5 4 3 2 1

Permissions:
University of North Texas Press
1155 Union Circle #311336
Denton, TX 76203-5017

The paper used in this book meets the minimum requirements of the American National Standard for Permanence of Paper for Printed Library Materials, z39.48.1984. Binding materials have been chosen for durability.

Library of Congress Cataloging-in-Publication Data
Dubbs, Chris (Military historian), editor. | Trout, Steven, 1963–
          American women report World War I : an anthology of their journalism / edited by Chris Dubbs; foreword by Steven Trout. | "Book is collection of newspaper articles written about World War I by American women journalists"— Provided by publisher.
          pages cm.
Includes bibliographical references and index.
          ISBN-13 978-1-57441-825-5 (hardcover)
          ISBN-13 978-1-57441-833-0 (ebook)
1. World War, 1914–1918—Press coverage—United States—Women authors. 2. World War, 1914–1918—Women—United States. 3. Women war correspondents—United States. 4. American newspapers—Sections, columns, etc.—War.

D632 .A73 2021
940.3–dc23
2020053134

The electronic edition of this book was made possible
by the support of the Vick Family Foundation.
Typeset by vPrompt eServices.

Contents

List of Illustrations ix

Foreword by Steven Trout.. xi

Introduction xv

Chapter 1 On the Front Lines 1
    Mary Boyle O'Reilly, "Woman Writer Sees
        Horrors of Battle," *The Seattle Star* 3
    Mary Roberts Rinehart, "For King and Country,
        No Man's Land," *The Saturday Evening Post*................ 9
    Edith Wharton, "In Lorraine and the Vosges,"
        Scribner's Magazine 19

Chapter 2 Reporting from France 27
    Madeleine Zabriskie Doty, "War Cripples,"
        The New Republic.. 29
    Jessica Lozier Payne, "Soldiers' Graves Dot Farms
        on Marne Battlefield," *Brooklyn Daily Eagle* 35
    Mary Heaton Vorse, "The Sinistrées of France,"
        The Century Magazine 37
    Maude Radford Warren, "Madame, C'est la Guerre!"
        The Outlook 49

Chapter 3 Women's Role 55
    Ellen Adair, "Women and the War,"
        Evening Public Ledger 57
    Sophie Treadwell, "Women in Black,"
        Harper's Weekly 60
    Mary Boyle O'Reilly, "Baby's Value in Europe,"
        Bismarck Daily Tribune 67
    Jessica Lozier Payne, "Women Work Tirelessly
        Making Shells for the Front," *What I Saw in
        England and France*.. 68
    Ruth Wright Kauffman, "The Woman Ambulance-
        Driver in France," *The Outlook*................................... 71

Chapter 4 Reporting the Central Powers 79
    Alice Rohe, "Once Gay Vienna Now City of Gloom,"
        The Washington Times 81

Nellie Bly, "Paints Horrors of War's Work,"
Tensas Gazette 86

Eleanor Franklin Egan, "Behind the Smoke of Battle,"
The Saturday Evening Post 89

Madeleine Zabriskie Doty, "War's Burden Thrown
on Poor of Germany as Food Supply Dwindles,"
New York Tribune 102

Chapter 5 Pacifists 113

Madeleine Zabriskie Doty, "At The Hague,"
*Short Rations: Experiences of an American
Woman in Germany* 114

Mary Chamberlain, "The Women at The Hague,"
The Survey 120

Alice Hamilton, "At the War Capitals," *The Survey* 130

Helen Ring Robinson, "Confessions of a Peace Pilgrim,"
The Independent 137

Chapter 6 Wartime Adventures 143

Mildred Farwell, "Americans Try a Big Bluff to Save
Serb Food" and "Bulgars Seize Serb Food Left
with Americans," *Chicago Tribune* 145

Eleanor Franklin Egan, "In the Danger Zone,"
The Saturday Evening Post 150

Mary Boyle O'Reilly, "Star Woman Runs Blockade,"
Seattle Star 162

Elizabeth Shepley Sergeant, *Shadow-Shapes:
The Journal of a Wounded Woman, October
1918–May 1919* 165

Chapter 7 Russian Revolution 171

Louise Bryant, "From the Frontier to Petrograd,"
Six Red Months in Russia 172

Rheta Childe Dorr, "Women Soldiers of Russia
May Rescue the Republic," *The Sunday Star* 178

Bessie Beatty, "The Rise of the Proletariat,"
Asia: Journal of the American Asiatic Association 186

Chapter 8 Americans in France 199

Dorothy Canfield Fisher, "The Sammies in Paris,"
Everybody's Magazine 200

Elizabeth Shepley Sergeant, "America Meets France,"
The New Republic 205

Rheta Childe Dorr, A Soldier's Mother in France:
"'A.P.M.' Magic Letters that Help Our Boys
in Straight Path Abroad," *The Courier-Journal* 211
Clara Savage, "The First Word from France,"
Good Housekeeping 216
Chapter 9 Americans in the Fight 225
Clara Savage, "Behind the Scenes in France,"
Good Housekeeping 226
Mary Brush Williams, "When Mothers Ask News
of Their Boys in France," *New York Tribune* 236
Maude Radford Warren, "We Took the Hill,"
The Saturday Evening Post 240
Chapter 10 After the Fighting 255
Peggy Hull, "Allied Troops Unpopular Now
in Vladivostok," *The Tampa Times* 256
Peggy Hull, "Peggy Hull Tells 'Death Train'
of Russian Bolshevik," *Battle Creek Enquirer*............. 258
Maude Radford Warren, "The First Invasion,"
Good Housekeeping 261
Elizabeth Frazer, "The Signature," *The Saturday
Evening Post* 276

Appendix 287

Bibliography 293

Index 297

List of Illustrations

Illustrations
1. Mary Boyle O'Reilly 4
2. Mary Roberts Rinehart 10
3. Edith Wharton with French officers 21
4. Madeleine Zabriskie Doty 31
5. Mary Heaton Vorse.. 39
6. Refuge family 46
7. Ellen Adair 58
8. Sophie Treadwell 61
9. Women munition workers 70
10. British women ambulance drivers................................ 75
11. Alice Rohe...82
12. Nellie Bly.. 87
13. Armenian woman with dead child............................ 98
14. Bismarck monument 105
15. American delegation to the Women's Peace Congress 116
16. Alice Hamilton.. 132
17. Helen Robinson 139
18. Eleanor Franklin Egan 152
19. Elizabeth Shepley Sergeant with nurses........................ 169
20. Louise Bryant 174
21. Rheta Childe Dorr... 179
22. Maria Botchkareva.. 180
23. Dorothy Canfield Fisher 202
24. American soldiers in Paris................................... 203
25. Traffic jam behind American lines in the Argonne 227
26. American Red Cross entertainment tent...................... 232
27. American soldiers in the destroyed town of Vaux 250
28. Peggy Hull 259
29. Maude Radford Warren with American officers............... 265

Foreword

This extraordinary anthology showcases the talents of some thirty women journalists, most of them long forgotten, who reported on World War I for various American newspapers and periodicals. Vivid, fast-moving, and often humorous, their work comes as a revelation, its freshness and verve undiminished by the passage of a century.

Much of the writing that Chris Dubbs has collected here might never have happened were it not for incredible perseverance. Women journalists who wished to cover the biggest story of the era had to outsmart governments and military organizations determined to thwart independent reporting. And they had to learn how to operate within a writerly realm long defined as exclusively masculine. After all, in the early twentieth century, female reporters were tolerated primarily as authors of lightweight "human interest" stories and frivolous pieces for the fashion and society pages. By 1914, women had made progress in the profession, but writing about history in the making still belonged to men, or so it was widely thought. Most editors believed that war reporting was best conducted by the likes of Richard Harding Davis, the dashing architect of the Rough Riders legend and a manly icon of the strenuous life, not by delicate members of the fairer sex.

What stands out in the journalism collected here are the extraordinary lengths to which women reporters went to get their stories and just how much chauvinistic nonsense they had to endure in the process. Gender, one quickly realizes, defined everything about a woman reporter's experience. Depending on the situation, men in uniform responded to female war correspondents and their requests for information with chivalry, patronizing familiarity, derision, contempt, open hostility, and, on rare occasions, respect.

Ultimately, the women represented in this anthology outmaneuvered their male opponents by turning seeming disadvantages to their advantage. Blocked from witnessing military violence firsthand, they focused on the conflict's human collateral damage. Denied membership in the US military's official press corps, they made their way to France (and more exotic realms) by other means, which exposed them to stories they would never have discovered otherwise. This was, after all, a total war that touched everyone. Good war stories were everywhere, both at the front lines and far from the sound of the guns, a fact that women reporters comprehended far more fully than did their male colleagues.

Beyond exposing the gendered dynamics of reporting a century ago, this collection also gives us insight into the global nature of the world's first *world war* and the modernist texture of wartime writing. Many of the selections show just how far-ranging the fighting was in World War I and just how many fronts, many of them scarcely thought of today, existed beyond the familiar theater of operations in France and Belgium. American women journalists received assignments that placed them, for example, in the Balkans, the Middle East, and Civil-War torn Russia, and aboard ships crisscrossing the Atlantic, itself a battlefield, as several of the stories make clear. Readers will also be struck by the richly varied voices and prose styles of these maverick reporters. Some of the pieces speak to nineteenth-century sensibilities, but many of them come across as boldly modernist. The writers employ clipped sentences (managing to sound, at times, almost Hemingwayesque), multiple levels of irony, and passages of impressionistic details (often rendered in the present tense) that come close to the stylings of the literary avant-garde.

A number of selections lift journalism to the level of art. These include Eleanor Franklin Egan's harrowing account of surviving a submarine attack in the Mediterranean (as well as her groundbreaking coverage of the Armenian Genocide); Elizabeth Shepley Sergeant's narrative of her accidental wounding during the tour of an ordnance-strewn former battlefield on the Western Front; Bessie Beatty's eyewitness report on the Bolshevik Revolution; Maude Radford Warren's deeply moving piece on German-American relations in the occupied Rhineland; and Elizabeth Frazer's bitingly sardonic treatment of the Paris Peace Conference, the banality of which she brilliantly underscores through a quiet scene featuring ordinary French citizens. The latter offers the perfect ending to this anthology, a poignant coda that resonates, hauntingly, long after one has finished the book.

Reading these pieces today, one senses what an overwhelming experience the Great War was for everyone swept up in it, including and especially the journalists who tried to make sense of the chaos all around them. And who could say what would come after the terrible conflict finally ran its course? The world, Radford Warren proclaimed in 1919, was "rolling on about its big concerns" after the war, "but surely it could never be the same world." She speaks for all of the writers represented in this volume. And for the anthology's twenty-first century readers as well. Once again, we find ourselves in the midst of a world war, this time against an insidious viral enemy. Like these pioneering reporters of a century ago, we wonder how long the conflict will last, what the final casualty count will be, and what kind of world we (those of us who survive) will inhabit afterwards. Normality has given way to an unwelcome sense of being part of history.

The writers featured in this collection threw themselves into their own turbulent historical moment with gusto, ingenuity, and conviction. They would not accept a print version of the Great War crafted entirely by men; they had to see for themselves. And once they reached their overseas destinations, they changed the nature of war correspondence. In the supposed margins of the conflict, outside the physical arena of combat, they found stories that revealed the complexities and infinite tragedies of total war as it affected ordinary people. One-hundred years later, their journalistic testimony is still moving, stylistically audacious, and startlingly relevant.

Steven Trout

Introduction

On 3 August 1914, one day into World War I, George Lorimer, editor of *The Saturday Evening Post*, sent a telegram to writer Corra Harris: "How would you like to spend a few days in London for us doing woman's side of war?" Lorimer had already recruited two men to cover the war: Samuel Blythe would report from the warring capitals and Irvin Cobb from the front lines. Harris would be expected to fill out the picture with articles about women.

The concept of a "woman's side of war" had existed at least since the Spanish-American War, when several newspapers sent women to report on behind-the-scene activities in Cuba. But Lorimer was the first editor to embrace the concept in WWI and to enshrine it as editorial policy throughout the conflict. In the first year alone, he dispatched five women to England, Canada, Russia, France, Serbia, and Turkey for war stories.

The genius of George Lorimer was an ability to measure the pulse of Progressive Era America. Lorimer had grown the *Post* into the largest circulation magazine in America, in part by broadening its appeal to women. The *Post* embraced the cause of women's suffrage, highlighted the expanding role of women in the workforce, and published many women writers. A larger female readership attracted larger advertising revenue. Lorimer wanted war content that appealed to his female readers. What he wanted for the "woman's side of war" were human-interest stories. What he got was a good deal more. What he set in motion changed the way we still view the Great War.

Collectively, these first five *Post* writers, published twenty-five articles in the two-million-circulation *The Saturday Evening Post* in 1914–15. They not only captured the woman's angle, but got first-time interviews with generals and royalty and gained exclusive access to the war zone and frontline trenches. And they began to draw into sharp focus the significant wartime role being played by women. In short, they demonstrated to the public—and to other female journalists—that being a woman was no bar to reporting the biggest war in history.

The fact that George Lorimer—and the many editors who followed his lead—assigned women to cover the war was clearly a reflection of women's evolving role in society and in the profession of journalism. That generation of women that came of age between 1890 and the start of WWI began to assert itself in the public sphere through work, higher education, social activism, entertainment, and consumer culture. The umbrella term "New Woman" had entered the lexicon to describe a host of evolving traits of modern feminism that pushed the limits set by male-dominated society. The campaign for women's suffrage took center stage, but a new vision of women began to appear in publications—professional, courageous, independent, assertive, and ambitious.

A similar emergence occurred in journalism. In 1914, women were still novelties at most American newspapers, often relegated to writing about fashion, society, and domestic topics for the paper's Women's Page. However, in the decades leading up to WWI, women had begun to grow their visibility in journalism through "stunt" reporting and that brand of investigative reportage known as muckraking. By going undercover or through in-depth reporting, they exposed many ills of society, such as poorly-run public institutions, unscrupulous doctors, unsafe working conditions, corporate monopolies, political corruption, or other deceptive, criminal, or dangerous conditions. Such investigative or participatory journalism often ran as a front-page series of articles that captivated readers and turned reporters into celebrities.

Seen in this context, the jump to women covering war seemed less of a jolt, especially since the initial role of female war correspondents was seen largely as operating behind the scenes, uncovering stories on the home front. The same careful scrutiny they had given to social, economic, and political topics at home, they could now give to such topics in the belligerent countries.

Home front reporting rose to prominence in the Great War. Traditional war reporting focused on armies and battles. However, the world's first "total war" redefined the type of news that qualified as war reporting. When the line between combatants and noncombatants blurs, when cities are bombed, when every individual and national resource is subordinated to the war effort, *everything* is war news: battles, the economy, politics, civilian morale, food shortages, medical care, the personal story of every soldier, wife, and mother. Suddenly the home front was as critical to the war effort as the battle line.

Not that the women war correspondents of WWI confined themselves to the home fronts. Prior to the entry of the United States into the war, its women journalists reported from all the warring countries. Some made brief visits to England, France, or Germany and wrote impressionistic articles about what they experienced. Mary Roberts Rinehart and Edith Wharton were well-known fiction writers, but in 1915 they won privileged access to the war zone to report on the activities of the British, French, and Belgium armies. Nellie Bly reported from a besieged city on the Eastern Front. Several women reporters dodged bullets on the streets of revolution-gripped Petrograd. Eleanor Franklin Egan reported from typhus-ravaged Serbia, came under U-boat attack, and smuggled secret documents out of Turkey to expose the Armenian Genocide. Mary Boyle O'Reilly and Alice Rohe, who worked for news syndication services, remained in warring Europe and wrote on numerous topics in the opening years of the war.

After the United States entered the war in April 1917, the number of women covering the conflict increased dramatically. Now that America was sending its own sons into harm's way, readers wanted to know everything about what they experienced. Every mother, wife, and girlfriend was suddenly intensely interested in what was happening to their loved one and wanted to know how the women of warring Europe managed to cope. For the first time, women's magazines, such as *Good Housekeeping, Woman's Home Companion, The Delineator, Pictorial Review*, and *Ladies' Home Journal*, sent their own correspondents to Europe. In the summer of 1917, Rheta Childe Dorr reported on women soldiers fighting for Russia, but when her son joined the army, she shifted focus. In a series of syndicated newspaper articles titled "A Soldier's Mother in France," she offered herself as a mother reporting for other mothers about the things that most concerned them. This collection includes several articles written for women's magazines and a Dorr article reassuring the mothers of America that their sons were being well cared for by the U.S. army.

Female reporters did not always receive the warmest welcome from military press offices. When the AEF selected fifteen journalists to be officially credentialled to cover U.S. forces, none of them were women. Likewise, civil and military authorities in England and France were often reluctant to assist women correspondents, especially those from smaller-circulation newspapers and women's magazines. Did the French military really need to waste time, reasoning went, to escort to the front lines a writer from *Good Housekeeping* magazine?

To evade military restrictions and ingrained prejudice, many women reporters employed the effective newsgathering strategy of volunteering with aid organizations. Charitable groups such as the Red Cross, YMCA, and Salvation Army, conducted extensive activities to support U.S. troops. Working with such organization gave women reporters access to prime newsgathering locations at or near the front lines and put them in close contact with soldiers. They rode with soldiers in ambulances and nursed them in hospitals. They helped wounded soldiers write letters to mothers and sweethearts. They traveled with entertainment units to training camps and served hot chocolate in the trenches. From these experiences, they gathered intimate portraits of the war that were not available to their male counterparts.

The American women who reported the Great War gathered their stories in all the belligerent countries, on the home front, in the trenches and front-line hospitals, in the most difficult and dangerous locales, amid the chaos of the Russian Revolution, in the sprawling enterprise of American involvement, and in the disorderly post-war period. Veteran journalist Eleanor Franklin Egan wrote more than sixty-five feature articles for *The Saturday Evening Post*. Two of Egan's articles are included here.

The articles in this collection saw publication in newspapers, magazines, or books published during the war and in the immediate post-war period. Some of the authors worked as professional journalists, others, who took on freelance assignments, were fiction writers, social reformers, suffragists, political activists, or peace advocates. Because the articles source from different publications, their style, usage, grammar, and spelling vary, and are sometimes as idiosyncratic as the authors who wrote them. For the most part those idiosyncrasies have been retained, with only an occasional correction of an obvious misspelling or typographical error.

Throughout the four long years of WWI and the post-armistice chaos, women journalists carved out a distinctive role and voice for themselves. The articles in this collection illustrate only a small sampling of their rich contribution to the history of the Great War.

Chapter 1

On the Front Lines

On August 27, 1914, a train departed German-occupied Brussels, carrying five frustrated American journalists, including Mary Boyle O'Reilly, the London bureau chief of Newspaper Enterprise Association. For nearly two weeks, the correspondents had been struggling, without success, to report on the German invasion of neutral Belgium. Allied newspapers published sketchy war office communiques and wild stories about German atrocities. But military restrictions, censorship, and the fluid landscape of the invasion made it impossible to find the fighting or report on the exact nature of this modern war.

Ironically, the train taking the reporters out of the war zone, carried them into a confrontation with a shocking element of the fighting war that none of them had ever imagined. The train stopped for a two-hour layover in Louvain, Belgium, just as it was being destroyed by the German army. From their train, the reporters watched the systematic demolition of a town, a "war on civilians," as they would describe it: the burning of houses and buildings, the reprisal execution of prominent citizens, and the destitute residents forced to become refugees. Given military restrictions on journalists, it was the first eyewitness view any reporters had gotten of the invasion.

When the journalists finally reached the safety of neutral Holland, four of the reporters rushed out stories to tell the outside world about Louvain. Only Mary Boyle O'Reilly returned to the war zone for the rest of the story. In Louvain she joined a group of refugees traveling through the region devastated by the German invasion. The shocking account of her return to Louvain and her subsequent refugee odyssey—included here—grabbed headlines in hundreds of U.S. newspapers.

O'Reilly's sensational eyewitness account of the invasion and its aftermath was very much the exception rather than the rule for journalistic access. For the first six months of the Great War, the "front," where all the fighting occurred, was a restricted area, off limits to journalists. Most war correspondents remained bottled up in London or Paris, forced to write their war stories from rumors and the official war office pronouncements that provided few details.

When the warring nations finally realized that news was as critical a component of war as men and armaments, they began to allow select journalists to make limited, guided visits to the front lines. Britain did not conduct its first official front line tour for reporters until February 1915, six months into the war. When that group of journalists arrived at the front for a one-day, supervised visit, the reporters were surprised to discover that a middle-aged, female, American novelist—Mary Roberts Rinehart—had been touring the front for several weeks. At this same time, another American novelist had gained similar access to the French lines. Their privileged access to the front was unique at that point in the war.

At this turning point in news coverage of the war, America's most popular mystery writer—Mary Roberts Rinehart—and its leading literary novelist—Edith Wharton—were given guided VIP tours of the war zone. Allied governments had clearly identified both women as having the stature and the sympathies to plead their case in the neutral United States. On assignment for *The Saturday Evening Post* and *Scribner's Magazine*, the two writers wrote a series of articles that thoroughly mapped the landscape of the war. They suffered inconveniences, dangers, came under enemy fire, witnessed combat, visited towns destroyed by the fighting, interviewed royalty and generals, and made it to the most advanced frontline trenches. Their mix of emotions—shock, awe, excitement, compassion, horror, and glory—so perfectly reflected the response of an innocent observer learning about the character of the war. In the process, these two novelists helped to shape American public opinion at this critical juncture in the conflict.

In the two articles excerpted here, both Rinehart and Wharton write about their visit to the front lines. Rinehart took a perilous walk into No Man's Land, the empty, free-fire zone between opposing trenches. She was the first journalist in the war to be granted such access and to paint so graphic a picture of activities along the Front. American expatriate novelist Edith Wharton had been living in Paris for seven years when war began in August 1914. Early in 1915, French authorities granted her unprecedented visits to the entire 400 miles of the Western Front. In this excerpt she describes her arduous trek to see where the French and German lines faced each other in the Vosges Mountains.

Mary Boyle O'Reilly (1873–1939)

Near the road two old men hang from a tree, hostages whose lives were taken by the enemy. I passed that tree, but never as long as I live will I be able to erase from memory the dead faces of those two old men.

"Woman Writer Sees Horrors of Battle"
Mary Boyle O'Reilly
The Seattle Star, September 23, 1914

I am just back from a pilgrimage of that part of Belgium around which the German war machine has ringed its belt of iron. Between Brussels and Liege, Louvain and Vise, lies roughly a parallelogram of country about 60 miles long by 30 miles wide. Here were fought all the early battles of Germany's advance upon France.

Out of this smoke-shadowed district came such stories of sacked villages and slaughtered non-combatants as to horrify mankind. To prove these stories untrue, I became a refugee inside the Prussian lines. For some dreadful days I lost myself in the piteous crowds which fled from Tirlemont to Tongres. I had, to save myself at the worse, the pass which the German vice consul in Holland had given me. In the following I will tell the story of what I saw on that pilgrimage.

Mary Boyle O'Reilly, London bureau chief for the Newspaper Enterprise Association. *Source:* Harris & Ewing Collection, Prints and Photographs Division, Library of Congress, LC-DIG-hec-01937.

West of Tirlemont, where the smoke of burning Herent and Hangarde darkens the sky, stands an ancient church, white flags of peace still hanging from its bombarded belfry.

On the shell-shattered steps lies the dog of Flanders,[1] his Red Cross blanket and first-aid barrel shot to pieces by the invader's bullet. The two are sign and symbol of a Prussian army passing.

Herent was fired because a father resented a Uhlan's[2] insult to his daughter.

The heart of prosperous Hangarde was bombarded because the peasants destroyed the bridge over the village brook. There was neither rifle nor ammunition in either place; probably never had been.

1. The northern region of Belgium
2. Uhlans were light cavalry units.

The town of Tirlemont, where small arms were stored in a desperate desire of self-protection, has been badly shot up but still stands.

In Brussels and [in] Belgium, where Prussian soldiers are exposed to foreign observation, they conceal their regimental numbers while the officers refuse to give their names. Thus atrocities are the work of anonymous men.

Within the German cordon such safeguards seem unnecessary. Sacked Tirlemont is filled by dragoons[3] of the 66th, 26th, and 34th Regiments of the Line. The Place du Marchi is crowded with machine guns, on whose steel shields are chalked each gun crew's record so far in the war. On the walls of the Thirteenth Century church the Prussian army has pasted posters printed in three languages, giving us the following exact news of the war:

"The English are being driven into the sea."

"The French have retreated to Paris."

"Germany's campaign is all over but collecting the indemnity."

Two refugee women at my shoulder sobbed piteously. A sentry reproved them with blows in the abdomen from the butt of his gun.

Utterly cowed, we turned away. Tirlemont is not Belgian any more, is—reads the Prussian placard—now part of a conquered German province.

The straight, tree-shaded road to Grinde is crowded with homeless wanderers; hundreds of wan-faced women, children whimpering at their skirts; scores of aging men in self-respecting home-spun, a determined little boy carrying his pet kid, a girl [c]lasping her bolt of wedding linen, youths with the essential parts of their textile tools strapped to their backs, strong old women staggering under huge jars, dogs tugging at over-laden trucks, a cart with a white flag, a dying child in its father's arms, a paralytic, a blind man—all of them homeless, penniless, heart-broken.

Yet in their misery they find pity for sharper sorrow. That delirious woman lying in the wheelbarrow is the sister of the army scout, John Markin, whom, it is charged, dragoons buried alive, head downward, and whom Belgian chasseurs discovered and disinterred—too late.

In silence, in terror, we crowd down the once peaceful road hands raised, passports humbly held before us. Every few yards

3. Cavalry

there is a sentry to be passed, perhaps placated, an over-strained, sullen soldier who commands with a bayonet and argues with a gun butt.

The villagers had disappeared. Only three dead peasants. Bayoneted in their doorways and a few horses killed in the small main street remain. I see men of the 18th German Dragoons, white crosses on their gold starred caps, loot at their leisure.

We refugees speak in whispers, plodding on to poor little Bandersea. From far off we can see that the village has been shelled, its houses leveled by artillery. Near the road two old men hang from a tree, hostages whose lives were taken by the enemy. I passed that tree, but never as long as I live will I be able to erase from memory the dead faces of those two old men.

In the roadside ditch the father of a day-old babe has built a wigwam of tentpoles and straw. Last week he had a nice, pretty Belgium house—a prosperous farmer, the master of flocks and kine.[4]

"Louvendane is utterly destroyed," he says, grimly. "Germans fighting west of Mechlin were repulsed by the Belgians. A hundred 55th Lancers of the Rhine fell back here. Some of them, mad with blood, insulted the women of our village. In a dozen houses vials were burst which spread strangling fumes. Then our houses were fired. If you want to see worse, go to the chateau below."

The suggestion is good, but impracticable. A seemingly endless convoy of guns block the road---siege guns moving toward the east. Fifty drivers flourish taunting whips to chalked inscriptions. We read as they pass:

"Nach (to) Brussels—nach Lille—nach Paris."

Wayside Shrine Used as Target

While we wait perforce, Uhlans off duty amuse themselves by firing at a wayside shrine. Women who have borne catastrophe bravely break down as they watch the wanton shooting of the crucified.

In what was so lately the little town of Corbeek-Loo stands what was a chateau. Both are ruins, for Corbeek-Loo suffered annihilation by artillery. No one knows why, assailants and people having disappeared. Only the patient old cure remains to tell his story.

---

4. Cows

"We were merely a village, quite harmless and peaceful," says the cure. "Our thoughts were of the crops and of God. The war, of which we heard vaguely, seemed far away. Not one of my people ever owned a rifle or ever fired a rifle. My church and the chateau dominated Corbeek-Loo. Baron Ernst lived in the chateau. He is an elderly man, retiring and scholarly. Both of his sons are in the diplomatic service. With him lived his six daughters—ladies of a certain age—all unmarried. The good angels of our village.

"Come, that I show you what these barbarians do to a Belgian home."

Something Doing in the Chateau

We enter the once stately gates now shattered by shells. The acres-wide formal garden is strewn with fragments of statuary, with broken graphaphone[5] disks, wine glasses, slippers, shattered fans—a hundred womanly trifles.

In the long drawing rooms every family portrait has been slashed from its gilded frame, every cabinet rifled of its treasures, hundreds of books torn page from page.

Amid piles of broken furniture lie sleeping rugs hacked from old Turkish carpets. Dogs have been kenneled in the Louis XIV boudoir, the dining room is ankle deep with shattered glass and porcelain, the family chapel has served as a shooting gallery, debris makes the bedrooms impassable.

Heaps of women's delicate clothing is strewn about or strung up for obscenity. In all the stately home no breakable thing is left unbroken, no valuable thing unruined, no sacred thing unsacrificed.

The chateau is the epitome of wanton, pitiless, disgusting destruction.

"Rich and poor, gentle and simple, we Belgians are paying the price to protect Europe," sighs the cure.

Emperor Sowing Tares, Says Priest

"The emperor is the enemy sowing tares![6] If we are to be a conquered province, will not all this pitiless devastation make us

---

5. An early version of the phonograph
6. Weeds

hateful vassals? If Belgium is to remain independent, will not this make us hateful neighbors for a century?"

Heart-sick I walked toward St. Trond, the little town which Kommandantur Blihoofer has "subdued" ruthlessly. The Mobile Stappen is crowded with dragoons from the 85th, 88th and 26th regiments.

In the shadow of the ancient church, "sacred to God and fatherland," are gathered the seized crops and farm wagons of the district. The town is ringed round with field pieces—guns' crews lying ready. Motor cars filled with soldiers facing four ways, their rifles cocked, dash about incessantly. It is two weeks since the nine-hour cavalry battle ended in a Prussian repulse. There is quiet now in St. Trond. It is the peace of Warsaw.[7]

"St. Trond was rebel, WAS, you understand," boast the Uhlan commanders.

Men Are Gone—None Know Where

Today the population is made up of women and children. No one seems to know what has become of the men—no one will ever know, I am afraid.

A mile down the St. Trond road we refugees pause that some may pray. It was right here that five priests were shot dead—all hostages (none of them young), whose lives were forfeited because peasants who had fowling pieces did the Lexington and Concord act.[8] Just beyond lies the road to Tongres where these peasants made their last stand. The elm trees, felled as a barricade by these citizen sharpshooters, are hardly dead.

In the broad, sunlit square of Tongres troopers of the 12th and 52nd Brandenburg regiments haggle over their loot. For Tongres (i.e. a fort), which had been a place of defense since the days of Caesar, resisted invasion and was, for reprisal, given shell and sack. Today no one may leave his or her house without a military pass; no one may light a candle after nightfall.

In the twilight the shattered streets echo with the agonizing sobbing of heart-broken women. The burghers have been driven by Uhlans none save their captives know where.

7. An unclear reference, perhaps to one of the treaties between Prussia and Poland, in which Poland ceded territory in exchange for military assistance in a war.
8. The first military engagements of the American Revolution, in which civilians fought the British.

"Halt!—or I fire!"

It is the last sentinel on the way of sorrow. We stand submissively to show our papers. Beyond, just two miles away, rise the spires of Maastricht in Holland.

Holland and Safety at Last

A pearl gray evening mist shrouds the stricken land. Only one little mile now between us and safety. Men and women who have faced death with fortitude walk on blinded with tears.

In the dusk, we can see a spectral barrier, a lantern, and the tri-color of Queen Wilhelmina's delightful Holland.[9]

"Stand!—friends or enemies?"

The refugees' voice answer.

Slowly, so slowly that the last sink down exhausted, our sad little company crosses the frontier.

Mary Roberts Rinehart (1876–1958)

I had been to the front. I had been far beyond the front, indeed, and I had seen such a picture of war and its desolation there in the center of No Man's Land as perhaps no one not connected with an army had seen before; such a picture as would live in my mind forever.

"For King and Country, No Man's Land"
Mary Roberts Rinehart
The Saturday Evening Post, May 8, 1915

Until now our excursion to the trenches, aside from the discomfort of the weather and the mud, had been fairly safe, although there was always the chance of a shell. To that now was to be added a fresh hazard—the sniping that goes on all night long.

Our car moved quietly for a mile, paralleling the trenches. Then it stopped. The rest of the journey was to be on foot.

All traces of the storm had passed, except for the pools of mud which, gleaming like small lakes, filled shell holes in the road.

9. Holland was a neutral country and thus safe haven, its queen Wilhelmina Helena Pauline Maria.

Mary Roberts Rinehart, a famous writer of mystery fiction, became a war correspondent for *The Saturday Evening Post*. With the endorsement of the Belgian Red Cross, she won unprecedented access to the war zone and became the first journalist to visit the frontline trenches. *Source:* George Grantham Bain Collection, Prints and Photographs Division, Library of Congress, LC-B2- 4007-13.

An ammunition lorry had drawn up in the shadow of a hedge and was cautiously unloading. Evidently the night's movement of troops was over, for the roads were empty.

A few feet beyond the lorry we came up to the trenches. We were behind them, only head and shoulders above. There was no sign of life or movement, except for the silent *fusées*[10] that burst

10. A bright flare shot into the air and descending on a parachute, to illuminate the area between opposing trenches

occasionally a little to our right. Walking was bad. The Belgian blocks of the road were coated with slippery mud, and from long use and erosion the stones themselves were rounded, so that our feet slipped over them. At the right was a shallow ditch three or four feet wide. Beyond that the railway embankment where, as Captain Fastrez had explained, the Belgian Army had taken up its position after being driven back across the Yser.[11]

The embankment loomed shoulder high, and between it and the ditch were the trenches. There was no sound from them, but sentries halted us frequently. On such occasions the party stopped abruptly—for here sentries are apt to fire first and investigate afterward—and one officer advanced with the password. There is always something grim and menacing about the attitude of the sentry as he waits on such occasions. His carbine is not over his shoulder, but in his hands, ready for use. The bayonet gleams. His eyes are fixed watchfully on the advance. A false move, and his overstrained nerves may send the carbine to his shoulder.

The House of the Barrier

We walked just behind the trenches in the moonlight for a mile. No one said anything. The wind was icy. Across the railroad embankment it chopped the inundation[12] into small crested waves. Only by putting one's head down was it possible to battle ahead. From Dixmude came the intermittent red flashes of guns. But the trenches beside us were entirely silent.

At the end of a mile we stopped. The road turned abruptly to the right and crossed the railroad embankment, and at this crossing was the ruin of what had been the House of the Barrier, where in peaceful times the crossing tender lived.

It had been almost destroyed. The side towards the German lines was indeed a ruin, but one room was fairly whole. However, the door had been shot away. To enter, it was necessary to lift away an extemporized one of planks roughly nailed together, which leaned against the aperture.

---

11. The Yser River
12. The Belgians intentionally flooded parts of their lowlands in order to halt the German advance and maintain control of a small portion of their country.

The moving of the door showed more firelight, and a very small, shaded and smoky lamp on a stand. There were officers here again. The little house is slightly in advance of the trenches, and once inside it was possible to realize its exposed position. Standing as it does on the elevation of the railroad, it is constantly under fire. It is surrounded by barbed wire and flanked by trenches in which are mitrailleuses.[13]

The walls were full of shell holes, stuffed with sacks of straw or boarded over. What had been windows were now jagged openings, similarly closed. The wind came through steadily, smoking the chimney of the lamp and making the flame flicker.

There was one chair.

I wish I could go farther. I wish I could say that shells were bursting overhead, and that I sat calmly in the one chair and made notes. I sat, true enough, but I sat because I was tired and my feet were wet. And instead of making notes I examined my new six-guinea silk rubber rain cape for barbed wire tears. Not a shell came near. The German battery across had ceased firing at dusk that evening, and was playing pinochle four hundred yards away across the inundation. The snipers were writing letters home.

It is true that at any time an artillery man might lose a game and go out and fire a gun to vent his spleen or to keep his hand in. And the snipers might begin to notice that the rain was over, and that there was suspicious activity at the House of the Barrier. And, to take away the impression of perfect peace, big guns were busy just north and south of us. Also, just where we were the Germans had made a terrific charge three nights before to capture an outpost. But the fact remains that I brought away not even a bullet hole through the crown of my soft felt hat.

When I had been thawed out they took me into the trenches. Because of the inundation directly in front, they are rather shallow, and at this point were built against the railroad embankment with earth, boards, and here and there a steel rail from the track. Some of them were covered, too, but not with bomb proof material. The tops were merely shelters from the rain and biting wind. The men lay or sat in them—it was impossible to stand. Some of them were like tiny houses into which the men crawled from the

13. Machine guns

rear, and by placing a board, which served as a door, managed to keep out at least a part of the bitter wind.

Evening in the Trench

In the first trench I was presented to a bearded major. He was lying flat and apologized for not being able to rise. There was a machine gun beside him. He told me with some pride that it was an American gun, and that it never jammed. When a machine gun jams the man in charge of it dies and his comrades die, and things happen with great rapidity. On the other side of him was a cat, curled up and sound asleep. There was a telephone instrument there. It was necessary to step over the wire that was strung up on the ground.

All night long he lies there with his gun, watching for the first movement in the trenches across. For here, near the House of the Barrier, has taken place some of the most furious fighting of this part of the line.

In the next division of the trench were three men. They were cleaning and oiling their rifles round a candle. The surprise of all of these men at seeing a woman was almost absurd. Word went down the trenches that a woman was visiting. Heads popped out and cautious comments were made. It was concluded that I was visiting royalty, but the excitement died when it was discovered that I was not the Queen. Now and then, when a trench looked clean and dry, I was invited in. It was necessary to get down and crawl in on hands and knees.

Here was a man warming his hands over a tiny fire kindled in a tin pail. He had bored holes in the bottom of the pail for air, and was shielding the glow carefully with his overcoat.

Many people have written about the trenches—the mud, the odors, the inhumanity of compelling men to live under such foul conditions. Nothing that they have said can be too strong. Under the best conditions the life is ghastly, horrible, impossible.

That night, when from a semishielded position I could look across to the German line, the contrast between the condition of the men in the trenches and the beauty of the scenery was appalling. In each direction, as far as one could see, lay a gleaming lagoon of water. The moon made a silver path across it, and here and there on its borders were broken and twisted winter trees.

"It is beautiful," said Captain Fastrez beside me, in a low voice. "But it is full of the dead. They are taken out whenever it is possible, but it is not often possible."

"And when there is an attack the attacking side must go through the water?"

"Not always, but in many places."

"What will happen if it freezes over?"

He explained that it was salt water, and would not freeze easily. And the cold of that part of the country is not the cold of America in the same latitude. It is not a cold of low temperature; it is a damp, penetrating cold that goes through garments of every weight and seems to chill the very blood in a man's body.

"How deep is the water?" I asked.

"It varies—from two to eight feet. Here it is shallow."

"I should think they would come over."

"The water is full of barbed wire," he said grimly. "And some, a great many, have tried—and failed."

As of the trenches, many have written of the stenches of this war. But the odor of that beautiful lagoon was horrible. I do not care to emphasize it. It is one of the things best forgotten. But any lingering belief I may have had in the grandeur and glory of war died that night beside that silver lake—died of an odor, and will never live again.

And now came a discussion.

The road crossing the railroad embankment turned sharply to the left and proceeded in front of the trenches. There was no shelter on that side of the embankment. The inundation bordered the road, and just beyond the inundation were the German trenches.

There were no trees, no shrubbery, no houses; just a flat road, paved with Belgian blocks, that gleamed in the moonlight.

At last the decision was made. We would go along the road, provided I realized from the first that it was dangerous. One or two could walk there with a good chance for safety, but not more. The little group had been augmented. It must break up; two might walk together, and then two a safe distance behind. Four would certainly be fired on.

I wanted to go. It was not a matter of courage. I had simply, parrot-fashion, mimicked the attitude of mind of the officers.

One after another I had seen men go into danger with a shrug of the shoulders.

"If it comes it comes!" they said, and went on. So I, too, had become a fatalist. If I was to be shot it would happen, if I had to buy a rifle and try to clean it myself to fulfill my destiny.

The Sentry Agreement

So they let me go. I went farther than they expected, as it turned out. There was a great deal of indignation and relief when it was over. But that is later on.

A very tall Belgian officer took me in charge. It was necessary to work through a barbed-wire barricade, twisting and turning through its mazes. The moonlight helped. It was at once a comfort and an anxiety, for it seemed to me that my khaki-colored suit gleamed in it. The Belgian officers in their dark blue were less conspicuous. I thought they had an unfair advantage of me, and that it was idiotic of the British to wear and advocate anything so absurd as khaki. My cape ballooned like a sail in the wind. I felt at least double my ordinary size, and that even a sniper with a squint could hardly miss me. And, by way of comfort, I had one last instruction before I started:

"If a *fusée* goes up, stand perfectly still. If you move they will fire."

The entire safety of the excursion depended on a sort of tacit agreement that, in part at least, obtains as to sentries.

This is a new warfare, one of artillery, supported by infantry in trenches. And it has been necessary to make new laws for it. The winter deadlock has given rise to one of the most curious. It is a sort of *modus vivendi*[14] by which each side protects its own sentries by leaving the enemy's sentries unmolested so long as there is no active fighting. They are always in plain view before the trenches. In case of a charge they are the first to be shot, of course. But long winter nights and days have gone by along certain parts of the front where the hostile trenches are close together, and the sentries, keeping their monotonous lookout, have been undisturbed.

---

14. An arrangement accepted by both sides

No doubt by the time this article is published the situation will have changed to a certain extent; there will be more active fighting, larger bodies of men will be involved. The spring floods south of the inundation will have dried up. No Man's Land[15] will have ceased to be a swamp and the deadlock will be broken.

But on that February night I put my faith in this agreement and it held.

The tall Belgian officer asked me if I was frightened. I said I was not. This was not the truth; but it was no time for the truth.

"They are not shooting," I said. "It looks perfectly safe."

He shrugged his shoulders and glanced toward the German trenches. "They have been sleeping during the rain," he said briefly. "But when one of them wakes up, look out!"

After that there was little conversation, and what there was was in whispers.

As we proceeded the stench from the beautiful moonlit water grew overpowering. The officer told me the reason.

A little farther along a path of fascines[16] had been built out over the inundation to an outpost halfway to the German trenches. The building of this narrow roadway had cost many lives.

Half a mile along the road we were sharply challenged by a sentry. When he had received the password he stood back and let us pass. Alone, in that bleak and exposed position, always in full view as he paced back and forward, carbine on shoulder, with not even a tree trunk or a hedge for shelter, the first to go at the whim of some German sniper or at any indication of an attack, he was a pathetic, almost a tragic, figure. He looked very young too. I stopped and asked him in a whisper how old he was.

He said he was nineteen!

He may have been. I know something about boys, and I think he was seventeen at the most. There are plenty of boys of that age doing just what that lad was doing.

Afterward I learned that it was no part of the original plan to take a woman over the fascine path to the outpost; that Captain Fastrez ground his teeth in impotent rage when he saw where I was being taken. But it was not possible to call or even to come

---

15. The unoccupied land between opposing trenches
16. Bundles of sticks used to create a path through the water or mud

up to us. So, blithely and unconsciously the tall Belgian officer and I turned to the right, and I was innocently on my way to the German trenches.

After a little I realized that this was rather more war than I had expected. The fascines were slippery; the path only four or five feet wide. On each side was the water, hideous with many secrets.

I stopped, a third of the way out, and looked back. It looked about as dangerous in one direction as another. So we went on. Once I slipped and fell. And now, looming out of the moonlight, I could see the outpost which was the object of our visit.

I have always been grateful to that Belgian lieutenant for his mistake. Just how grateful I might have been had anything untoward happened, I cannot say. But the excursion was worth all the risk, and more.

The Soldier Monk in His Tower

On a bit of high ground stands what was once the tiny hamlet of Oudstuyvenskerke—the ruins of two small white houses and the tower of the destroyed church—hardly a tower any more, for only three sides of it are standing and they are riddled with great shell holes.

Six hundred feet beyond this tower were the German trenches. The little island was hardly a hundred feet in its greatest dimension.

I wish I could make those people who think that war is good for a country see that Belgian outpost as I saw it that night under the moonlight. Perhaps we were under suspicion; I do not know. Suddenly the *fusées*, which had ceased for a time, began again, and with their white light added to that of the moon the desolate picture of that tiny island was a picture of the war. There was nothing lacking. There was the beauty of the moonlit waters, there was the tragedy of the destroyed houses and the church, and there was the horror of unburied bodies.

There was heroism, too, of the kind that will make Belgium live in history. For in the top of that church tower for three months a Capuchin monk has held his position alone and unrelieved. He has a telephone, and he gains access to his position in the tower by means of a rope ladder which he draws up after him.

Furious fighting has taken place again and again round the base of the tower. The German shells assail it constantly. But when I left Belgium the Capuchin monk, who has become a soldier, was still on duty; still telephoning the ranges of the gun; still notifying headquarters of German preparations for a charge.

Some day the church tower will fall and he will go with it, or it will be captured; one or the other is inevitable. Perhaps it has already happened; for not long ago I saw in the newspapers that furious fighting was taking place at this very spot.

He came down and I talked to him—a little man, regarding his situation as quite ordinary, and looking quaintly unpriestlike in his uniform of a Belgian officer with its tasseled cap. Some day a great story will be written of these priests of Belgium who have left their churches to fight.

We spoke in whispers. There was after all very little to say. It would have embarrassed him horribly had anyone told him that he was a heroic figure. And the ordinary small talk is not currency in such a situation.

We shook hands and I think I wished him luck. Then he went back again to the long hours and days of waiting.

I passed under his telephone wires. Some day he will telephone that a charge is coming. He will give all the particulars calmly, concisely. Then the message will break off abruptly. He will have sent his last warning. For that is the way these men at the advance posts die.

As we started again I was no longer frightened. Something of his courage had communicated itself to me, his courage and his philosophy, perhaps his faith.

The priest had become a soldier; but he was still a priest in his heart. For he had buried the German dead in one great grave before the church, and over them had put the cross of his belief.

It was rather absurd on the way back over that path of death to be escorted by a cat. It led the way over the fascines, treading daintily and cautiously. Perhaps one of the destroyed houses at the outpost had been its home, and with a cat's fondness for places it remained there, though everything it knew had gone; though battle and sudden death had usurped the place of its peaceful fireside, though that very fireside was become a heap of stone and plaster, open to winds and rain.

Back to Headquarters

Again and again in destroyed towns I have seen these forlorn cats stalking about, trying vainly to adjust themselves to new conditions, cold and hungry and homeless. We were challenged repeatedly on the way back. Coming from the direction we did we were open to suspicion. It was necessary each time to halt some forty feet from the sentry, who stood with his rifle pointed at us. Then the officer advanced with the word.

Back again, then, along the road, past the youthful sentry, past other sentries, winding through the barbed-wire barricade, and at last, quite whole, to the House of the Barrier again. We had walked three miles in front of the Belgian advanced trenches, in full view of the Germans. There had been no protecting hedge or bank or tree between us and that ominous line across. And nothing whatever had happened.

Captain Fastrez was indignant. The officers in the House of the Barrier held up their hands. For men such a risk was legitimate, necessary. In a woman it was foolhardy. Nevertheless, now that it was safely over, they were keenly interested and rather amused. But I have learned that the gallant captain and the officer with him had arranged, in case shooting began, to jump into the water, and by splashing about draw the fire in their direction!

We went back to the automobile, a long walk over the shell-eaten roads in the teeth of a biting wind. But a glow of exultation kept me warm. I had been to the front. I had been far beyond the front, indeed, and I had seen such a picture of war and its desolation there in the center of No Man's Land as perhaps no one not connected with an army had seen before; such a picture as would live in my mind forever.

Edith Wharton (1862–1937)

Here we were, then, actually and literally in the front lines!
The knowledge made one's heart tick a little.

"In Lorraine and the Vosges"
Edith Wharton
Scribner's Magazine, October 1916
May 17th

Today we started with an intenser sense of adventure. Hitherto we had always been told beforehand where we were going and how much we were to be allowed to see; but now we were being launched into the unknown. Beyond a certain point all was conjecture—we knew only that what happened after that would depend on the good-will of a Colonel of Chasseurs-à-pied[17] whom we were to go a long way to find, up into the folds of the mountains on our south-east horizon.

We picked up a staff-officer at Head-quarters and flew on to a battered town on the edge of the hills. From there we wound up through a narrowing valley, under wooded cliffs, to a little settlement where the Colonel of the Brigade was to be found. There was a short conference between the Colonel and our staff-officer, and then we annexed a Captain of Chasseurs and spun away again. Our road lay through a town so exposed that our companion from Head-quarters suggested the advisability of avoiding it; but our guide hadn't the heart to inflict such a disappointment on his new acquaintances. "Oh, we won't stop the motor—we'll just dash through," he said indulgently; and in the excess of his indulgence he even permitted us to dash slowly.

Oh, that poor town—when we reached it, along a road ploughed with fresh obus-holes,[18] I didn't want to stop the motor; I wanted to hurry on and blot the picture from my memory! It was doubly sad to look at because of the fact that it wasn't *quite dead*; faint spasms of life still quivered through it. A few children played in the ravaged streets; a few pale mothers watched them from cellar doorways. "They oughtn't to be here," our guide explained; "but about a hundred and fifty begged so hard to stay that the General gave them leave. The officer in command has an eye on them, and whenever he gives the signal they dive down into their burrows. He says they are perfectly obedient. It was he who asked that they might stay ... "

Up and up into the hills. The vision of human pain and ruin was lost in beauty. We were among the firs, and the air was full of balm. The mossy banks gave out a scent of rain, and little waterfalls from the heights set the branches trembling over secret pools. At each turn of the road, forest, and always more forest,

17. Light infantry
18. A crater caused by an exploding artillery shell

Novelist Edith Wharton with French officers. The French army took Wharton on several guided war tours in 1915, which resulted in a series of articles and a book that helped to publicize the French war effort. *Source:* Edith Wharton Collection, Beinecke Rare Book and Manuscript Library, Yale University.

climbing with us as we climbed, and dropping away from us to narrow valleys that converged on slate-blue distances. At one of these turns we overtook a company of soldiers, spade on shoulder and bags of tools across their backs—"trench- workers" swinging up to the heights to which we were bound. Life must be a better thing in this crystal air than in the mud-welter of the Argonne and the fogs of the North; and these men's faces were fresh with wind and weather.

Higher still … and presently a halt on a ridge, in another "black village," this time almost a town! The soldiers gathered round us as the motor stopped—throngs of *chasseurs-à-pied* in faded, trench-stained uniforms—for few visitors climb to this point, and their pleasure at the sight of new faces was presently expressed in a large *"Vive l'Amérique!"*[19] scrawled on the door of the car. *L'Amérique* was glad and proud to be there, and instantly conscious of breathing an air saturated with courage and the dogged determination to endure. The men were all reservists: that is to say, mostly married, and all beyond the first fighting age. For many months there has not been much active work along this front, no great adventure to rouse the blood and wing the imagination: it has just been month after month of monotonous watching and holding on. And the soldiers' faces showed it: there was no light of heady enterprise in their eyes, but the look of men who knew their job, had thought it over, and were there to hold their bit of France till the day of victory or extermination.

Meanwhile, they had made the best of the situation and turned their quarters into a forest colony that would enchant any normal boy. Their village architecture was more elaborate than any we had yet seen. In the Colonel's "dug out" a long table decked with lilacs and tulips was spread for tea. In other cheery catacombs we found neat rows of bunks, mess-tables, sizzling sauce-pans over kitchen-fires. Everywhere were endless ingenuities in the way of camp furniture and household decoration. Farther down the road a path between fir-boughs led to a hidden hospital, a marvel of underground compactness. While we chatted with the surgeon a soldier came in from the trenches: an elderly, bearded man, with a good average civilian face—the kind one runs against by hundreds in any French crowd. He had a scalp wound which had just been dressed, and was very pale. The Colonel stopped to ask a few questions, and then, turning to him, said: "Feeling rather better now?"

"Yes, sir."

"Good. In a day or two you'll be thinking about going back to the trenches, eh?"

"I'm going now, sir." It was said quite simply, and received in the same way. "Oh, all right," the Colonel merely rejoined; but he laid his hand on the man's shoulder as we went out.

Our next visit was to a sod-thatched hut, "At the sign of the Ambulant Artisans," where two or three soldiers were modelling and chiselling all kinds of trinkets from the aluminium of enemy shells.

19. "Long live America!"

One of the ambulant artisans was just finishing a ring with beautifully modelled Fauns' heads, another offered me a "Pickelhaube"[20] small enough for Mustard-seed's wear, but complete in every detail, and inlaid with the bronze eagle from an Imperial pfennig.[21] There are many such ringsmiths among the privates at the front, and the severe, somewhat archaic design of their rings is a proof of the sureness of French taste; but the two we visited happened to be Paris jewellers, for whom "artisan" was really too modest a pseudonym. Officers and men were evidently proud of their work, and as they stood hammering away in their cramped smithy, a red gleam lighting up the intentness of their faces, they seemed to be beating out the cheerful rhythm of "I too will something make, and joy in the making."

Up the hillside, in deeper shadow, was another little structure; a wooden shed with an open gable sheltering an altar with candles and flowers. Here mass is said by one of the conscript priests of the regiment, while his congregation kneel between the fir-trunks, giving life to the old metaphor of the cathedral-forest. Nearby was the grave-yard, where day by day these quiet elderly men lay their comrades, the *pères de famille*[22] who don't go back. The care of this woodland cemetery is left entirely to the soldiers, and they have spent treasures of piety on the inscriptions and decorations of the graves. Fresh flowers are brought up from the valleys to cover them, and when some favourite comrade goes, the men, scorning ephemeral tributes, club together to buy a monstrous indestructible wreath with emblazoned streamers. It was near the end of the afternoon, and many soldiers were strolling along the paths between the graves. "It's their favourite walk at this hour," the Colonel said. He stopped to look down on a grave mothered in beady tokens, the grave of the last pal to fall. "He was mentioned in the Order of the Day," the Colonel explained; and the group of soldiers standing near looked at us proudly, as if sharing their comrade's honour, and wanting to be sure that we understood the reason of their pride ...

"And now," said our Captain of Chasseurs, "that you've seen the second-line trenches, what do you say to taking a look at the first?"

---

20. A spiked helmet worn by German soldiers in the early years of the war
21. German coin
22. "Fathers of the family"

We followed him to a point higher up the hill, where we plunged into a deep ditch of red earth—the "bowel" leading to the first lines. It climbed still higher, under the wet firs, and then, turning, dipped over the edge and began to wind in sharp loops down the other side of the ridge. Down we scrambled, single file, our chins on a level with the top of the passage, the close green covert above us. The "bowel" went twisting down more and more sharply into a deep ravine; and presently, at a bend, we came to a fir-thatched outlook, where a soldier stood with his back to us, his eye glued to a peep-hole in the wattled[23] wall. Another turn, and another outlook; but here it was the iron-rimmed eye of the mitraille-use that stared across the ravine. By this time we were within a hundred yards or so of the German lines, hidden, like ours, on the other side of the narrowing hollow; and as we stole down and down, the hush and secrecy of the scene, and the sense of that imminent lurking hatred only a few branch-lengths away, seemed to fill the silence with mysterious pulsations. Suddenly a sharp noise broke on them: the rap of a rifle-shot against a tree-trunk a few yards ahead.

"Ah, the sharp-shooter," said our guide. "No more talking, please—he's over there, in a tree somewhere, and whenever he hears voices he fires. Some day we shall spot his tree."

We went on in silence to a point where a few soldiers were sitting on a ledge of rock in a widening of the "bowel." They looked as quiet as if they had been waiting for their bocks[24] before a Boulevard café. "Not beyond, please," said the officer, holding me back; and I stopped.

Here we were, then, actually and literally in the first lines! The knowledge made one's heart tick a little; but, except for another shot or two from our arboreal listener, and the motionless intentness of the soldier's back at the peep-hole, there was nothing to show that we were not a dozen miles away.

Perhaps the thought occurred to our Captain of Chasseurs; for just as I was turning back he said with his friendliest twinkle: "Do you want awfully to go a little farther? Well, then, come on."

We went past the soldiers sitting on the ledge and stole down and down, to where the trees ended at the bottom of the ravine.

23. A wall made of intertwined sticks
24. Beers

The sharp-shooter had stopped firing, and nothing disturbed the leafy silence but an intermittent drip of rain. We were at the end of the burrow, and the Captain signed to me that I might take a cautious peep round its corner. I looked out and saw a strip of intensely green meadow just under me, and a wooded cliff rising abruptly on its other side. That was all. The wooded cliff swarmed with "them," and a few steps would have carried us across the interval; yet all about us was silence, and the peace of the forest. Again, for a minute, I had the sense of an all-pervading, invisible power of evil, a saturation of the whole landscape with some hidden vitriol of hate. Then the reaction of unbelief set in, and I felt myself in a harmless ordinary glen, like a million others on an untroubled earth. We turned and began to climb again, loop by loop, up the "bowel"—we passed the lolling soldiers, the silent mitrailleuse, we came again to the watcher at his peep-hole. He heard us, let the officer pass, and turned his head with a little sign of understanding.

"Do you want to look down?"

He moved a step away from his window. The look-out projected over the ravine, raking its depths; and here, with one's eye to the leaf-lashed hole, one saw at last ... saw, at the bottom of the harmless glen, half way between cliff and cliff, a grey uniform huddled in a dead heap. "He's been there for days: they can't fetch him away," said the watcher, reglueing his eye to the hole; and it was almost a relief to find it was after all a tangible enemy hidden over there across the meadow ...

The sun had set when we got back to our starting-point in the underground village. The chasseurs-à-pied were lounging along the roadside and standing in gossiping groups about the motor. It was long since they had seen faces from the other life, the life they had left nearly a year earlier and had not been allowed to go back to for a day; and under all their jokes and good-humour their farewell had a tinge of wistfulness. But one felt that this fugitive reminder of a world they had put behind them would pass like a dream, and their minds revert without effort to the one reality: the business of holding their bit of France.

It is hard to say why this sense of the French soldier's single-mindedness is so strong in all who have had even a glimpse of the front; perhaps it is gathered less from what the men say than from the look in their eyes. Even while they are accepting cigarettes and exchanging trench jokes, the look is there; and when one comes on them unaware it is there also. In the dusk of the forest that look followed us down the mountain; and as we skirted the edge of the ravine between the armies, we felt that on the far side of that dividing line were the men who had made the war, and on the near side the men who had been made by it.

Chapter 2

✦
✦
✦
✦

Reporting from France

By the summer of 1915, deep into the first year of the Great War, it had become apparent that the outcome of the conflict would have less to do with military victories than with a national test of endurance. The struggle of the civilian population to endure every blow of the war and to meet every additional sacrifice, hardship, and obligation, captured the attention of women journalists. Several of them visited France in the years before America entered the conflict to offer sobering accounts of what a nation at war had to suffer.

Madeleine Zabriskie Doty was so moved by her first impressions of France *in extremis*—cripples, widows, overflowing hospitals— that she volunteered temporarily as a nurse. "The heart and life of France is being crushed. It is impossible to see this and do nothing," she explained. The move allowed this *New York Tribune/Chicago Tribune* reporter to capture intimate cameos of wounded soldiers. From her encounters with soldiers and civilians, Doty drew a picture of a country that was "proud, suffering and resolute." But she couldn't resist ending on a cynical note, by describing a ceremony in which a hundred "legless, armless and blind men" assembled in a hospital courtyard to receive medals from a general, while proud, weeping relatives looked on.

When Mary Heaton Vorse arrived in Paris in May 1915 she was shocked by the civilian victims of war, *les sinistrées*, those displaced by the German invasion. Some resided now in German-occupied territory; many others had been scattered across France. They had lost their communities, homes, and possessions and been separated from loved ones. A vast bureau sprang up in Paris that attempted to gather news of the dispossessed and answer thousands of queries from people trying to locate and learn the fate of their relatives.

At a time when correspondents were given only short-duration, escorted visits to the war zone, Vorse got French permission to travel on her own to three towns near the front lines. There she encountered "pitiful bands of homeless people wandering about the roads of France" and the makeshift efforts to support them. In her article "The Sinistrées of France," Vorse chronicled her "strange and heart-breaking" excursion into the devastated regions to tell the story of these civilian victims of war and the inspiring women of France who shouldered the burdens of sustaining civilization.

In the second year of the war, when it became clear that the war would not end quickly—as some had predicted—France eased its restrictions on journalists. To win the sympathies of neutral nations, particularly the United States, France began to offer packaged war tours to reporters and VIP opinion-makers. Two locations high on the list of visited sites to give reporters a taste of the war: Reims Cathedral and the Marne Battlefield. The fourteenth-century cathedral at Reims had been damaged by German shelling early in the war, and the French liked to show visitors how Germany made war on the world's cultural treasures.

The Marne battlefield ranked number one for war tours. One month into the war, French and British forces successfully halted the German invasion at the Battle of the Marne, within miles of Paris. The iconic battle became emblematic of French spirit and hope. Reporters could visit that site, see trenches, graves, and the scarred landscape, and then write about their first-hand glimpse of the war. As part of her coverage of England and France for the *Brooklyn Daily Eagle*, Jessica Lozier Payne visited the Marne battlefield in the fall of 1916. Her brief article reads a bit like a travel itinerary: the grave-dotted battlefield, a ruined town and church, a glimpse of German prisoners of war, and the opportunity to walk in the abandoned trenches.

Maude Radford Warren's article, "Madame, C'est la Guerre!" that appeared only two months after America entered the conflict, took a more light-hearted look at French war sacrifice. In the excerpt included here, she describes how every hardship and sacrifice, from food shortages, to the high cost of living, even personal loss, are likely to be accepted with a shrug of the shoulders as the unavoidable cost of the war.

Madeleine Zabriskie Doty (1877–1963)

In the hospital the truth is spoken. No soldier wants to go back to battle. Yet he goes and every man in France goes willingly. What else is there to do? The enemy is in the land and must be driven out.

"War Cripples"
Madeleine Z. Doty
The New Republic, November 13, 1915

It was late evening when I reached Paris. There was not a ray of light in the street when I stepped from the cab to my lodging place; in that one glance I knew Paris was no longer Paris. The next day I began to explore. The Opera House sparkled in the sunshine, the driver's whip snapped; the streets were crowded, but a shadow lay across the city. Sorrowing black-clad people filled the streets. I saw that practically every woman was in mourning. And the men, where were they? Grey-haired men drove cabs, white-haired, bent shouldered waiters served drinks; but straight, upstanding young men there were none. A one-legged Turk, scarcely more than a boy, went hustling by on crutches with an empty red trouser-leg flapping aimlessly. Paris is full of cripples. Legless, armless, blind men, all young, passed in a steady stream. Every able-bodied man in France under forty-eight has gone to war. Cripples, widows and ambulances, these are the dominant notes. Unceasingly grey auto-ambulances emblazoned with red crosses dash by, bearing their burdens to hospitals all over Paris.

France says little and does much. She is proud; she is heroic; she fights on. But the heart and life of France is being crushed. It is impossible to see this and do nothing. I offer my services as assistant nurse at the American ambulance[1] and am accepted. At eight every morning a hospital car takes me to the American ambulance where I work until six. It is a busy life. At first I turn in horror from those swollen, red, raw, pus-flowing wounds, occupying the place of an arm or leg or a portion of a face. But in twenty-four hours I am dressing these wounds, self-forgotten. It is good to be working instead of waiting—waiting for unknown horrors. But when a man's wound heals and his strength returns I rebel at sending him back to battle. Is the labor all to be lost? Faster than women can save, men go out and kill. Fortunately or unfortunately, not many men leave the ambulance for the front. Generally they have been too terribly wounded. They come to us with the jaw and lower face blown away or a lung ripped. But science is marvelous. Ribs are cut from the patient and new jaws made, arms, legs and eyes amputated and artificial ones substituted. The ambulance loses by death but six per cent of its cases, yet only one in ten of the men in my ward will be able to return to the front. This accounts for the endless procession of cripples.

On the second morning as I hurry down a long hospital corridor I see a familiar face. A short, dark-haired, dark-eyed young man is coming toward me. He is one of the wounded and his right arm is gone. His eye catches mine. He stops bewildered. Then comes recognition. It is Zeni Peshkoff—Maxime Gorki's[2] adopted son. Eight years ago when this man was a boy I had known him in America. I grasp the left hand and my eyes drop before the empty right sleeve. But Zeni Peshkoff is still gay, laughing Zeni. He makes light of his trouble. Not until later do I understand the terrible suffering there is from the missing arm or realize how he struggles to use that which is not. Peshkoff had been in the trenches for months. He had been through battles and bayonet charges and escaped unhurt, but at last his day came. A bursting shell destroyed the right arm. He knew the danger, and struggling to his feet, walked from the battlefield. With the left hand he supported the bleeding, broken right arm. As he stumbled back past trenches full of German prisoners his plight was so pitiful, his pluck so great, that instinctively these men saluted. At the Place de

1. War hospitals in France were called ambulances.
2. A popular Russian writer

Lawyer Madeleine Zabriskie Doty made three trips to warring Europe to report for various newspapers and magazines. *Source:* Madeleine Z. Doty Papers, Sophia Smith Collection, Smith College (Northampton, Massachusetts).

Secours[3] eight hundred wounded had been brought in. There were accommodations for one hundred and fifty.

All night young Peshkoff lay unattended, for there were others worse hurt. Gangrene developed, and he watched it spread from fingers to hand and from hand to arm. In the morning a friendly lieutenant noticed him. "There's one chance," he said, "and that's

3. Emergency care station

a hospital. If you can walk, come with me." Slowly young Peshkoff arose. Half fainting he dressed and went with the lieutenant—first by taxi to the train and then twelve torturing hours to Paris. As the hours passed the gangrene crept higher and higher. The sick man grew giddy with fever. At each station his carriage companions, fearing death, wished to leave him upon the platform. But the lieutenant was firm. The one chance for life was the hospital. Finally Paris was reached; a waiting ambulance rushed him to the hospital. Immediately he was taken to the operating room and the arm amputated. A half hour more and his life could not have been saved. But this dramatic incident is only one of many. The pluck of the average soldier is unbelievable. Operations are accepted without question. There are no protests—only the murmured "C'est la guerre, que voulez-vous?"[4]

The wounded do not like to talk war. Their experiences have been too terrible. They try to forget. War is no longer a series of gallant deeds, it is a matter of bursting shells. One man with leg blown off had never even seen the enemy. Bayonet charges after months of waiting are almost a relief. But a normal man does not enjoy running his bayonet into his fellow-man. It can be done only under intense excitement. Self-defense and stimulants are the aids.

Only one soldier spoke with gusto of the Germans he had killed. This man had had his lower face shot away. A wounded German lying on the ground had risen on his elbow and shot him. "Then," said the Frenchman, "I took my bayonet and ran him clear through." He said: "Ugh, I ran him through again and he was dead." To most men those bayonet charges are like mad dreams.

I asked Zeni Peshkoff, socialist, what his sensations were when he went out to kill. "It didn't seem real, it doesn't now. Before my last charge the lieutenant and I were filled with the beauty of the night. We sat gazing at the stars. Then the command came and we rushed forward. It did not seem possible I was killing human beings." It is this unreality that sustains men. Germans are not human beings—only the enemy. For the wounded French soldier will tell you he loathes war and longs for peace. He fights for one object—a permanent peace. He fights to save his children from fighting.

---

4. "It's war, what do you want?"

"Have you any children?" I asked one soldier. "No, thank God," is the reply. "But why?" "Because," comes the fierce answer, "if I had a son I would rather he deserted than see what I have seen." This man is not unusual. The soldiers—not the women—are beginning to say: "We will have no more children unless there is no more war."

In the hospital the truth is spoken. No soldier wants to go back to battle. Yet he goes and every man in France goes willingly. What else is there to do? The enemy is in the land and must be driven out. It may be the Frenchman will smash himself and his house, but as he says, with a significant shrug: "C'est la guerre, que voulez-vous?" How often that phrase struck my ears. In the operating room, at the death-bed, in the presence of hundreds of little white crosses on a bloody battlefield, wearily, cynically, despairingly, I hear the voice of the soldier proclaiming: "C'est la guerre, que voulez-vous?"

Yet out of the suffering of war has come gentleness. Ready hands help one another. Strangers talk in the street. Wherever I go my little red cross sign of the hospital wins favor. A torn skirt is humbly mended on bended knees, and when I offer a fee the money is pushed back into my hands with the words: "Pour les blessés."[5] This is the language of the women—"pour les blessés." No service is too great for the wounded. Weeping women stop to tell each other their stories. Vainly I search for signs of heartlessness or gayety. The Montmartre district is closed. The paint is peeling from the front of the Moulin Rouge, and the theatre door sags on its hinges. The Folies Bergéres[6] was open and I went there. But it was a dreary performance—no lightness, no gay little jokes, no evening dresses. Even the street women wore black and plied their trade cheerlessly. I remember the conversation of my neighbors in a restaurant. Unknown woman to soldier home on leave: "Can't you stay over this evening?" Soldier: "No." Woman: "I don't want any money; I want to be with you and talk." Soldier: "Why?" Woman: "Paris is so boring; there are no men."

It is a curious anomaly that in all Paris there is no "peace movement," yet there is nowhere else one can talk peace. The soldiers in the hospital listen eagerly to my tales of the social democrats in Germany. I suggest internal revolution rather than smashing

5. "For the wounded."
6. A popular cabaret music hall

by an outside force as a way of ending war and militarism. To this they agree. But how [to] reach the social democrats and start revolution? That is the problem. To negotiate with the German government they believe impossible. The government is not to be trusted. It would lie and there would be another war. Germany must be defeated because that will defeat militarism, end war, and bring permanent peace. Germany bitter, relentless, ugly and at bay; France tragic, proud, suffering and resolute; England annoyed, reluctant, capable and sure; and all determined to fight the thing through to a finish. Is there a way out? When will it end? "I don't know when the war will end," says a soldier, "but I know where it will end—in the trenches." More and more it grows clear that the test is to be endurance, not victories.

One day I visited the battlefield of the Marne. This is twenty miles or more from the front. Yet at Marne new trenches are being dug. France is covered with trenches; as my train sped to Boulogne soldiers were building them to the railroad track. From day to day as battle rages a trench may be taken. But how can either side beat back over miles and miles of trenches? Meanwhile human life ebbs out. The fields of Marne are one vast cemetery. The land is dotted with little white crosses. Yet from this land the peasant gathers his crop. Never has the ground been more fertile. With a crack of his whip the driver points to a great open meadow. "There," he says, "four thousand Germans were burned to death, and to-day we are gathering the biggest hay crop the land has known."

On one of my last days in Paris I went to the Invalides.[7] Some wounded soldiers were being decorated. The place was packed. Weeping relatives came to honor their brave men. A mother with a baby stands beside me. Tears are on her cheeks, but pride shines in her eyes as a blind husband is led to his place. Then a band strikes up, and out across the courtyard move a hundred legless, armless and blind men. The Commander-in-Chief is bestowing kisses and pinning on medals. I shut my eyes. I see France as she will be in a few years—swarming with cripples. I see young men made old and helpless, sitting in chimney corners, silently fingering medals.

----

7. A complex of buildings and monuments, including a hospital, related to the military history of France

Jessica Lozier Payne (1870–1951)

"I climbed down into them and walked along in the slippery mud, for I wanted the experience of being in a real trench."

"Soldiers' Graves Dot Farms on Marne Battlefield"
Jessica Lozier Payne
Brooklyn Daily Eagle, November 14, 1916

It was a day late in September and a soft misty rain was falling when I took the train from Paris to Meaux to visit the battlefield of the Marne and to note how the scars of battle were being effaced from a countryside where less than two years before there had been fought one of the most hotly disputed and bloodiest battles of the war. For this was the high water mark of the German invasion. It was to this place on the River Marne that Gallieni[8] rushed his troops from Paris by rail, on foot, in taxicabs, omnibuses, motor lines, private automobiles and carriages to stem the advancing tide of German soldiers before they could get within striking distance of Paris.

The twenty-eight mile run took about an hour from Paris, and it did not need much of an effort of the imagination to again people the long straight roads with a hurrying throng of soldiers in every conceivable type of vehicle, rushing with stern faces and grim determination to turn the enemy who had almost reached the gates of Paris. As we drew into the station I smiled at the recollection of the struggles of the English Tommies to pronounce the name Meaux; they called it "Mee-yow"—like a cat—just as they stumbled over Vielle Chapelle, which they called "Veal Chapel," and Ypres, which they pronounced "Wipers."

A military pass is necessary in order to go out to the battlefield, but this had been duly obtained in Paris, by the foreign correspondent of The Eagle, with whom I made the trip, and bore on the front cover a duplicate of the photograph that was on my passport.

The straight French road, with its occasional rows of poplars, ran through fields that had just been harvested—they were dotted like a golf course with small tri-colored flags, each denoting a

8. French general Joseph Gallieni

soldier's grave, sometimes several soldiers in one grave, forty-three in one place. At the head of the grave a white cross bearing the name of the soldier and his regimental number, and back of it the flag. There must have been thousands of them, and many Germans buried there, too; their graves marked with a black square on an upright, and labelled with their marks of identity. They were buried as they fell, and you could visualize the attack and repulse, by following the advancing line of German graves until it is met by a group of French graves and the two rows lie facing each other—peacefully enough now.

I noticed a corked bottle containing a card tied on many of the French crosses, and I was deeply touched on reading one to find it was the prayer of a French mother to any French soldier to give her news of her son, who is missing and whom she believed to have been killed at the Battle of the Marne.

Farmers have respected these graves, each with its little barbed wire fence, and have ploughed and planted and have harvested around them—but perhaps in a few years they will be obliterated unless the war ends and the French Government can remove the bones to Paris and give them dignified sepulture. Nature heals more quickly than man—already the torn battle fields ploughed with shot and shell have yielded a bountiful harvest, but for what man has sowed of his kind there will be no fruition on earth.

The little villages still bear the scars of war, their walled buildings were deeply pitted by shells and the roofs tell the tale of recent reparation by patches of fresh terra-cotta tiles, or still have gaping holes.

Barcy, with its ancient church seems to have been the center of some special conflict. The churches were always made the first point of attack by the machine guns of the enemy, since there was danger that the belfries would serve as observation towers for the villagers, who could thus give warning of their approach.

The church at Barcy is a complete ruin; a shell squarely hit the belfry and dislodged the bell, and the clock fell crashing through the tower to the pavement below. The beautiful bronze bell lies there unhurt, but the clock is a jangled mass of rusting springs and wheels.

The high altar is a wreck, and through the bare rafters one can see the sky. As I turned from the ruined church I looked down the ancient cobbled street, with its gray houses of stone and cement, and saw a pastoral scene—a flock of sheep on its homeward way, followed by an ancient shepherdess, in weather bleached cape, and accompanied by her well trained, faithful dog.

Our driver was filled with the true dramatic instinct, and, leaning back from his high seat, he asked in mysterious tones if we desired to see "les Boches." Assenting, we dismounted, and to his repeated "doucement,"[9] we crept like conspirators to a small stone house with padlocked doors, and through the window we saw three German prisoners quite cheerfully and peacefully repairing some chairs.

After this thrilling spectacle we went to see the trenches. I had always imagined trenches to be ditches dug in [a] straight line. I was astounded to find them a maze of zig zags not more than eight or ten feet without a sharp bend or turn. The driver said they were built that way so no machine gun getting the range could make a clean sweep of the trench.

I climbed down into them and walked along in the slippery mud, for I wanted the experience of being in a real trench. They were about seven feet deep and four feet wide; their sides were protected from caving in by roughly woven willow withes like coarse basket work; and on the side facing the enemy there ran a ledge about a foot high on which the soldier could stand to fire.

As we drove back through the flag-studded fields to the train I realized we were looking in the graves of men who had really saved France, and from every mound came the sentiment:

"Mon corps a la terre,
Mon ame a Dieu,
Mon coeur a la France."[10]

Mary Heaton Vorse (1874–1966)

War, which had welded the men of the country into an engine of destruction, had sent its women forth on countless works of mercy and reconstruction, and this work I had come to France to witness.

9. Slowly
10. My body to the earth, My soul to God, My heart to France.

"The Sinistrées of France"
Mary Heaton Vorse
The Century Magazine, January 1917

It is a smiling, fruitful country over the surface of which graves are everywhere scattered,—men died fast along this country lane,—in the grain are crosses, in the dooryards of what once were peasants' houses are more crosses. Here and there in the pleasant wood trees have been mown down as by a scythe, and when the road leads to a town, heaps of brick, tortured ironwork, and shapeless mounds of stone confront one, and in strange contrast to the general desolation, scattered seemingly at random, are occasional wooden houses, temporary dwellings which the English Quakers in cooperation with the French Government have been building in what is aptly named "the devastated areas."

In these districts, over which the full fury of war passed, they will tell one, as they do in Paris, that "things are more normal now." In these areas of destroyed towns and grave-strewn fields live the *sinistrées,* a sinister name for those war victims. These, again, are divided into three classes: the refugees, the burned, and the pillaged.

It is strange and terrible to visit Paris,—and no one can be happy,—but to one who has loved France it is far worse to visit the lovely Northern country. There is here a sense of emptiness, as if terror still hushed the normal cheerful noises of mankind. The people of these regions have lost everything: their houses are burned; their animals, even the rabbits, are gone; their farm implements are shapeless pieces of grotesquely melted iron. They live in temporary, patched shelters and in the houses built by the Society of Friends,[11] or mass themselves in some nearby village that escaped destruction at the hands of the crown prince's retreating army.[12] After a time in this silent country one gets the sense that destruction is normal, and tears start to one's eyes at the sight of an undestroyed French village smiling in the sun. So changed are all values that I could feel nothing strange in the words of the woman who told me, "Fortunately, my husband is a hunchback."

11. The pacifist Quakers were conscientious objectors during WWI. However, they were very active in non-combatant roles, such as ambulance drivers, medical care, and building temporary housing.
12. German Crown Prince Wilhelm commanded the 5th Army during the opening hostilities on the Western Front.

Mary Heaton Vorse as she appeared in 1915 when traveling to the Women's Peace Congress. A suffragist and labor journalist, Vorse wrote about the refugees of France and the efforts to support them. *Source:* George Grantham Bain Collection, Prints and Photographs Division, Library of Congress, LC-B2- 3443-11.

Then through the empty country-side come a few soldiers, or a band of wounded men stagger and grope their way on their first walk forth from the hospital gates; and the thought comes to one that in the world there are always devastated areas and men wounded in battle.

It is in the devastated areas, from the *sinistrées* themselves, that one will learn how simple women feel toward war. It is there one will hear more fully expressed the thought that I had already heard in different languages and in different countries.

"We do not live in the world in which we believed that we were living. None of us thought that it could happen to us, in our time, to the lands we knew, to our husbands and our sons. No one could believe that the world was like this and continue to bear children. And all the time, like some hideous growing plant, war was preparing; it was there waiting for us a few years away, a few months away, a few days away, and no woman believed it could be.

"Then came the horror that we refused to believe in: war came."

War held up a hand and said, "Stop!" Civilization stood still. Suddenly men and women went separate ways; common life was cleft in two by war.

When war called all the able-bodied men to the blood-stained ditches and burrows that rend France from the channel to Alsace and gave the command, "Destroy!" it also said to the women: "Go your fruitful way, bear more children, bind up your men's wounds, bind up the wounds of the country. See, beside your own work of children and home, I give into your hands the families of a million refugees. Bind up the wounds of their spirits, put hope into the hearts of the old, save the lives of the little children, put together those countless families that have been torn apart; then the work that your man has left I give to you to do, and later I may come and destroy the fruitful fields you have planted, and in a day undo the work of careful centuries. I will kill your men and your old people and little children, and when I have done this, you must again rise up and again bear children and again repair the ruin I have wrought."

A well-known writer[13] who has had unusual opportunities for observation has searched almost in vain among the wounded and among those men who have suffered most in war for men who hated it, and has found discouragingly few. Had the search been among women, he would have had a different story.

The simple man accepts war as he accepts birth and death. It does not show its face to him as a monstrous and bleeding horror. Among the many wounded men I talked with, the emotion I found often was a naive self-congratulation that they had been through so much. They, too, when they were old, could tell of their adventures in the great war.

No woman in France could speak this way, but the women of the devastated districts, educated or simple, have a special

13. The reference here may be to the English writer Rudyard Kipling, who was a staunch supporter of the British and French war efforts. His book *France at War: On the Frontier of Civilization*, appeared in 1915.

loathing of war and a bitter and intelligent hatred of the conditions which make war possible. As they talk about it, one feels that there has surged into their fruitful, painstaking lives a hideous monster having no connection with the civilization of which they were a part, a terrible and indecent anachronism, as though from some hidden place of slimy ooze some primeval creature had reared its head and come forth to ravage a country-side.

It is in the quiet of the devastated areas, where from one week's end to another you will see no young man, that you will find the sharpest contrasts between women's and men's parts of the world's work in war-time. In the foremost ranks of what one might call mobilized women have been the schoolmistresses. In one little village, which is recorded as totally destroyed, one house has been rebuilt. This one house serves as school-house and *mairie*.[14] The schoolmistress was a youngish woman, frail and delicate, with lines of sorrow and overwork on her intelligent face. She and an assistant teacher instructed eighty children. It was her energy and resourcefulness that caused the reconstruction of this one house.

She also acts as mayor of the village. The mayor himself is of course mobilized; so is the cure. This means that she takes upon herself much of the relief work that the cure would naturally have performed. The acting mayor is an old man who comes from a village at some distance as infrequently as possible, only to sign the papers necessary for giving receipts for money from the Government, etc.; for the French Government gives to all *sinistrées* twenty-five cents a day for every grown person and ten cents for all children under sixteen years of age. The distribution of this fund, as well as the private charities, falls, therefore, into her hands. She sat there in her little office and talked about the various sides of her work, and said in a tone of apology:

"You see, there is really more to do than I can do well. There are eighty children to care for, and their families, and I have an immense correspondence." She motioned to some vast portfolios. "Two thousand French soldiers fell on the battle-field over there,"—she nodded out of the open window,—"and I am of course still answering the inquiries of their families."

She was of course still answering the inquiries of their families, and she was of course teaching eighty children; she was of course

14. Town hall

doing all manner of relief work; she was of course giving all sorts of comfort and kindness, making a circle of light in the desolation in which she lived. And as I looked at her, I realized that there were hundreds of women like her who were of course doing the same thing through all the vast, desolated country of the north of France, merely standing by their posts as the telephone and telegraph girls had done during the invasion, unwitting heroines performing their tasks of incredible difficulty. This woman did not mention that she was merely doing her duty; there comes a pressure in human affairs where one ceases to think in terms of duty for one's self, where one works to the limit of endurance and then beyond that limit.

During the war there have been thrown to the surface extraordinary women like the "Mayor of Soissons," but even more characteristic of the spirit of the people are the unusual qualities that have been called up in those who are merely the nation's ordinary women.

I looked out of the window. Here indeed was the biblical word fulfilled, "There shall not be left one stone upon another." What had been an orderly and sweet French village was a nameless heap of stones and rubble, only rearing their heads, gaunt and fireless amid the general destruction, were the chimneys and the hearthstones, as though the *foyer*, the hearth, of France, refused to be destroyed. Pompeii, beside it, was habitable. It looked as if some great natural calamity, known as an act of God, had passed over it. So it seemed.

Then came to me the intolerable thought, Man did this thing. No incredible cataclysm of nature, but man, more relentless than the sea in his hideous self-destruction.

I looked from this work of man to the toil-burdened schoolmistress who in the midst of this desolation had assembled her children together, and contrasted her work with that for which the men of Europe had been preparing, and one nation so supremely well and with such loving care. The careful Germans had brought with them petroleum cans, solid and German, with which to burn the villages through which they passed. An old man, standing in his flowering garden, showed me a can that had escaped in the general conflagration; he called it his "little souvenir which the Prussians had left him." They even brought with them paraffin with which to burn the manure heaps, so that, in case they should not hold the land, the civil population might suffer to the utmost, as they have indeed suffered, but with what unshakable gallantry it is impossible to express.

This unquenchable spirit was forever being interpreted to me by some person like an old woman whom I found working in her flower garden. No dwelling of man was now near that garden, only the shapeless ruins of what had once been houses. All about was the quiet of the country and fields, fields studded with graves—graves and ruins, and there was that garden, bright with peonies and other flowering things, and the old woman working it. She looked up from her weeding to offer me flowers.

"Of course my garden is not what it may be another year," she told me, "for I have walked eight miles to get here, and I cannot always come; but I cannot bear the thought of losing them altogether. Flowers, you know, require cultivation."

This blooming garden in the midst of the unspeakable desolation of a ruined village was a part of this old woman's contribution toward reestablishing order. Whether there has been war or not, the education of the little children must go on, and flower gardens must go on, and all the blooming, graceful things of French life must go on, as much as they can.

Among all the *sinistrées*, only once did I come across the suggestion from any woman that there was no use in going on. This woman had lost all her sons in battle, and her husband had been ill all the winter as the result of exposure. She sat with hands folded in her lap; when a woman from the Society of Friends asked her if she did not wish to put in an application for a temporary house, she said:

"There is no use in it for us."

Her husband, beaten by illness and the loss of his sons, sat there as though still stunned by the immensity of his misfortunes. These two people were so apathetic, so detached from life, that they seemed to be only waiting for death; and it came to me that they were the first I had seen whom the Germans had beaten. But I had reckoned without their eight-year-old daughter Rose.

"Madame," she said as we were leaving, "they want this house." She came forward, her face flushed. She stood there before us, her little head erect, her eyes shining, the embodiment of the courage of the women of France. "I will go with you," she said, "to the *mairie*, and we will put in our application."

She knew what she wanted; she knew the cost of the house; she knew the business details connected with it. "For I can read," she said; "I have been reading about these houses upon the posters."

She had sat there amidst her mother's tears, her father's dumb despair; she had watched them relax their hold on life, and, baby though she was, there had come into her heart the resolve of a woman: she would have their little house; she would reestablish their family.

And now, at this writing, Rose's house will already have been built, and her parents will again be re-awakening to life. For such a heroic child they can do nothing else.

I left the country of the *sinistrées* with the words of a friend of mine echoing in my heart:

"I have seen so much beauty, so much mutual aid, so much self-sacrifice since the beginning of this war that I can never distrust human nature again."

But above this thought is another one. Must heroic and great qualities of men and women be organized forever only for war and for repairing the destruction that war causes?

There is an office through which passes a procession of dark-clothed men and women, where all day long the words, "We regret there is as yet no news," are heard. Once this had been a language school; to-day it houses the Bureau de Renseignements pour les Familles Dispersees.[15] This is one of the thousands of familiar places in Paris that war has changed to its uses.

The red cross floats over the place where there had been a club for girl students; a favorite restaurant houses a workshop. The reception-rooms of hotels are turned into *vestiaires;*[16] schools house the most miserable of all *sinistrées*, the refugees. The altered use of public and private buildings is the outward sign which tells you that all through France the thought of anything except war has ceased. Life in its ordinary course has ceased. People get up and go to bed, pursue their various businesses, as in a vacuum. The ordinary business of life has no longer any meaning; nothing

15. Office of Information for Dispersed Families
16. Locker rooms

has meaning except that unnatural and ghastly work of killing; nothing counts that is not connected with this work of destruction. The complete spiritual isolation of a whole nation from all subjects that do not concern killing and being killed, or the contemplation of the destruction attendant on war, is another of war's least negligible by-products.

In the strange and nightmare country of the trenches where the men of France live, the real lives of the women of France are passed.

There is not a single little family on the remote border of France whose eyes are not fixed on that long, narrow strip of blood-stained country, that tormented and tortured country of barb-wire, of mitrailleuses, of shell, of great guns and trenches. The state of soul of a nation which has subordinated the fruitful industries of life to the subject of killing and being killed is a strange thing. The spirit of a nation which sees its young manhood and its youth surge up to the country of death and then ebb back wounded and dead is strange and grave; so strange and so grave that, if you had lived there before, the unfamiliarity of its familiar aspect is a terrifying thing.

As I went about among my friends, I became aware of the overpowering sense of something that was almost more poignant than grief; a nerve-racking spiritual discomfort overwhelmed me, outsider though I was; and presently the meaning of this discomfort translated itself into words: suspense was what brooded over all the men and women whom I met. They were waiting; they gave the effect of a whole nation listening to invisible voices; and while the surface of conversation was as normal as it could be, since it dealt with such abnormal things as war and the lamentable by-products of war, they were all of them waiting, waiting, for news from the front, waiting to learn if sons and husbands were still alive, waiting for the end of the war.

Suspense was everywhere, but it brooded more closely in that office where once people went to learn languages and where they now go to wait for tidings of their mothers, of their children, lost years ago, in the time when the German army overran France and created the army of the *sinistrées*.

In the vast confusion that occurred when the German army swept down upon Paris—a confusion which affected a civil

A refugee family in France, fleeing an area devastated by the fighting. *Source:* American National Red Cross photograph collection, Prints and Photographs Division, Library of Congress, LC-DIG-anrc-06249.

population of millions of people, members of families lost one another. In the vast card-catalogues of the Bureau de Renseignement les Familles Dispersees is concentrated the suspense and anguish of a nation.

Of this vast suspense, this anguished searching of mothers for children, of daughters for mothers, of fathers, of sons for all their families, nothing is heard in the outside world. This calamity of the tearing asunder of thousands upon thousands of families, which, had it come at another time, as the result of some cataclysm of nature, would have caused the pity of the whole civilized world to stream forth, is now only a little incident for the world at large, an incident for everyone except those concerned in its hideous tragedy.

There are many little children in France, tiny youngsters, babies so young that they cannot speak, who have strayed on the roads, and of whose parents no trace has yet been heard. The newspapers in France also contain advertisements of fathers searching for their children, and wives for their husbands, and soldiers for their families.

So to-day when I think of France, I cannot think merely in the terms of a country invaded. Another great, shadowy army fills my mind—the army of mothers searching for their children, of daughters searching for their old parents, waiting day by day for news of those whom they love, wondering among what strangers they are living, and then, perhaps mercifully and perhaps sadly, after months, again united. My mind reverts to this group of women searching continuously for the lost, and helping to reunite the members of those families.

War, which had welded the men of the country into an engine of destruction, had sent its women forth on countless works of mercy and reconstruction, and this work I had come to France to witness. As I went about on this strange and heartbreaking sight-seeing, as I visited barracks in which not wounded soldiers, but wounded families, lived and ate, saw workshops, hospitals, there came to me a vision of what a total disorganization war meant to the civil population.

Day by day among the *sinistrées* I heard stories of flight from burning villages, until such a flight seemed a usual experience. I heard tales of lost relatives. I saw families cut in half by war. I saw women searching for old mothers. I saw refugees who had lost little children. I listened to the dreadful prattle of children who talked of killing. I saw listless, sad-eyed young girls who had witnessed the death of all dear to them. I saw women sitting with folded hands, their means of livelihood gone, their husbands gone, their reason for living gone.

I saw little children below the age of speech, who had been found wandering on the roads by soldiers, and two Belgian children who had been found in the very trenches where they had fled terrified during the bombardment. No one can ever know who they are; their mothers will never see them again.

I saw women, in deepest grief over the loss of their sons, stay by their posts unflinching, never stopping in their work, and everywhere I saw beauty and un-quenchable courage, even though many walked with the weary air of those whose illusions have been killed and with them their inner reason for living. High and low worked with the desperate activity of ants whose ant-hill had been stepped on. I looked and listened until I was drowned by what I saw, until I could see no more and hear no more.

And as I saw these things, all the vast, restless stirring of women, which, when it is self-conscious, we call feminism, seemed to me to have supremely gained in significance; it seemed that its very roots lay in women's age-old mute protest against war.

I had, in the weeks that preceded my journey into France, heard a great deal of talk concerning the basic racial and economic causes of war. Here is the contribution to these reasons of a very simple woman, and it seems to me that in it there is a very profound truth.

The name of this woman is Mme. Etienne, and she was once my concierge. I always go to see her when I am in Paris, for I love her homely wit and her gaiety. Her three boys had been almost young men when I had last seen her, and I wondered if she had joined the women in mourning. She met me dry-eyed. She seemed, indeed, as if turned to stone, for she told me in a hard and steady voice:

"They are all dead, all. All three died within six weeks. Since then I have read no papers. There is no victory for me. There can be no victory for those whose sons are dead."

From the streets came the sound of singing, cabs rattled by decorated with Italian flags. War had called to something deep in the hearts of these men, and found there a response. We watched them in silence a moment. Then Mme. Etienne stretched out her hand toward them and cried:

"As long as men love war like that, there will be war, and when they hate it as we hate it, there will be no more war."

And at her words the oppression that had followed me since the beginning of the war found its meaning. She had said the thing that I had seen since I had realized to the full the terrific cleavage war had brought between men's affairs and our affairs, but had not wished to put into words.

Since the war, even the men at home had turned to me the faces of strangers. They thought negligible what women thought important. The things we asked one another as we talked about the war held no interest for them. The sense of men's strangeness has bred a fear in me that had no name and no face. Now at last I saw the reason with terrible clearness.

Now I knew why even the men of my own country had seemed so alien to me, and the reason is that the difference between men and women is the difference between birth and death. I had thought that the profound differences between men and women became trivial in the face of their still profounder similarity. But now it seems to me that our deepest experience is giving life and their intensest moment is when they are called on by war to go out and destroy the lives for which we have risked our own.

Man plays a very small part in the supreme adventure of birth. When a woman goes down to death to give life she goes alone. Man is nothing to her then. Her husband, the father of the child to be born, cannot share in her pain. Her intensest moment she lives by herself. The great miracle of birth is no concern of his, and he can only shrink back, a frightened witness, and wait and wait interminably and pray that all is well. The great experience for her, and for him only the permission to wait.

When men go out to fight they, too, go alone. We cannot go with them; we only wait while they risk their lives that other men may die. Men and women go alone to their supreme adventures.

Maude Radford Warren (1875–1934)

I requested a napkin. The waiter looked amused, shrugged his shoulders, thrust out his hands palms upward, and said:

"Ah, madame, c'est impossible: c'est la guerre!"

"Madame, C'est la Guerre!"
Maude Radford Warren
The Outlook, June 27, 1917

Happily, the expression *"C'est la Guerre!"* (It's war) does not invariably stand for horrors. In Paris it has its amusing side. Paris, the beautiful, is no longer gay. Some day it will come back into its heritage, for it ought to be the setting solely for joy; to all the world the very words Bois de Boulogne, Champs-Élysées, Tuileries, Rue de Rivoli, mean leisure, elegance and charm, sunshine and color. But to-day in all these places the chief notes of color are the horizon blue of the uniforms of the soldiers and the black of the long crape veils and dresses of women. Through the wide Paris streets and gardens pass too many soldiers with an arm or a leg gone (perhaps both); with eyes gone. They are brave. I saw two soldiers, one with a cork leg and one with a wooden leg, hobbling a race. and roaring with laughter when cork-leg won. But laughter is rare and smiles mean only courage and serenity, not joy.

So when the Parisian can say, lightly, "C'est la guerre," he likes to do it, especially to a stranger. Every time it was said to me it had some connection, superficial or vital, with the food question and the high cost of living, though in the beginning I did not perceive this. The first time it was said to me was the day after I reached Paris. I drifted into a little tea-shop with the idea one has that where there is the sign "English spoken" the tea will be unusually good. As per usual, the person who spoke English was out, and the tea was good. But there was no napkin and the wonderful French cakes were sticky. I requested a napkin. The waiter looked amused, shrugged his shoulders, thrust out his hands palms upward, and said:

"*Ah, madame, c'est impossible: c'est la guerre!*"

He spoke and looked over his smile with just the faintest touch of reproach, just enough to induce in me the remorseful thought that I wanted luxuries when there were soldiers in the trenches who did not have common comforts. I saw other people surreptitiously wiping their fingers on the table-cloth, looking dreamily the while across the room or else leaning forward chatting animatedly as if to disguise what they were doing, and so—.

That same evening I went to dine in a restaurant in the Rue Léopold Robert, famous the Latin Quarter over for the frescoes and pictures on the walls done by New York and Chicago artists, for a signed portrait of Victor Hugo, and for other unexpected pleasures. I sat down at a table from which four people had risen, and, my mind being on linen, noticed the good yeoman service the table-cloth had done. From all signs it had been used for luncheon as well as dinner. I dined, being joined by three strangers, who ate frugally and departed. At the cheese stage I felt eyes, and, looking up, saw four people waiting for my table. They were gazing hungrily right through me, just wanting my place, hypnotized by their own desire. Under that stare nothing but the laws of gravity could have kept me in my seat. I fled and let them sit down, standing by the kitchenette till my bill was made out. There was one illegible item for which I could not account—ten cents for what?

"What is this that I have eaten. Henriette?" I asked.

"Ah, madame, 'courrir'—chiefly for the table-cloth. The laundry assassinates me with the charges. *C'est la guerre!*"

I counted, say, eight people at the cloth for luncheon, and the twelve I had seen with my own eyes at dinner—two dollars. That diligent cloth paid for itself every day.

When I entered my hotel that night, I discovered that the ceiling light was none too bright and that there was no reading lamp. I rang for the *garçon* and ordered one. He said that he would speak *toute suite* to the housekeeper, who was now dining. I allowed her plenty of time to dine, and then went in search of her. She was all plump obligingness.

"But yes, madame; I will find a lamp for madame."

Madame thought it prudent to accompany her on the search, and was led to a closet, on the top shelf of which sat two lamps. The housekeeper greeted them with an exclamation of approval. I did not, for I saw that the connection of each was broken. She acted as if she had discovered this only when she took them down.

"Ah, unhappily they are broken! I am so sorry that madame cannot have a lamp."

"Get them mended," suggested madame.

"Ah, but impossible! C'est la—"

"Yes, I know, it's the war; but are there no electricians left in Paris?"

I gathered that they were all at the front except a few, who somehow could not repair lamps because it was the war.

The next morning was evidently the time for weekly presentations of bills at the hotel. There was the sum per diem which the proprietor had mentioned to me, and at the bottom a neat little addition of ten per cent. I sought this man, an agreeable person whose charm took the edge from all financial transactions.

"What is this ten per cent item for?" I asked.

"Ah, madame, c'est la guerre."

He indicated, delicately, a notice on the wall, none too conspicuously placed. It announced that on a certain date the hotel proprietors had met at the Palais d'Orsay, and, in view of the increased cost of living and to save themselves from disaster, had decided to increase their charges by ten per cent.

The notice added that at the meeting nearly all the hotel proprietors agreed to the proposition that guests should be informed
of the change by signs placed in the establishment—a pleasant
muffled way of doing things.

"*C'est la guerre*" was by this time associated in my mind with
the high cost of living. I went to call upon a friend who kept house.
On my way I passed a coal-yard. A long line of people stood beside
it, carrying baskets and sacks. There were stout housewives in blue
aprons, some with little girls beside them; there were bareheaded
bent old women; there were old men on canes; there were little
boys in long black aprons. All of them had the look of having been
waiting a long time, but they were very patient. They had the air
one sees in the soldiers—brave, weary, tenacious; it is the spirit of
all France. When I spoke to some of them, they said they had been
standing for hours, that none of them could have more than twenty
pounds of coal, and that coal was fifty dollars a ton.

"Coal! I should think so!" commented my housekeeping friend.
"And the laundresses say that because of the increased cost of it,
and of soap, soda, and other materials, laundry work is going to
cost sixty per cent more. Think of my problems with having
to use sugar tickets, with butter tickets threatened, with butter
seventy-five cents a pound, bread a third more than it was, eggs
from eighty cents to a dollar the dozen. Certain kinds of paper
have gone up four hundred per cent; alcohol, seven hundred per
cent. It's appalling!"

She talked vigorously; people do, and the Government does.

"Oh, la, la!" said my mending woman, old Jeanne. "How they
talk, these people, and France, wasting, wasting. Do not I know?
Did they not waste my only son, Pierre, wounded in the leg at the
battle of the Marne? A little, little wound that I could have cured!
But they sent him, not to a hospital in Paris, seventeen miles from
the place where he was shot, but to the very borders of Spain. In all
those days of travel the wound was not cared for, and at times he
had to walk."

Old Jeanne's wrinkled face was grim.

"It is to laugh," she said, her voice hard; "they say we must
close the shops at six to save light and heat; but they close them
from twelve to two for luncheon; no saving there, because they
choose to eat long, long meals! Madame has eaten the luncheon

and dinners of these civilians who are telling the soldiers to fight to the end. Two and three meat courses, always. Waste there, eh, madame? But my neighbor, Elise, threw herself and her three children out of the window last Friday because there was not enough to eat and she could not get work. Madame read of it in the papers. And the Apaches,[17] who were good enough soldiers—they have come back discharged from the army without pensions, because they were only consumptive, or had heart trouble, or were not very badly wounded. They too are hungry, madame. The soldiers waste their blood, and the rich waste meat and cake, and the poor have not enough food, and the Government talks of what it will do to save! Ah, la, la! My Pierre dead, and France dying, and the Government talking!"

17. Criminals

Chapter 3

✦

✦

✦

✦

✦

Women's Role

Mention of the war did not typically appear in the traditional location for news concerning women—a newspaper's Woman's Page. The Woman's Page had become a popular department for newspapers by the start of the twentieth century, featuring articles about society, fashion, romance, and domestic issues. But in December 1914, the war put in an appearance in Ellen Adair's Woman's Page column in the Philadelphia *Evening Public Ledger*. She shared a letter she had received from a British nurse, confessing a most unladylike thrill at her involvement in the war and the danger she faced. It struck a discordant note on the Woman's Page, but it was also a prelude to the large role women would play in the war and its impact on women's rights.

War notes began to regularly appear in Adair's column: the war-awakened women of England, children in the war zone, women leading protest riots after the sinking of the liner *Lusitania*. Growing interest in such topics culminated with an announcement by the *Ledger* that its Woman's Page editor, Ellen Adair, would travel to warring Europe to write about issues of interest to women. Adair's December 1914 column is included here.

From the opening months of the war, women journalists chronicled the evolving role of women. That storyline developed as a valuable counterpoint to the male, horror-of-the-trenches experience of war and demonstrated that women had their own unique sacrifices, challenges, and triumphs. A recurrent theme dealt with by many women war correspondents was the sacrifice by women in the warring countries, in particular the loss of loved ones. Women dressed in the black of mourning were the most visible sign of that sacrifice. In the article "Women in Black" Sophie Treadwell shares a train ride with a grieving mother who had lost one son in the trenches and had two others at the front.

But the war impacted women's lives in many other ways, as their roles on the home front evolved. In her article "Baby's Value in Europe," Mary Boyle O'Reilly reports the alarming drop in the birth rate in the warring countries. With the men away, with women employed in industry and unable to afford another mouth to feed, the British and German birth rates dropped to the lowest ever recorded. "Childless marriages, once 'smart,' will now be considered high treason." As O'Reilly points out, it was not a question whether parents wanted children, but that the nations needed children.

Jessica Lozier Payne's reporting from Britain and France in the summer of 1916 proved so popular with the readers of the *Brooklyn Eagle* that the newspaper collected her articles into the booklet *What I Saw in England and France*. Payne wrote about wartime life in these countries and the difficulty of travel. One topic that interested her was the changing role of women. Women were working in many positions in business and industry from which they had previously been excluded, bringing home their first paychecks, living on their own, and enjoying their new-found independence. It was a truly astonishing social development.

In the article included here, Payne visits a munitions factory in Edinburgh, Scotland that employed women in the manufacture of artillery shells. She marvels at the "young Amazons" operating hydraulic presses and other heavy equipment, work that had previously been done only by men.

In addition to their employment on the home front, women took on roles at or near the fighting front. Ruth Wright Kauffman's article takes us into the war zone by featuring the work of women in the British Volunteer Ambulance Drivers (V.A.D.). Working under demanding and dangerous conditions, they transported wounded, evacuated ambulance trains, and loaded hospital ships. By riding along in an ambulance with one of the woman drivers, Kauffman gets insight into their difficult and dangerous work and the personality of the V.A.D. drivers.

Ellen Adair (May Christie) (1890–1946)

"My present life is thrilling in the extreme," writes the nurse. "I just feel that up to the present time I have never truly lived! But, indeed, I am living now, and am enjoying it all immensely, although we are running very great risks of being blown to atoms."

"Women and the War"
Ellen Adair
Evening Public Ledger, December 18, 1914

The heroism of women during the present war frequently passes unnoticed, but as gallant actions are being performed daily by them as any on the actual field of battle.

The life of the nurse on board the ship running between the Continent and Great Britain is thrilling in its adventure. At any moment during the passage across, a mine may be struck, and the ship, nurses and wounded men blown into a million pieces.

I have just received an interesting letter from an English nurse who is acting as sister on board the English boat, Oxfordshire, of the Bibby Line. The Oxfordshire has been turned into a hospital ship and runs between the Continent and Great Britain, carrying hundreds of wounded men home to hospital and friends.

* * *

"My present life is thrilling in the extreme," writes the nurse. "I just feel that up to the present time I have never truly lived! But, indeed, I am living now, and am enjoying it all immensely, although we are running very great risks of being blown to atoms. At any time we may strike a mine or be torpedoed by the Germans or be fired upon by their ships.

"I am doing night duty, and you cannot picture what it is like. Imagine six of us nurses attending in darkness to 700 wounded men, a great part of who are quite delirious and are muttering and

May Christie, who wrote under the name Ellen Adair, was the editor of a newspaper Women's Page when the war began. She traveled to warring Europe several times to report on the role of women. *Source:* George Grantham Bain Collection, Prints and Photographs Division, Library of Congress, LC-DIG-ggbain-37599.

moaning somewhere in the depths! At first it was the most 'creepy' sensation to go around the ward with my little lantern. Not that I felt nervous, one feels so dreadfully sorry for the poor fellows that one has no nerves at all, but yet—.

"Lights have to be out at 10 o'clock every night, and so we just work among the wounded in the dark. I make my rounds with a tiny lantern, bending over each cot and throwing the light on the patient's face to watch for sudden collapse or any change. Most of them are pretty bad cases, and there they lie, moaning and calling.

* * *

"At first it was terribly eerie. You see, lots of them are delirious and get out of bed. It is a queer sensation to hear a pattering of feet behind you in the darkness and to hear the breathing and panting of some poor wounded fellow, knowing as you do, that he is not responsible for his actions. The first time that happened, I did feel a little bit nervous, I confess it. If I could have seen where my patient was, I shouldn't have minded—but then, you see, I couldn't locate him, at first in the darkness of the place, and he kept wandering around, muttering and talking, till I got hold of him and persuaded him to go back to bed. He was in no state to get out of bed, poor soul, as he was terribly smashed up.

"We have an orderly to each ward, of course, but working in the dark is a difficult business. Of course, we cannot show a light, so one makes the best of it. Six nurses to 700 wounded men means busy work all the time.

* * *

"My boat has been to St. Nazar,[1] Havre, and Boulogne for the wounded, and had taken them to Queenstown, Ireland, to Dublin, but mostly to Southhampton. Next time we will probably go as far as Scotland calling at Glasgow. We never know where we are going till the last moment, and often don't get orders till actually out at sea.

"We carry wounded Germans, too, and they get on excellently with the English and the French. It is most amusing to see the great friendships struck up between the English and French soldiers, for they cannot understand each other's talk! The gesticulating that goes on is ludicrous!

"The colonel in charge of us nurses is exceedingly kind and nice. I am having a splendid time and my only fear is that I may be transferred to shore duty! Hard work and exciting work are the two things I enjoy best, and, indeed, I am getting them now to the full!"

* * *

A letter such as this brings home to one the horrors and the hardships of war. Certainly there is an excitement in the nurse's work, but the strain must be tremendous. The night work in particular must be very hard for any woman. The anxiety and responsibility are immense—yet these nurses glory in the work. Imagine working

---

1. Saint-Nazaire

among hundreds of wounded and delirious men in the darkness. Carrying her small lantern and groping from cot to cot, the nurse hurries from one poor soul to another, feeling the pulse here, applying the morphine syringe there, giving a quick restorative to the dying, and watching for that curious gray look that betokens a failing heart.

"Water, water, nurse," comes echoing from every dark corner, and many times she wishes that she had 20 pairs of hands and feet to answer all the calls and cries. Truly the nurse on board the hospital ship is heroic and utterly self-forgetful of her bravery.

Sophie Treadwell (1885–1970)

"My neighbors tell me if one had to be taken, it is better Jeanjean, because he is not married, he does not leave the wife and the children."

"Women in Black"
Sophie Treadwell
Harper's Weekly, July 31, 1915

Women in black. They are all over this land. It is late spring—spring in France! But the fall sowing was lead and powder; the winter rains, blood and tears; and the spring has its flowering in women in black. The cities are great silent plains, where they grow close. In the empty country they seem to be the only harvest. They look out at you from every nook and corner of France—the women in black.

We rode together in a third class compartment from Angouleme to Poitiers. Her strong body was hardened and stooped with work, her hands were seared and knotted with it. Her face was dumb with it—except her eyes. Her eyes were very bright. The black she wore was clumsy, much too large. And yet it had an air somehow of dimly belonging to her; as though she had cut it out from an old pattern that had been hers once—in ampler days.

We rode a long time together in silence through that lovely land; through the delicate green meadows, through the vineyards, past the little low houses of old white stone, past the great chateau high above the river's bank—all shimmering in sunshine, all glittering in spring—and yet, all grey in loneliness, in emptiness. An old man

When Sophie Treadwell reported from Paris in 1915, she wrote about women who lost their loved ones in the war. *Source:* Sophia Treadwell Papers, Special Collections, The University of Arizona Library.

slowly following an ancient horse down a feeble furrow in the field, a woman bending in the vineyard, a child playing in the courtyard of one of the little low houses of old white stone, an old woman beating her donkey up the road to the chateau—but nowhere a strong man lustily at work.

It was after two when she brought out of her *panier*[2] a piece of bread and some cheese. She began to eat, but slowly, without enjoyment, as though troubled about something. Finally she held her luncheon out to me.

"Will you, madame?" she said. I took a bit. "Take plenty, madame. Take plenty." I offered her some chocolate from my bag; and as we ate together, we talked together—the war. It is always the war.

2. Basket

"It has taken no one from you, madame—the war? No? You are of the few, madame. A stranger? Then you cannot understand. I have three sons in the war, madame. Two are in the trenches. One is dead! Oh yes, it is sure. It is certain. I have had the word. No I do not know where it was exactly. It is difficult to know. Some where in the north. When the war is over I will know perhaps. The youngest—and he goes the first. Always so gay, madame, always the most gay. I got one letter. I will show it to you, madame, if you wish, that you may see with your own eyes, how fine he could write. No! I do not know where it was from. They do not let them say. Somewhere in the north.

She lifted her clumsy black skirt above her black petticoat beneath, and unpinned from the pocket there a piece of folded paper and a little purse. She held the paper out to me.

"Is it not so, madame? Is that not beautiful writing? And think, no pen, no ink, no desk! Is it not well done?" They were just a few lines, written with cramped care. They said: "Dear mama, I am in good health. Do not worry. We are going to lick them. Jeanjean. P. S. Tell papa to keep straight or when I come home I will lick him, too. Jeanjean."

"It is indeed well done, madame," I said, handing her little letter back to her. "It is indeed well done." She looked at it for a moment nodding, and then she folded it up carefully and pinned it and the little purse back in the pocket of the petticoat. She settled her clumsy black skirt about her, and sat for a while, quite still, her hands folded in her lap. Finally she went on.

"He was always so gay, madame, always the most gay. Only eighteen. My neighbors tell me if one had to be taken, it is better Jeanjean, because he is not married, he does not leave the wife and the children. But he was so gay, madame, always the song to the lips. The other two, they are both married. One has three children, fine big goslings. The other one was just married when the war began—three months, madame, and now—a little rabbit that he has never seen, a little girl, madame, and not too strong. I think it is because the mother was all the time so sad. She spent all the time in the church praying to St. Genivieve[3] for her man to be brought back safe to her—

---

3. Treadwell misspells the name of St. Genevieve, a woman who dedicated her life to prayer, practices of devotion, and acts of penance.

"'Better,' I told her, 'that you sit at home in the doorway and sew, and leave the candle in the church—before the blessed Mary to send you a son.' But she would not listen.

"'I am the best candle,' she would say, 'I will stay in the church and burn for him.' They are not healthy. Those thoughts, madame—and just a girl of seventeen. It is as I told her. The little rabbit is not strong and it is not a boy, but—it's a sweet little chicken, all the same, madame."

She folded what was left of the cheese in a piece of the paper that she had brought it in, and put it carefully into the *panier*.

"We are all in one house together," she went on. "These wives of my sons with their children, and my children, the younger ones, and my husband. Everything is taken from us—our good horse. Oh, they paid us, the government. It is very good—the government, it pays us for all. But he is gone, our good horse, and we cannot do our work in the fields without him. No, my husband is not at the war. He is too old, and he has drunk too much. He is sick. But perhaps later he will have to go. If he goes we will be better off. The government will pay us. It is one franc twenty-five each day for the husband at the war, and a half a franc for each child left at home. He costs us dear. The wine and the boots are dear, madame—the wine in the shops. My daughter-in-law, she with the three children, she says better he go. But yet, I do not want him to be called. You can understand that, madame, can you not? I do not want him to be called."

She got off the train at Poitiers. I had the compartment to myself until Tours, where it filled with soldiers, from the military hospital there, going back to the front.

A few nights ago, I dined at the home of a lady in black, Mme. de V. There were but two other guests, Madame L, and Madame R, two ladies in black. No one in Paris is receiving now, but these three women are very old friends. Since the war, since they are alone, they dine together several nights each week. And I was a stranger, the friend of a friend, and so one to whom some little courtesy was due.

Somehow we seemed a pitifully inadequate little gathering—that table there in that big and beautiful room—the massive carved buffet, the enormous old clock, the towering fireplace, the tall windows curtained and shuttered from the lovely garden without—a room that needed men and bare shoulders and *valets-de-pied*[4]— and we were just three women, three of us in black—(but three of us trained from earliest childhood in the necessity in life for charm, for gaiety, for pride; three of us trained not to bring grief to table, and three of us trained, too, always to dine well in spite of all.)

Mme de—is the wife of a Colonel of heavy artillery now under fire at—. She wears black for a brother killed at Ypres. The war death has reached its hand into the hearts of the other two women in black as well; yet it was only in the something that lay deep in their eyes, that you could tell the suffering, the suspense, that they are day and night enduring. And, now and then, as something was inadvertently said that stirred perhaps some different memory, a sudden mist would fill the eyes of little Mme de V but she didn't quiver an eye lid. Not a tear fell.

She is a small woman, Mme de V, pretty not much over thirty, smartly turned out, with tiny feet and hands. (She wore but one ring, this night, except, of course, her wedding band—a ring that many of the women in black are wearing. It is made of aluminum from the German shells that fall into the French trenches. You cannot buy one of these rings. You must have some one "at the front" who sends it to you—just for you, with your initials cut into it.) She is altogether chic is Mme de V, but somehow the black she wears seems too snug for her. It seems to suffocate, to choke her small tense body. I noticed it when she would be going about the table deftly clearing away each course, while her friends made little jokes about the *service de guerre* and the *personnel*.

"As *femme de chamber*, I assure you, Simone, you are perfect," said Mme L, as our little hostess went about. "I really prefer dining here since you lost that fearful *valet de chambre*[5] you used to inflict on us."

"Naturally!" cried Mme R. "He was so serious, so depressing! Now with you—there is something light, something appetizing about you in this capacity!"

"I'm glad I amuse you, my dears," laughed Mme de V. "I assure you I do not amuse myself."

---

4. Servants
5. The terms *femme de chamber* and *valet de chamber* refer to a female and male servant.

—"But it is good for you Simone. You were always the spoiled little wife."

—"And, before that, the spoiled little child!"

"*Eh bien*, now I am the spoiled little cook! The way you are eating my dinner, my old girls, would spoil a *maitre d'hotel*.

"But it is you, Simone, who have made this *veau marengo*?"

"Who else? The *bonne*[6] who now decorates my bedroom as well as my kitchen, lacks, I can tell you, the touch in all."

"But this veal is delicious!"

"*Ravissante!*"[7]

"*Eh bien*, another little piece—*tout petit*, eh?"

At nine we were through coffee but we did not move. Mme de V's home, as most of the houses in Paris now, is almost entirely closed. The dining room serves also as salon. The table was quickly cleared, and seated round the heavy board that threw off soft lights and thick shadows from its rich wood, we began folding bits of white gauze into compresses. Pile upon pile, the little badges of pain grew under our hands.

"We cannot knit now," explained Mme R. "All the things we made for the winter are of no more use. The call is now for hospital supplies. We dread that means the grand coup, the great advance to gain a decisive victory and end this terrible war. If it is, the loss of life will be horrible, and the wounded—anyway we make these!"

Again that quick mist that I had noticed come and go before, filled the eyes of Mme de V.

"Tell us," she put in quickly to me, "Tell us honestly, have you seen one pretty, one really *chic* woman since you came to Paris?"

"No, I haven't, and it's a bitter disappointment."

"But you should not have expected to see them," cried Mme R. "There are no men. Why be beautiful?"

"Then too," said Mme L. "We have much to do! It not only takes heart, but it takes time to be beautiful!"

"And money," said Mme de V.

"Oh of course, money! And we have other uses for that than the friction, the massage, the marcel. France can make better use of our money than that!"

6. Nursemaid or female servant
7. Delightful

"And of us, too!" said Mme R.

"Perhaps," sighed little Mme de V, "But to be honest—I miss the pretty women, the women *soigné*.[8] If M de T could see me now! could see my hands!"

"And if you could see him, Simone!" Again the tears swam in Mme de V's eyes. Again she turned quickly to me.

"For seven months now, my husband has had his clothes off only to make the change of linen. He sleeps like that—in the straw!"

"In straw because he is an officer, Simone! The men sleep in the dirt and mud and water! They have not even the change of linen! You must think of that!"

"I know!" breathed little Mme de V, "I should not complain. You are right. Straw is something! It is a great deal!"

"If you could see them!" said Mme L, turning to me, "the wounded when they first arrive here at the hospitals—filthy, crawling in vermin! the smell is terrible! nice boys too, some only seventeen!"

"This war! this war!" cried Mme de—, pressing down the tall piles of gauze that threatened to topple over.

"All for nothing!" breathed Mme L. "When will it ever end!" asked Mme R. There was silence.

Suddenly Mme de— jumped to her feet.

"You have done very well, my children," she said gaily, looking at the neat piles of compresses standing in rows before us.—"A good point for each!"

"And we must hurry, Simone."

"Yes! It is almost ten. The Metro will be closed!"

"All our cars are gone," exclaimed Mme de V. smiling. "Taken in the first days."

"And Simone had just a new one. It was a first prize at the last show."

"*Eh bien*," laughed little Simone de V. "The Metro still runs!"

"And at this hour" went on Mme L. "When there is nobody, one finds oneself very well in the second class."

"But certainly!" She was opening the outer door for us, our little hostess. "That is understood. These days, for all of us—it is the second class!"

----

8. Well-dressed

Mary Boyle O'Reilly (1873–1939)

Childless marriages, once "smart," will now
be considered high treason.

"Baby's Value in Europe"
Mary Boyle O'Reilly
Bismarck Daily Tribune,[9] July 26, 1916

London, England, July 24.—France is buying babies. The value of the baby rises as the size of the family increases: $100 for the first two in a family, $200 for the third, $400 for the fourth, is payable to the mother from the treasury of the republic when the baby is one year old.

To keep her place among the great nations France must ask her mothers to give "la Patrie"[10] four children each for the next 25 years.

The French chamber of deputies is now considering a plan to provide every mother of four with a life annuity, the necessary funds to be supplied by taxing bachelors, childless people and the parents of an only child. In one suburb of Paris a new baby pays the rent for a quarter.

All Europe will soon be race recruiting.

Germany, now preparing to endow children and to legitimatise children of unwed mothers, has lowered the legal age for marriage to 16 years.

The war and the unprecedented employment of women in industry have brought about a startling fall in the birth rate. Babies have become the most perplexing question that ever faced a state.

It is not a question whether parents want children: The nations need children.

It is folly to wage war if no rising generation is left to profit.

For 35 years the birth rate of Europe has declined one per cent annually. For every three English babies born in 1876, only two were born in 1913.

Since 1900 the birth rate in Germany has fallen from 35 to 27 per thousand.

---

9. O'Reilly reported for the Newspaper Enterprise Association, a news syndication service. Therefore her articles appeared in many newspapers.

10. The country

Meantime conquering Russia leads the world with a birth rate of 42 babies per thousand papulation.

Last winter the English and German birth rates were the lowest ever recorded, and war had swept away a generation of baby Belgians and Poles and Serbs.

The decay of the Roman empire began that way.

Women must save the race. Every war puts a new valuation on motherhood.

But the pith of the problem is economic: Children are expensive luxuries. Poor people must consider the penalties of parenthood.

One-third of the adult male workers of England earn $6.25 a week, and one-tenth earn less than $5 in a country where living has increased 49 per cent, above pre-war prices.

If the state needs children, the state must pay for them.

With war debts taking one-fourth of every man's income, ordinary wages cannot feed eight children as well as four. Even a poor woman's baby costs $1.25 a week.

Premiums for mothers and state bonus for fathers are a necessity.

A Ministry of Maternity is more needed than a Ministry of Commerce.

Childless marriages, once "smart," will now be considered high treason.

The standard of luxury will be lowered, and the standard of living raised.

A decent living wage without which healthy children are impossible, the encouragement and honoring of an efficient motherhood by the state, rest from household or industrial labor before and after childbirth with free medical attendance and the institution of a ministry of maternity with a woman director controlling hospitals are the initial factors in a national system by which France hopes to double the number of births at a nominal cost.

Jessica Lozier Payne (1870–1951)

The heaviest work I saw women doing was operating the hydraulic press, which, under tremendous pressure, welds the copper band on the shells. Three young Amazons were doing this and were jesting and laughing and apparently enjoying it.

"Women Work Tirelessly Making Shells for the Front"
Jessica Lozier Payne
What I Saw in England and France[11]

Among all the changes which the war has caused in industry none has been more spectacular than those brought about by the ever-increasing demand for shot and shells. In the many new employments for women it is the munition story that is the wonderful one.

The government called on every machine shop and foundry in the United Kingdom to turn out munitions. In addition, old warehouses were hastily fitted with lathes and tools and new buildings run up and equipped as speedily as possible. Where were the workers to be found? The men were needed at the front and there was nothing for it but to call upon the women to do their bit and serve their country and their flag. A tremendous army of women was needed to serve as machine hands, and no readier patriotism has been shown than the way in which they responded to the call. By the thousands they came trooping in and are still coming, although the tide has swelled beyond the quarter of a million mark.

In Edinburgh I was eager to see and talk to these women munition workers, but it is very difficult to get on the inside of these plants doing government work, for naturally they do not desire visitors.

But through the influence of friends, who vouched for my innocuousness, an appointment was made for me to visit the works of Bruce, Peebles & Co., the largest engineering works in Scotland, and now employing 150 girls on munition work, and also the shops of David Thomson, engaged before the war in manufacturing bakery machinery, but now doing nothing but government work and employing over 200 girls.

Entering Bruce, Peebles & Co. I found myself surrounded by the hum and throb of speeding machinery. Long aisles of electrically driven tools, each with a woman worker before it absorbed in her task. There were many young girls, pretty and rosy cheeked, and all dressed in a uniform of lavender cotton

---

11. Payne reported for the *Brooklyn Daily Eagle*. Her articles proved so popular that the newspaper collected all her war articles into this booklet.

British women inspecting artillery shells. By 1917, two million people worked in the manufacture of munitions in Britain; nearly 90 percent of them were women. George Grantham Bain Collection, Prints and Photographs Division, Library of Congress, LC-DIG-ggbain-25850.

goods which completely covered them, and on their heads were shirred mob caps of the same to keep their hair from dust and from being caught in the machinery. The age seemed to range from 18 to 25, and they seemed very interested when the forewoman told them that I was a lady from America who wanted to see the women working.

I spoke to one smiling, blue-eyed girl, whose tool was making grooves in a core. She had only one part of this operation to complete, and it did not require special skill, since the tool was set to perform this task automatically.

"Don't you get tired of doing this ten hours every day?" I asked her.

"No, I like to watch my tool cut the metal, just as if it were cheese, and every shell I pass along I say, 'there goes another for our boys at the front.'"

That seems to be the spirit that carries the work along, and you can feel it as you walk by these rows of women, each faithfully doing her bit to help, for, without doubt, every woman there had some man belonging to her out on the fighting line.

The heaviest work I saw women doing was operating the hydraulic press, which, under tremendous pressure, welds the copper band on the shells. Three young Amazons were doing this and were jesting and laughing and apparently enjoying it.

The government inspectors were young women, too, and had instruments for measuring each shell before it was passed for test. Those that did not come up to requirements were rejected.

Ruth Wright Kauffman (1885–1952)

"Each girl has her own ambulance," he said, as he pointed them out one by one; "and she takes entire care of it herself. There are no night shifts, so she must be ready for duty at any time within the twenty-four hours at a few minutes' notice."

"The Woman Ambulance-Driver in France"
Ruth Wright Kauffman
The Outlook, October 3, 1917

It's a dusty business riding at a good clip in an ambulance for twenty or thirty miles on one of those long white French roads—the kind they have so much poetry about. I was glad I wasn't a stretcher case—but let me tell you how it happened.

I was to be driven by the only sort of conveyance in that part of the world to a large military hospital in northern France. The only sort of conveyance was an ambulance.

I waited at base headquarters until I saw the great gray creature with its scarlet cross pull up on the other side of the street. For a moment I thought that the driver, who walked toward me in motor cap and rubber coat and high boots, must be a man, a stocky and alert and somewhat young man. Then I saw my mistake.

"You're to come with me, I think," she said, holding out a strong hand. "Wait a minute, please. I've kept the cushions doubled over, so they wouldn't get dusty, but I shall have to dust them, after all. I hope you don't mind not starting for another hour. I've a lot of calls to make."

I did not mind. But I was glad that she invited me to go with her while she made them. None the less, I took my place gingerly within the ambulance. I had never stepped inside an ambulance before, and this one, which had carried so many wounded soldiers, four by four—the last batch only yesterday—made me hold back for an instant.

My driver delivered her messages here and collected her mail there, slinging, without the slightest hesitation, heavy bags of it that would have been beyond my strength. Soldiers saluted her, but she was left alone to hoist boxes and big sacks. She wasted no time, her manner was businesslike, and she performed her errands with military precision.

For the first half of the trip I stayed back with an over-age Red Cross man, who spent his time hunting up missing soldiers and questioning the wounded for details of their comrades. There were two other passengers —two rosy-cheeked young women in the V.A.D. (Volunteer Ambulance Drivers) uniform that one comes soon to recognize, returning from a fortnight's leave to England. They were bubbling over with chatter of their holiday, and were anticipating seeing their old friends again. They had been doing Red Cross work in France for over a year, and were practical enough not to look on the dark side of their clouds. They reminded me more of school-girls returning after holidays than anything else, for they must have been very young.

Then, for I was white from the dust sucked up from the road, I changed to a seat beside the driver, where she thought it might be cleaner.

We moved at top speed and rattled over all the back roads while we executed our various official orders. We passed numbers of German prisoners. A group of three of them smiled good-morning to us. I saw a Tommy[12] give a light to another German. My driver told me that she had driven many Germans to and from the hospital, but it made no apparent difference to her; they were wounded when she had to do with them.

She was looking forward to the summer, and called my attention to the luxuriant Lombardy poplars and the masses of flowers that miraculously grew and kept in order: roses that hung over walls, huge clusters of peonies. Not that it would have any effect on the amount of work. The hospital had always been full since she arrived, although there had been depressing occasions when it had suddenly become crowded to twice its capacity; but summer meant

12. British soldiers were referred to generically as Tommy Atkins, or Tommy for short.

easy weather conditions, and motor-drivers perforce consider the weather conditions. The winter had been incredibly cold. For the nursing members, who lived in practically unheated huts, it must have been almost unbearable; but what could be done when there was a shortage of fuel? The drivers had a charming house set in a lovely garden. It used to belong to a French Deputy. In winter, however, it was conspicuous for its single open fireplace, around which eighteen girls could not comfortably toast themselves.

"There's one good thing about that," I was cheerfully told. When you're kept pretty cold all the time, you don't feel the outside cold nearly so much. Most of our work this winter had a way of coming along between two and three o'clock in the morning. Now that it's fine weather and makes no difference, the trains generally arrive about six. It is perverse of them!"

There had been snow for long periods from November until April, sometimes several feet deep. My driver had once run into a drift during a storm and stuck there. Fortunately, she was quite alone at the time. She had walked back, got another ambulance, returned to find the snow so banked up that there was no digging her first car out, and she finally had to tow it home. She has now made it a rule never to go out without a shovel.

I wondered if she had to know much about mechanics.

"Well, you see," she explained, "I had my own car and had been running it for five years, so I had no trouble in qualifying. I can do any road work, but I'm not a skilled mechanician. I mean, if the car completely broke down it would have to go to the garage for repairs. Several men are kept there to attend to the more serious troubles."

"Do you have to take up Red Cross work before you qualify as a driver?" I asked.

"Yes, now. But I was in the original lot, so I've never taken a course in Home Nursing or First Aid. It wasn't required then. Now they have to take courses both in First Aid and in motor-driving. The First Aid is very important. We never have an orderly with us, you know, and when we come this way it's about twenty miles. We've often had to transfer men when they were really in too dangerous a condition to be moved, so as to make room for incoming train-loads, and it's rather awful not to know what to do if one of them faints or has a hemorrhage."

"You don't carry them at this pace, do you?" I gasped.

"We crawl," she laughed.

"I suppose pulling down that flap at the rear keeps out the dust?"

"No; not a bit. There doesn't seem to be any way to avoid the dust. Sometimes the stretcher cases have dust all over their eyelids when we get them to the end of the journey."

In the town itself—a town once overflowing with summer tourists from all parts of the world, and gayly picturesque with its mixture of old France and new, with its hotels and golf and tennis and white cliffs and sands where the brightly dressed children used to play—I saw first the lolling soldiers in their blue invalid uniforms on the promenade by the sea, their figures silhouetted against a brilliant sky. Casino [sic] and hotels are now hospitals, but for a space I lost sight of that side of things, and, with the gracious permission of the commanding officer, I was taken to see the motor-drivers' headquarters and their immaculate garage.

The officer under whom the girls directly work showed me, with an air of pride, the fourteen cars.

"Each girl has her own ambulance," he said, as he pointed them out one by one; "and she takes entire care of it herself. There are no night shifts, so she must be ready for duty at any time within the twenty-four hours at a few minutes' notice. Generally, the girls are working here the better part of each morning, except that two or three of the cars are nearly always on the road. The duties consist in a good deal more than transporting the wounded. The drivers are under orders to go whenever they are sent, wherever they are sent, for whatever purpose they are sent, and that means carrying mails, bringing passengers, collecting stores, concert parties—anything that must be brought or transferred. The girls never complain. I've never heard one say she was tired. And the ambulances are kept in much better condition than when the men had them—we are forced to admit that. The girls take a pride in them, you see."

I pointed to a toy monkey perched in front of one ambulance.

"Oh, that's a mascot. They all like mascots. Curious, isn't it? You'll be going back with that car, I expect."

At the Deputy's house we came upon the girls eating lunch, a sturdy-looking assemblage, their faces ruddy from the winds, their eyes spirited, their whole bearing enthusiastic. As most of them had held their jobs for at least a year, the newness and adventure

British women ambulance drivers. *Source:* George Grantham Bain Collection, Prints and Photographs Division, Library of Congress, LC-DIG-ggbain-25045.

of their work had worn off. They were not in France through any war hysteria. One girl said to me that after three months comes the hardest strain; for by that time you are sick of just the same roads and the same stones day in and day out. Afterwards you get used to it and forget the monotony.

"Don't a lot of you break down?" I asked.

"No; surprisingly few. One girl went home to-day because the doctor thought she wasn't fit. The winter was pretty hard on her. But we're all strong to begin with, and of course we have a severe medical examination before we are accepted. We're supposed to have nothing to do besides driving, though in the end we do a great many other things, because nobody is within reach, and things that must be done must be done at once."

"What do you do when work's over?"

"We never know when it's over! That's the worst of it. You can't count on the hour when anything's going to happen in a war. If the Germans wound our men or gas our men, and there's a train-load to come, we must be there. We have a regular route to and from the station, so we never get in one another's way. For instance, yesterday, we brought the entire four hundred and fifty men—and they were mostly lying cases—in an hour and a half. The first train we unloaded and deposited at the casino in twenty-eight minutes, but we were delayed by the second train; they generally arrive in two sections."

"How long does it take to bring in one load from the local station?"

"Six or seven minutes. But the return trip takes no time; we shoot along with the empties."

"But," I persisted, "it isn't only driving these ambulances that keeps you looking so well." "Oh, no," said another driver, the most rosy-cheeked of all, I think. "We're great believers in exercise and open air. Whenever we get a moment off, we go out. Tennis and walking and golf and bathing when it's at all safe. There's a swift current, and we're not allowed to bathe without a boat. We never go so far away that we can't be found quickly. That's the really hard thing, that awful feeling of responsibility. But we do manage to take a lot of exercise. And then we don't worry. It's a rule not to worry."

In the beginning the girls had come as a unit of fourteen motor-drivers only. They were the pioneers, for this was the first place in France where women ambulance-drivers were used, and one can well imagine the struggle that must have ensued with the military authorities before they could be persuaded that women were as capable as men for driving ambulances. For some months this unit of fourteen did its own cooking and housekeeping in odd leisure moments; but the odd moments were few and far between. The girls had no energy left to cook and keep house, so finally the unit was increased to consist of eighteen members, including two cooks, a housemaid, and a parlor-maid—all voluntary. The unit is on half Government rations and receives enough money to pay for laundry. Tickets to England for the semi-annual fortnightly leave are provided, but in the end the girls are out of pocket, because they buy some of their food. A great deal of the food they receive is tinned, as if they were soldiers; and tinned butter, I can well believe, is more than one can pleasantly endure.

My return journey—in the ambulance with the monkey—showed an instance of skill. We had barely entered the town of our destination when one of the tires collapsed. In five minutes exactly, without any fuss, but with the usual idle crowd that collects in a country at war as well as in a country at peace, a fresh tire was in place and we were again on our way.

What, I think, made me see most clearly into the lives of these girls was a sort of diary, kept in very brief form, into which their commandant let me take a glimpse. It gave me what the spoken words could not of themselves give, and showed, through its very lack of intent to show, the rare courage of these young women, set among conditions that not so long ago would have been considered impossible for women to bear, especially as these motor-drivers belong to a class that have never dreamed of earning their living, and were certainly unused to hardships before they "signed on" for their present work. The bald statements of fact from the diary are the more poignant because they are expressed as mere commonplaces. I quote bits lifted here and there, without dates:

"The rush of work for this unit began on Sunday and continued roughly ten days. All the unit without exception worked splendidly, and besides being many hours on the road kept their cars in such excellent condition that, in spite of hard usage, not a car suffered from neglect.—and— joined the unit to assist with housework, as all the drivers were wanted. Within the fortnight we carried 2,115 lying cases, 719 sitting cases. The mileage was 8,718 miles....

"In one day two ambulance trains were evacuated and three hospital ships were loaded....

"The latter half of the last fortnight has been very busy. Three trains have been met, and, though the men have not been able to be evacuated to England, ... large numbers of sitting cases have been carried by the convoy to convalescent camps. The garage has been converted into a temporary hospital, and the cars are at present parked on the square. Several members of the unit have volunteered to help with the patients in the garage, and their offer has been very gratefully accepted by the matron, as the increased number of beds has been a great strain on the nursing staff. The assistance rendered in getting patients' meals, cutting up dressings, making beds, etc., by the unit, especially by those who hold the Home Nursing certificates, has been most appreciated....

"The weather has been intensely cold, and it has been difficult to prevent the cars from freezing during the night....

"Transport has been difficult owing to the state of the roads, which in places have been several feet thick in snow. On more than one occasion drivers have had to dig their cars out of the drifts....

"Repairs have again been heavy, and have been done by the unit themselves. Most of the evacuations have taken place in the night, and this has frequently entailed a full day's work in the workshop being followed by a night on the road. Notwithstanding this, the health of the unit is excellent...."

What struck me most was the fact that mention was made of the possibility of the cars freezing, while nothing was said of hands and feet. That is the essential quality of these drivers; they are so much more distressed over their individual ambulances than over their personal discomforts.

I mentioned this to the commandant.

"Well, I don't know," she said, smiling deprecatingly. "When we had that huge lot of fifteen hundred instead of our nine hundred and fifty capacity, we were pretty sleepy. I don't know about most of the girls, though they couldn't have had it any easier than I did; I know that I got only three and a half hours' sleep in forty-eight hours, and as for food, I seized what I could when I saw it. We didn't need much rocking after that stretch of work was over."

And the colonel in command, who won his Victoria Cross[13] under heavy fire in the South African War long before the tradition of keeping women out of affairs military had ever been broken, confessed to me:

"I should feel a lot safer with those young women than with most men."

13. The highest British medal for bravery under fire

Chapter 4

✦

✦

✦

✦

Reporting the Central Powers

G iven the neutral status of the United States for the first two-plus years of the war, American correspondents could travel to any of the warring nations. Most of their attention focused on England and France, but in the fall of 1914 two women journalists brought American readers some of their first glimpses of war from Austria-Hungary and fighting on the Eastern Front.

As the newly appointed United Press bureau chief in Rome, Alice Rohe monitored war sentiment in neutral Italy. However, in October 1914 she visited Vienna, the capital of Italy's warring neighbor Austria-Hungary. Although Austrian newspapers carried only positive news about the war, Rohe saw how profoundly war had cast a pall over that once-gay city. Vienna's hospitals, schools, universities, hotels, and churches overflowed with 70,000 wounded. "I have seen trains arriving, every one crowded to suffocation, with the wounded and dying," she reported.

Austria-Hungary was unique among the warring nations in actually having in place a plan for how to handle war news. On July 28, 1914, the day it declared war against Serbia, it created the Imperial War Press Bureau, the Kriegspressequartier (KPQ). Austro-Hungarian and German journalists and artists could join the KPQ in lieu of military service. Foreign correspondents from neutral countries could join as well.

America's most-famous female journalist—Nellie Bly—happened to arrive in Vienna on private business a few days after the start of war. She had won fame in the 1880s-1890s for her "stunt" journalism. She masqueraded as a lunatic to expose the abusive treatment of the mentally ill and gained international fame by breaking the record for round-the-world travel. But by 1914 her byline had not appeared in any newspaper for the past twenty years. She took advantage of finding herself in a warring country to apply for a KPQ tour to the front lines.

In October 1914 she joined several other American journalists on a month-long KPQ tour that included visits to the fighting with Russia in Austria's northern province of Galicia, the Serbian front, and sojourns in Vienna and Budapest. Her articles about the tour describe some of the gruesome conditions in Galicia, but overall read more like travelogues than detailed war reporting. This chapter includes one of her articles from that tour, the one article that captures better than the others the moment she suffers the real shock of war by staring into the face of a dying soldier. Her mix of emotions—shock, horror, compassion—reflect the response of an innocent observer confronting the horrors of war, a response that mirrored that of her readers, learning about the conflict through Bly's eyewitness account.

As the war-weary nations slogged into the third year of the war, articles began to appear in the Allied press about food shortages in Germany. Rumors of bread riots in some German cities gave heart to Allied leaders that victory might depend less on success on the battlefield than on Germany's inability to feed its citizens. In the fall of 1916, the *New York Tribune* sent Madeleine Zabriskie Doty to investigate conditions in Germany. In a series of front-page articles, Doty described the hunger and bleak conditions she found.

Eleanor Franklin Egan reported from Turkey for *The Saturday Evening Post* during the Allies' ill-fated Gallipoli campaign. While writing several articles about life in Constantinople, she began to hear horrendous reports about atrocities committed by the Turkish government against its Armenian population. Armenians had long been a hated minority in the Ottoman Empire, but the current persecution came in response to some Armenians siding with Turkey's enemy Russia. Many military-aged men were murdered. Over two million Armenians were forced to "resettle," given five days to abandon their homes and all their possessions for long journeys through mountains and deserts to camps in the interior. No provisions were made for food, shelter, or safe conduct for the refugees. The new policy inflamed long-standing animosity toward Armenians, which led to widespread abuses, violence, and massacres. Estimates of deaths resulting from the Armenian genocide range from 800,000 to 1,500,000.

Through secrecy and censorship, the Turks took great pains to conceal their relocation policy and the resulting atrocities. In the article included here, "Behind the Smoke of Battle," Egan reveals Turkey's murderous policy to the outside world and her own heroic role in bringing it to world attention.

Alice Rohe (1876–1957)

"They have buried our dead in heaps," he said, tears coursing down his face. "They were killed like sheep driven to a slaughter yard. The Russian artillery had done unbelievable things."

"Once Gay Vienna Now City of Gloom"
Alice Rohe
The Washington Times,[1] October 23, 1914

Vienna, Oct. 6. (By Courier to Rome, thence by mail to New York)[2]—Vienna is a city of lost hope, of gloom, of gray despair.

Once the gayest and most beautiful capital of Europe, it is today the saddest, the most distressed. Silent, hopeless protests against the horrors of war, which have turned this wonderful, joyous city into a melancholy sepulcher for the living, permeated every stratum of society.

I have seen a procession of 4,000 mothers, whose husbands have died in Galicia,[3] carrying in their arms their fatherless babes. They filed past the great cold palace of the ministry of war.

It was their mute appeal for peace.

1. Rohe reported for the United Press, a news syndication service. Therefore her war articles appeared in hundreds of different newspapers.
2. This circuitous route was necessary to avoid Austrian censorship.
3. A northern province of Austria that saw heavy fighting early in the war, between Russia and Austria-Hungary.

Gray Wings of Dread

I have seen a procession of little children, plaintive and futile emissaries of life, silently protesting against needless death.

Alice Rohe became the Rome bureau chief for the United Press in September 1914 and reported from Vienna the following month. *Source:* Prints and Photographs Division, Library of Congress, LC-DIG-ppmsca-32096.

I have seen trains arriving, every one crowded to suffocation with the wounded and dying. From the midst of these maimed and mutilated, sickened and suffering men, I have seen uncomprehending soldiers, dazed by the horrors of war, crazed with joy at being home again, dragged from their companions and placed under arrest.

Their crime? Why, they cried out in the delirium of excitement their curses against the Russians who had brought such terrible defeat to the Austrian armies. For no news must be whispered by the wounded or the fugitive which reflects the truth of Austrian disasters.

And above these visual pictures of the melancholy Vienna of today, I have sensed the touch of those gray wings of dread which cast their shadow over the town—the soiled, the sordid, the horrible wings of Cholera.

I have felt with the people, stalking beside this hideous enemy—the Plague—its sister specter, Hunger.

Arrests Made Hourly

In Vienna today 70,000 wounded are being cared for in hospitals, schools, universities, hotels, churches.

The Red Cross admits its inability to care for all the wounded, and the sight of helpless men, suffering needlessly and hopelessly, is one which confronts the worker in the cause of humanity.

In all Europe there does not exist today another capital where the public is treated so inconsiderately in regard to war news. The newspapers publish nothing save the official statements—and their "news" can be guessed at. Arrests are made hourly of Viennese who whisper words of Austrian defeat. Spies are everywhere.

In a café on the Praterstrasse I sat in a nervous crowd and saw whispering refugees from Galicia passing their story on, furtively and fearfully. Suddenly I saw a young man, whose pale face told of recent suffering deserted by his companion, who went to the door, whispered to an officer and departed. In a moment the fugitive was arrested. He had talked to a spy.

At the same station, where the incoming trains bring new misery for gay Vienna that was, I talked with a young mother whose husband lay dead on the battlefield. She had fled to the capital to plead with the government which had taken her husband

and robbed her children of a father, for means of support and some of the necessities of life. She told in patient, resigned tones of her sufferings in bringing her three children from Galicia, where her home was to be her haven no longer, and where blood ran deep in the garden beds which she had tended so faithfully, waiting the return of her husband.

"When we arrived at the frontier," she said, "the scenes were awful. We were herded like animals and were treated worse than we treated our dogs. I was days in securing a place in the trains because I had no money. There was a police officer on the train, and he demanded our passports, such money as we had, and when we could show neither he refused for days to let us go on."

The natural impulse of these fugitives here is to speak of the evil days which have befallen them, of their losses and the carnage—and they cannot understand why they are arrested for it.

The sight of automobiles carrying wounded soldiers past the brilliant Hof theater, past the opera, past the Gothic splendor of St. Stephens, where formerly gay cars sped on, bent on pleasure, is one that moves the Viennese to despair.

I talked to one of these wounded soldiers as the car in which he was being carried was stopped in front of the Burge Theater for repairs. He told me in whispers, while the guards were busy with the car, of the frightful ravages made by the Russians and the Servians upon the Austrians.

"They have buried our dead in heaps," he said, tears coursing down his face. "They were killed like sheep driven to a slaughter yard. The Russian artillery had done unbelievable things. The Russians waste their ammunition as though it were free as air. Their infantry is not good, but how terrible is the artillery—how terrible."

Spirit of Patriotism

The spirit of patriotism in the Viennese runs to its highest flood when these wounded men are being conveyed through the streets.

Before the palace of the minister of war, beside the monument of Maria Theresa[4] and of Prince Schwarzenberg,[5] the cannons

4. The very capable ruler of Austria, Hungary, and Bohemia (1717–1780)
5. Prince Karl Philipp of Schwarzenberg (1771–1820) was an Austrian field marshal. He distinguished himself in wars against the Turks and Napoleon's armies.

and arms captured from the Russians are on view. They are insignificant arms, but the people do not tire of caressing them. The meager signs of Austrian success are like gleams of hope in a leaden sky of despair.

And patrolling the streets, one sees increasing in number daily, a nondescript army of uniforms. Every color and sort of ancient regalia has been brought forth from old storehouses.

In the hour when war and its horrors are keeping a pall over Vienna, the sight of religious processions, headed by priests praying for divine aid, brings out in relief the picture of faith. The churches are constantly filled with women and children praying for husbands and fathers and brothers who may never return.

In the time of sorrow too great to endure alone, the people are throwing themselves more and more upon the bosom of the church, which has offered them consolation so many times before.

Murmurs of Protest

While the devout are filling the churches and the wounded are filling the hospitals, while the wretched fugitives are bringing with them famine from Galicia, accusations and protests are rising above the murmurs of distress, against the rich.

On different subscription lists opened daily for the Red Cross, the sight of unbelievably small sums given by members of the nobility and by millionaires, has brought forth waves of indignation.

A feudal prince who is among the richest men in Europe has subscribed 20 crowns ($4).

Everywhere one hears criticism of the aristocracy, of the high nobility and their avarice. This selfishness, say the people, is traditional, but the public believed that in an hour like this even the tightened purses of the nobility would open.

It has been suggested that a list be published, giving the names of the nobility, of the rich who have been guilty of avarice, and who have added to the general public depression. Emperor Francis Joseph does not conceal his indignation against these grasping members of the nobility.

Nellie Bly (Elizabeth Jane Cochran Seaman) (1864–1922)

"I want you to get into a taxi and come here, Miss Bly," he said.
"I have received just now the worst cases I have ever seen
in my entire life. They may interest you."

"Paints Horrors of War's Work"
Nellie Bly
Tensas Gazette (St. Joseph, LA), February 26, 1915 (International
News Service)[6]

Budapest—Ten languages are spoken in the hospital, and nurses, German, Austrian, Gulitzin, Hungarian and Servian, are employed, so that patients will always have nurses who speak their language.

They have also a series of chapels, Catholic, Protestant and Hebrew. Off each ward are small soundproof rooms called "death chambers."

Patients on the point of death are removed to these rooms to spare the feelings of their fellow comrades. Smoking rooms, glass partitioned, are also an adjunct to each ward.

This hospital accommodates 2,000 wounded. The kitchen is superb and needs a column to properly describe it. They showed with pride a large American refrigerator. The doctors and nurses each have their sleeping, eating and rest departments. One large hall, gayly decorated with the national colors, is used for the amusement of the convalescent. Every kind of shows are given and concerts.

Men were being received from a train, so we went down to see them. We talked to them, as detachments of 20 were taken at a time to the bath.

I cannot praise too highly the wonderful executive ability of those who conceived and established the astounding perfection of these two hospitals. Nothing is wanting to aid and assist nature to save and heal what man is so inhumanly torturing and destroying.

We had scarcely reached the Astoria[7] when I had a telephone call from Doctor MacDonald.

6. Bly's war stories were syndicated by INS and thus appeared in many newspapers.
7. The Astoria Hotel where she stayed

Called to Hospital

"I want you to get into a taxi and come here, Miss Bly," he said. "I have received just now the worst cases I have ever seen in my entire life. They may interest you."

I rushed to the American Red Cross hospital. It is located in Mexico street in a large building, formerly used as a home for the blind. I flew in the door and up the stairs over which floats a 50-foot American flag.

Doctor MacDonald, grave and sad, met me at the head of the stairs. "Come into the operating room," he said, taking my hand. "I have the most frightful case I ever saw."

Nellie Bly's 1914 passport photo. The most famous woman journalist in the world in the nineteenth century, Bly reported on fighting on the Eastern Front in 1914. *Source:* Certificate no. 1250, U.S. Passport Certificates 1101–1500, 22 June 1915-24 June 1915, National Archives Record Group 59, Archives II, College Park, MD.

Mr. Schriner,[8] who had enough misery for one day, had tried to induce me not to come. Failing he had come along. Silently he kept at my side.

The operating room was in confusion. On the floor was blood. Filling pails and in piles were bloody bandages. I tried not to see. I began to wish I had not come.

Four American Red Cross nurses stood gravely around an operating table. Doctor MacDonald pointed to two bandaged stumps. I could see one foot was gone at the ankle, the other apparently half way to the knee.

"This is a Russian," said the doctor. "He was wounded by a shot through his body. For eight days he lay in the trench unattended. His feet froze. He was put on a freight train, and when we received him an hour ago his feet had dropped off, doubtless in the car, for we never saw them, and the last blood the poor fellow had was pouring from his open veins. We carried him here and bandaged him up, but he cannot live many minutes longer. He has no pulse now. Come, look at him."

A Dreadful Sight

Come, look, reader, with me! My whole soul shrank from the sight. The doctor took me by the hand. I kept my eyes away from the face I was afraid to look upon.

"Look at this body," said the doctor. I looked—I shuddered. The clay-pallor of death. The ribs cutting the skin. Bones, bones, no flesh anywhere.

The head turned. Great, hollow black eyes looked into mine. Transfixed. I stood, heartsick, soul-sad. Those great hollow eyes searched mine. They tried to question me. They spoke soul language to soul. The lips parted, a moan, a groan of more than physical agony. He spoke. I could not understand. His words were a sound my ears shall never forget. The appeal, the longing, the knowledge.

"What does he say?" I cried, unable to stand it. "Can no one understand? Can't you find someone to speak to him?"

A nurse smoothed his forehead. An attendant held fast the pale, pale hands.

---

8. Bly misspells the name of George Schreiner, a reporter for the Associated Press.

"The attendant understands" the doctor said: and to him, "What does he say?"

Asked for Children

"He is asking for his children," was the low reply.

The hollow, black eyes turned again to search mine. I could not endure their question. I had no answer to give.

"Let me go!" I said to the doctor.

The low moans seemed to call me back, but I walked steadfastly toward the door and down the corridor.

"Could emperors and czars and kings look on this torturing slaughter and ever sleep again?" I asked the doctor.

"They do not look," he said gently. "Only by witnessing such horrors can one realize them."

"Miss Bly," cried Von Leidenforst, running down the hall, "that poor fellow just died!"

This is only one case. Travel the roads from the scene of battle; search the trains; wounded, frozen, starved thousands are dying in agonizing torture—not hundreds, but thousands. And as they die thousands are being rushed into their pest-filled trenches to be slaughtered in the same way.

Eleanor Franklin Egan (1879–1925)

They began by gathering up the Armenians in Constantinople at the rate of about fifty a day, and among the first to go were many of the teachers and servants from the American schools.

"Behind the Smoke of Battle"
Eleanor Franklin Egan
The Saturday Evening Post, February 5, 1916

Behind the great curtain of battle across the entrance to the Dardanelles and on Gallipoli Peninsula[9] terrible things have been happening in Turkey these months past. When that curtain lifts, and not before, the full details will be revealed of one of the most

9. The Allies' ill-fated campaign on Turkey's Gallipoli peninsula extended from February 1915 to January 1916.

astounding scenes in history. The Committee of Union and Progress of the Young Turk Government, who are of the Company of
the House of Faith, which is Islam, are engaged in the congenial
task of dispersing two million Christian Ottoman subjects—the
Armenians.

However the performance may be referred to in the outside
world, that is what the Turks call it—"dispersing." Quietly, system-
atically, with a fixed intent, the work goes on; and already a million
and a half of the hated tribe have been driven from their homes,
with an incidental loss of life among them estimated at above
eight hundred thousand. An exaggeration? We must wait until the
curtain lifts. These were the figures whispered to me in Constantinople, always with an assurance that they minimized rather than
overstated the facts.

From the beginning Christian protest has not been wanting.
The Sublime Porte[10] has been repeatedly besieged by appeals and
approached with carefully guarded warnings of a future settlement;
but the Sublime Porte has been arrogant and immovable. Indeed,
the Sublime Porte is impatient of outside interference these days
and has answered warnings with threats.

In writing about this fearful thing one must, for obvious reasons,
be cautious. Names and exact localities cannot be mentioned without fear of getting somebody into trouble. Everything that is written
about Turkey and about Germany in Turkey gets back to Constantinople in some mysterious way almost as soon as it is published,
and information bureaus are organized in minutest detail. Specific
reference is not necessary anyhow; not yet. The scene of actual
atrocities embraces all Asia Minor, and there is not a town with
Armenians in it that has not long since felt the heavy hand of
government.

The reports came into Constantinople slowly and by devious
underground routes; and so ever present and breathless was the
fear of retaliatory massacre in the city itself that nobody would
speak freely, nobody would tell all he knew, and written commu-
nications were concealed or destroyed as though the possession
of them constituted the highest crime. I brought out with me, and
had with me through five days' detention on the border of Turkey,

10. Literally a gate into the Topkapi Palace, but it is used here as a figure of speech
denoting the Turkish (Ottoman) government.

a copy of the original order that was posted in Armenian towns and communities throughout Asia Minor sometime in June.

A Copy of the Proclamation

I was told in London and am assured by Armenian societies here that mine is the first copy of this document to be brought out of Turkey. I find it difficult to believe this, but after making careful inquiry I have decided that it must be true. I do know that bringing it out was for me a dangerous venture. I mentioned it in my story of five days in a Turkish prison and have since had a number of inquiries as to how I managed to conceal it. One stranger friend in the West hazards the guess that I had it between the lining and the leather of my shoe. No, nothing so easily guessable. I had it copied on the innermost inner margins of a perfectly harmless-looking book which I was more or less ostentatiously reading when the Turkish examiner came aboard my train. He picked the book up, shook it, ran its pages with his thumb a few times, and subjected it to what he doubtless considered a careful scrutiny, but none of the hazardous penciling revealed themselves and I was permitted to carry it off to prison with me, while the wholly uncompromising notes which were taken away from me went back to Constantinople to be passed on by the censor there.

I don't mind admitting that during my five days' suspense under the eyes of an armed guard that book became to me an object of curious dread. And with reason too. My keepers were ignorant Turks whose instructions were not to permit anybody to carry a written line across the border; I had outwitted them for the moment, a thing no Turk can stand in any case, and if by chance they had discovered my suspicious looking and so carefully hidden notes the word "perilous" would not have been too melodramatic to use in describing my situation. I think I should probably have figured as the party of the first part in a mysterious disappearance. The proclamation reads:

"Our fellow countrymen, the Armenians, who form one of the racial elements of the Ottoman Empire, having taken up, as a result of foreign instigation for many years past, with a lot of false ideas of a nature to disturb the public order; and because of the fact that they have brought about bloody happenings and have attempted to destroy the peace and security of the Ottoman state, the safety and interests of their fellow countrymen, as well as of themselves; and, moreover, as they have now dared to join themselves to the enemy of their existence"—Russia—"and to the enemies now at war with our state—our government is compelled to adopt extraordinary measures and sacrifices, both for the preservation of the order and security of the country and for the welfare and the continuation of the existence of the Armenian society. Therefore, as a measure to be applied until the conclusion of the war, the Armenians have to be sent away to places which have been prepared in the interior vilayets;[11] and a literal obedience to the following orders, in a categorical manner, is accordingly enjoined on all Ottomans:

"First—All Armenians, with the exception of the sick, are obliged to leave within five days from the date of this proclamation, by villages or quarters, and under the escort of the gendarmerie.

"Second—Though they are free to carry with them on their journey the articles of their movable property which they desire, they are forbidden to sell their lands and their extra effects, or to leave the latter here and there with other people, because their exile is only temporary and their landed property and the effects they will be unable to take with them will be taken care of under the supervision of the government, and stored in closed and protected buildings. Anyone who sells or attempts to take care of his movable effects or landed property in a manner contrary to this order shall be sent before the Court Martial. They are free to sell to the government only the articles which may answer the needs of the army.

"Third—Contains a promise of safe conduct.

"Fourth—A threat against anyone attempting to molest them on the way.

"Fifth—Since the Armenians are obliged to submit to this decision of the government, if some of them attempt to use arms against the soldiers or gendarmes, arms shall be employed against them and they shall be taken dead or alive. In like manner those who, in opposition to the government's decision, refrain from leaving or seek to hide themselves, if they are sheltered or given food and assistance, the persons who thus shelter or aid them shall be sent before the Court-Martial for execution."

11. Provinces

The Revolt at Van

It is not difficult to picture the reign of terror that ensued throughout Armenian Turkey and in all Armenian settlements on the posting of this proclamation. It struck down the hands of two million Christian people and left them in a state of helplessness beyond words to describe. It did not leave them even the refuge of friendship; and the promises of protection, both as to life and to property, were not to be taken seriously, as everybody knew. It was a literal order for banishment and confiscation, and the only way any Armenian could escape it was by turning Mohammedan.

It has always been the Turkish habit to make whole Christian communities within Ottoman borders pay for the offenses of individual citizens or of small rebellious groups; but this fact does not quite explain the present unprecedented movement.

At the beginning of the war some Armenians on the border between Turkey and Russia—Armenians who had felt the weight of Turkish oppression always, and many of whose people had been victims of the massacres of Abdul-Hamid[12]—went over and joined the Russian Army; while an organized body of them placed themselves in armed opposition to the Turkish forces at Van. This was unfortunate; and, since it was open rebellion, it called for the usual punishment, which no nation would deny Turkey the right to inflict. But the rebels represented but a handful of the great Armenian population, and the wholesale retaliation which has been meted out and is being meted out by the government now is so far beyond the bounds of necessity or reasonable excuse that it can be regarded only as another exhibition of the characteristic national shortsightedness and stupidity which have made so many pages of Turkey's modern history amazing to an intelligent world.

How the Armenians got arms nobody knows. It is and has been for many years a capital offense for any of them to carry weapons; but because there were arms along the eastern border it became expedient to assume that they were scattered throughout the country, and the methods of torture practiced on the luckless people to get them to reveal the hiding places of their mythical stores of guns and ammunition are too horrible to write about.

12. Massacres of Armenians and other Christians in the Ottoman Empire in the mid-1890s, named for the Ottoman ruler at the time, Sultan Abdul Hamid II.

One man, an American doing business in Turkey, tells of getting off a train at a station not far from Constantinople and of seeing a man behaving in a most extraordinary manner. He was dancing along on his toes and shrieking with what sounded like maniacal laughter. The American asked a bystander what the trouble was with him and was told that he had just been undergoing bastinado.[13] The bystander was a Turk and he delivered this information with a laugh.

Another man, an Armenian, in writing about the scenes of torture, says with a sort of plaintive simplicity: "In the old days anywhere from twenty-five to fifty strokes were considered enough, but now they don't stop under a hundred strokes and sometimes they give as many as two hundred. The calves of the legs swell and burst; the victim faints and is revived time and again, and many of them lose their reason under it."

Though the Armenian is a brave man if he has a fighting chance, aggressiveness in a political sense is conspicuously absent in the racial character. They are a people subdued by fear and desiring only to live in peace. If they had been capable of organized and general revolt against Turkish rule they would have risen long ago, if for no other purpose than to wreak vengeance on their age-long oppressors.

It is not fear of Armenian rebellion that is actuating the Young Turks now. It is the same jealousy, cupidity and fanatic racial hatred which, given free rein for longer than we know, has engendered in the very nature of the Turk a belief in his right to plunder and to persecute these people. The little rebellion on the far border of the country gave them a much-desired excuse for action at a time when all eyes are fixed on more far-reaching and important events; when great tragedies are dwarfed by greater tragedies and may be expected to strike soundlessly and resultless against the sensibilities of a tragedy-numbed world.

Everybody knows about the attempted launching of a Holy War when Turkey was drawn into this bewildering conflict. Throughout the Ottoman Empire the imams in the mosques read to the thronging, excited crowds the extraordinary declaration. It is a long and complicated address, but in every line it shrieks a fanatic hatred so

---

13. A form of corporal punishment that involves beating the soles of the feet

far removed from what used to be twentieth-century concepts that it sounds like nothing but medieval madness.

"It is necessary to form secret and public unions in the land of Islam," it says. "It is necessary that the people should know from to-day that the Holy War has become a sacred duty, and that the blood of infidels in Islamic lands may be shed with impunity, except those to whom the Moslem power has given security and those who are confederate with it....

"They must know that the killing of infidels has become a sacred duty, whether it be secretly or openly, as the great Koran declares in its word: 'Take them and kill them wherever you come across them, and we have given you a manifest power over them by revelation.' ...

"To whoever kills one single infidel of those who rule over Islamic lands, either secretly or openly, there is a reward like a reward from all the living ones of the Islamic world. And let every individual of the Islamic world, in whatever place he may be, take upon him an oath to kill at least three or four of the infidel enemies of God and enemies of religion. He must take upon him this oath before God Most High, expecting his reward from God alone; and let the Moslem be confident, if there be to him no other good deed than this, nevertheless, he will prosper in the Day of Judgment."

This declaration of a Holy War had nothing to do with the Armenian horrors in Turkey; but it preceded those horrors just long enough to have roused Mohammedan fanaticism to a point where few Turks have any compunction in carrying out the hideous orders of the government.

The Turks knew and have openly declared that the proclamation calling for the removal of all Armenians to the interior was intended for nothing but to give a color of justice to the procedure and to cover secret instructions which were sent throughout the districts marked for immediate depopulation, instructions that withdrew from the Armenians all protection of law.

I have already said that a million and a half have been removed, with a reported mortality among them of more than eight hundred thousand. No details could add to the frightfulness of the picture these figures present, but details are not wanting. The process of removal is a simple one, since it involves no responsibility on the part of the government for the welfare of the exiles. Secret agents are sent into the towns and villages, with powers that give them command over all local authorities; they post the proclamation and, with the aid of carefully organized and well-rewarded espionage, see that it is literally obeyed.

The pitiless sentence, "All Armenians must leave," does not mean that the government undertakes to gather them up and transport them to the places of exile. It means that they must report to a headquarters, learn where they are to go, either their final destination or a concentration camp, and then proceed on their own responsibility and entirely at their own expense. They must abandon their business, their affairs of all kinds, their homes, and every thing they possess that they cannot carry with them in their hands or on their backs; and they must submit without a murmur to any indignities that may be heaped on them.

It is said that when companies gather to start on the march, the Turks, their very neighbors, and especially Turkish women, crowd their trail like jackals and take away from them, without a chance of interference from the gendarmes, anything they may happen to want; so that many a helpless band goes off empty-handed, stripped of everything except such money and small treasures as they may happen to have concealed about them.

And it was not to be expected that some of the Moslem populations—Turks, Kurds and Arabs—would long be content with the monotony of dispersal. They soon grew tired of it and resorted in many places to the old and established methods of wholesale butchery. From various points have come reports of massacres as deliberate and complete as those Abdul-Hamid organized and directed during the years from 1894 to 1897. Whole towns have been wiped out, and when I left Turkey there was a growing fear that the slower process would be abandoned for more expeditious measures throughout the empire.

I might say here that it is generally believed that the Sultan, Mohammed V, is as strongly opposed to this performance as he is capable of being opposed to anything. Abdul-Hamid's massacres were his own, devised and ordered by himself; but his successor, who was his prisoner for thirty years, has milder and less cowardly views of things. He is not much in the way of a statesman or man of affairs. How could he be? He was only two years younger than his brother; he never had any real expectation of coming to the throne; and he was confined to his palace and about half a mile of territory round it during the entire time that Abdul-Hamid reigned.

Surrounded by spies and never permitted to see anybody or to know anything of the country's affairs, his favorite pastimes were playing the piano and drinking himself into a state of placid indifference. He plays the piano yet—very well, they say—and he has no taste for blood. He likes neither the war nor the massacres, and has uttered his feeble protest against both. This was told me by a man who knows the Sultan well, speaks his language, and has talked with him freely many times.

The Armenians are an industrious and prosperous element in the Ottoman population. They are the merchants, the bankers, the progressive students of modern life and methods, the teachers, the scientists. In humbler walks of life they are the capable and trusted servants, watchmen and guardians of property, while such advance in agriculture as has been made in Turkey is almost wholly due to their progressiveness and characteristic ambition. They accumulate wealth; and, though long familiarity with Turkish animosity has taught them the folly of ostentation, they house and clothe themselves in comfort and present an appearance of stable and admirable citizenship.

Being, as they undoubtedly are, the absolute sinew of the state, it is a natural question: Why is this thing being done to them? Nobody knows.

Ninety percent of all the business in the big towns on the Black Sea, and, indeed, all through Asia Minor, has been in the hands of Armenians, and their banishment has paralyzed the industrial life of the country. Removals may be made swiftly enough, but orderly confiscation of property and reorganization are slower processes. And those who know say the Turk is absolutely incapable of taking the place in the business life of the country the Armenian has so long occupied, to the country's very marked advantage. The colossal stupidity of it is its most inexplicable feature.

The proclamation speaks of "places which have been prepared in the interior vilayets." No preparation of any kind was ever made, so far as I could learn. The points to which the exiles are sent are to the southward, in the Arabian Desert, along the middle reaches of the Euphrates and in Mesopotamia.

One terrible account came through about eight hundred women and children who were separated from their husbands and fathers, and, with only a few old men among them, were started on a forty-five days' march from their home town to Aleppo, one of the big concentration centers. There were women of culture and refinement among them, who were forced, as the hardier peasants were, to carry on their backs all the necessaries to sustain life on the journey. They were in charge of Turkish gendarmes, whose instructions with regard to them seemed to include nothing about protection. Children were born on the way and the sick women were forced immediately to march on. One woman fell by the road-side in the throes of labor, only to be prodded by the bayonet of a gendarme, who said there was "no time for anything like that." This was reported by an eyewitness. She died and her body was abandoned.

An Armenian woman kneels above her dead child outside the city of Aleppo, in the Ottoman Empire. *Source:* George Grantham Bain Collection, Prints and Photographs Division, Library of Congress, LC-USZ62-48100.

One man wrote in August: "The roads to the south are strewn and stenched with rotting bodies, and the streams are clogged with them. Despairing mothers—insane, of course—throw their infants into the rivers or leave them in the camps to die. Women give up everything they possess—jewels, money, their very clothes and coverings—to buy immunity."

The women who are separated from their men and sent alone to the place of exile are promised that their men will rejoin them, will be marched on more rapidly to prepare places for them; but it seldom happens so. The men, by thousands, have been raided and massacred—"lost" by the way. One Armenian writes: "The purpose is our utter destruction. The Turks say so themselves. Destruction concealed from the world, cold-blooded, calculating! And methods are cunningly contrived to get from us at once all the money we have. We may buy our lives for the time being, but when our means are exhausted we die."

The Concentration Camps

At Ada Bazar there has long been established a concentration camp for about forty thousand people. Each family is given a small space, about eight by eight feet; and in this space every act of life must be performed. The camp is heavily guarded and no Armenian, unarmed and helpless though he be, is allowed outside its boundaries. This is not written about something that happened once on a time, but about something that is happening now. As you read these lines that camp exists. Your mind may dwell on it as one of the countless horrors the bitter winter wind is playing upon to-day in a heretofore comparatively happy world.

But how do these people live? Food and water venders demand exorbitant prices. For the rest one's imagination may give itself free rein. Exaggeration of miserable details is hardly possible. They are concentrated at Ada Bazar for deportation to remote points as rapidly as the authorities can handle them. They are transported in box cars on the Bagdad Railroad and the railroad running east from Smyrna as far as is possible; then come the weary marches. There is an added touch of irony, too, in the fact that everybody is made to pay railroad fare.

There were a number of women teachers and students from one of the American mission schools who were gathered up and sent to a point far down on the Bagdad Railroad from which they expected to be marched south into Mesopotamia. The American Ambassador, whose unceasing efforts in behalf of the Armenians would move heaven and earth if heaven and earth could be moved, entered a warm protest against this, and followed it up with sufficient pressure to induce Talat Bey[14] to promise that they should be sent back to their school. Under orders joyfully obeyed they got on a train and returned to Ada Bazar, only to find when they got there that there had been a change of the official mind. They were immediately ordered back to where they came from, and were made to pay for the journey the third time.

The great dispersal began out on the eastern border and in the Black Sea cities, but it moved very rapidly in the direction of Constantinople, until it embraced the whole of Asia Minor. American consuls and businessmen everywhere have seconded the splendid efforts of their Ambassador to mitigate the sufferings of the people in some degree, but their action has been met with threats of violence against themselves.

One young North Carolinian, representative of a large American concern with ramifications throughout the world, was arrested, treated with an entire lack of consideration and sent to Constantinople. The authorities assured him they would confiscate the valuable stores in his large warehouses, but his characteristic American answer was: "All right; there they are." When I saw him last, nothing had happened. He had committed no offense, he was merely in the way of contemplated large operations which they did not want him to see; so he was deported to Constantinople.

Talat Bey promised that Constantinople should not be touched. He even gave an intelligent reason, based on expediency, why it should not be touched. Tranquility in the capital and an orderly continuance of the city's business routine were too important to the situation to be disturbed for the time being; but something happened to change the Ministerial mind.

They began by gathering up the Armenians in Constantinople at the rate of about fifty a day, and among the first to go were many of the teachers and servants from the American schools. Nearly

14. Mehmed Talaat, (AKA Talaat Pasha, Talaat Bey) was the Grand Vizier of Turkey from February 1917 to October 1918. As Minister of Interior Affairs in 1915, Talaat initiated the Armenian Genocide. He fled the country in early November 1918 and was assassinated in Berlin in 1921 by a member of the Armenian Revolutionary Federation.

everybody one knew had lost or was in danger of losing some friend or valued retainer. The gatekeepers and watchmen at the Embassies and other foreign establishments were gathered up and sent into the interior regardless of the fact that they were men who could not be replaced.

I went with a party of friends a few days before I left to explore in a thorough manner the seventh-century Walls of Heraclius, from the Golden Horn up round the site of the ancient Palace of Blachernæ and on to Adrianople Gate. With us was a British clergyman who has been in Constantinople for a great many years, and who has a detailed and accurate knowledge of the city's history, which he is able and willing to impart in a manner to make such an expedition in his company a rare privilege. We were having a memorably pleasant afternoon.

We had followed a winding course for an hour or more through towers and underground passages, over crumbling ruins and past long, perfectly preserved stretches of the glorious old battlemented structure, when we came to a little wooden gate through which the reverend doctor said we must pass to get into the Tower of Anemas.

Mary Anderson Bereft

"And now," said the doctor, "we are going to see Mary Anderson. Mary is so ugly that the name was suggested to me by acute contrast; but she has a rare smile, Mary has, and I always like to see her, because she cheers me up."

He pulled a cord, which rang a little tinkling bell off somewhere behind the low house beyond the gateway, and pretty soon Mary came and admitted us.

She was trying hard to smile, but the tears were coursing down her poor old wrinkled face and she was sobbing under the most pitiful efforts at self-control ever witnessed.

"In goodness' name, what's the matter, Mary?" exclaimed the doctor.

Then she gave up and frankly wept, wept bitterly.

"They have just taken my son," she said; "he left not twenty minutes ago. If you had only been here! Maybe they would have let him stay for you. They took his father only last week, and I don't know where either of them has gone."

She spoke Turkish, which the doctor translated for us as she talked. She was left entirely alone, with no means of support, and she had no idea what was to become of her. She only knew that in all probability she had seen the last of both her husband and son, and she plaintively emphasized the fact that she was not given the comfort of having them taken at the same time, so that she might know they were together.

The worst of it is that such poor Armenians are not able to pay their way and in consequence their sufferings are increased a thousandfold. They are given neither food nor clothing, except by their fellow exiles, and they are not permitted to do anything to earn a living until they reach their destination. Does not the proclamation say "If they are sheltered or given food and assistance the persons who thus shelter or aid them shall be sent before the Court-Martial for execution"? This is meant to apply only to those who "refrain from leaving or seek to hide themselves"; but fear makes it applicable to all. Everywhere they are shunned as death's-heads.

Madeleine Zabriskie Doty (1877–1963)

The woman wants to sell her child. She says she hasn't anything to eat. She isn't a German mother. Of course, no German mother would do such a thing.

"War's Burden Thrown on Poor of Germany as Food Supply Dwindles"
Madeleine Z. Doty
New York Tribune, November 19, 1916

I awoke to find myself in Germany. I sprang from bed and crept to the window. Beneath lay an empty courtyard—quiet, still, no sign of life.

I press the electric button and order breakfast. A pale, worried little man arrives with a tray. There is the same undrinkable coffee of the night before, a tiny drop of blue watery-milk in a doll's pitcher no bigger than my thumb, no sugar, some black, sour, uneatable bread, and a small saucer of marmalade.

Irritation seizes me. How can I spend weeks in Germany without proper food? I remember my box of American crackers, and the Danish butter and sausage reposing in the hotel refrigerator. But I have the decency not to send for them. I have at most some weeks of discomfort, the German people months of patient suffering.

Poor Get Meat Allowance

The Danish food shall go to a German friend. By the time I am dressed, my traveling companion, No. 50, has joined me. We decide to make a tour of the city.

It is a gray, sunless day. The weather increases the gloom of the city. Only a few people are upon the street; old people or very young people and tiny children. But occasionally we pass a silent, dejected group lined up before a meat shop.

It is a meat day. Working women with babies in their arms, or tiny children carrying baskets, or old decrepit men and women clutching a Government meat card, patiently wait their turn. The shop door flies open, three or four are admitted, and a miserable half pound of meat portioned out to each.

Except for these food purchasers, the city seems actionless. We enter a book shop and ask for a map. But to sell a plan of Hamburg is verboten. So many things are verboten. Perhaps that accounts for the inactivity. Store windows present a fine display, but inside the shop is silent and empty.

Imperator Rusts in Disuse

Even in the business section there is little life. We find a small boat that makes a three hours' trip about the harbor, and take it. The great wharves are peopleless, no hurrying men, no swinging derricks, no smoke issuing from smoke stacks or funnels. In the docks lie big and little boats, rusty, paintless, deserted.

The great Imperator,[15] like a towering monster, commands the center. The paint is peeling from its sides. Its brass is dull, some dirty stained blankets flap on an upper deck. Like a thing alive it seems stricken with plague. Its proud title "Imperator" is gone, and in its place is the word "Cap Polonia."

Except for our tug and two others, no vessels move upon the water. There are no whistles, no chug-chug and swish of passing boats, no vibrant thrilling life. Hamburg is a city of sleepers. Its big hotels, its many stores, its impressive buildings stretch out endlessly, but within all is still.

---

15. A large passenger liner built in 1912 for the Hamburg America Line, a transatlantic shipping company. It sat idle in Hamburg during the war. As Doty notes, it fell into disrepair.

Like a Dying City

All that modern industry and the ingenuity of man can achieve has here been flung upon the land, and then the force that created it has vanished, leaving these great monuments to rot, to rust, and to crumble. The tragedy of unused treasures is as horrible as rows of dead. A city seems visibly dying.

Faint from want of food, we leave the boat to seek a restaurant. We find one directly opposite the Hamburg-American docks, on the hill side. We seat ourselves on the outdoor porch which commands the harbor. As we do so, we notice a long line of women and children filing into the big Hamburg-American buildings. Each bears a pail. When they emerge it is with steaming contents. The docks have been turned into big feeding kitchens.

When the women leave, a whistle blows. Then from every direction come old men and young boys. They come running, hopping, jumping, each striving to be first, driven by hunger, or by fear that the last may have nothing. The police keep them in order. They file into the big building to eat.

The meal furnished us is scanty, but after this scene it seems bountiful. There is soup, fish, meat, vegetables, fruit, and cheese. The bread and meat are to be had only with cards. Like the day before, the food is watery and tasteless. It is such food as is served in institutions. Prison diet does not promote health or strength. One can live on it, but patriotism and temper suffer.

Bread is of Two Kinds

I discovered there are two kinds of bread, one a small roll, its substance only slightly dark. This is very eatable, and quite different from the ordinary black bread. Six of these small rolls can be had on a daily bread card. This bread, with a piece of Swiss cheese, do much to restore me to cheerfulness.

When we have finished, No. 50 suggests a trip to the Bismarck Denkmal.[16] She is an ardent admirer of Bismarck and all German officials. It is only a short walk to the Denkmal. It is situated on a small hill, and the gigantic figure is further elevated by a high pedestal, till it towers over the city.

16. A monument to Otto von Bismarck (1815–1898), the first chancellor of the German Empire, created in 1871

The monument (*denkmal*) in Hamburg, Germany to Otto von Bismarck, who orchestrated the unification of Germany in 1871 and became the first chancellor of the German Empire. *Source:* Janet Hartl photograph, Wikimedia Commons.

There is something sinister in the figure. It is clad in armor, and leans on a gigantic sword. It seems to say "no force in the world shall deter me; I conquer all."

Yet there is weakness behind the strength. As a work of art it is a failure. It is made of square cut stone, placed on square cut stone. This endless multiplicity of exactly similar stones, well ordered and arranged, has the effect of massive greatness. But it is a greatness built from the outside. Beneath is no inspired central vein of strength.

"Germany Could Conquer All"

It is different with French sculpture. Rodin's figures, for instance, personify power. The power that arises from depicting the fire, energy, and originality of the human soul. But my companion is enthralled. This massive greatness of arrangements means to her strength.

"Isn't it wonderful?" she breathes. "If only he were alive, how different it would be! Germany would conquer all."

The words have hardly left her lips when we hear voices. A crowd of children is gathering just below. School is out, and they are surrounding an object of interest. One or two women join them. There is no passing populace to swell the throng.

We approach and see in the center of the crowd of children a woman crouched upon a bench. She is dirty, ragged, and dark in coloring. She may be Armenian or Italian. On the ground at her feet is a baby just big enough to walk. It also is dirty, and possesses only one ragged garment.

The mother sits listless, gazing at her child. It is evident she is soon to be a mother again. There is great chattering among the children. I turn to my companion for explanation.

Wants to Sell Child

"The woman wants to sell her child. She says she hasn't anything to eat. She isn't a German mother. Of course, no German mother would do such a thing. You can see she isn't good. She is going to have another baby."

A school-child gives the toddling baby some cherries. She eats them greedily. My hand goes to my pocket-book, but my companion pulls me away. If I bought the baby, what could I do with her on a trip through Germany?

Then my eyes rest on the Bismarck Denkmal. I gaze at that massive, methodical, stolid war god at whose feet this human tragedy is being enacted. Rage seizes me, and a brilliant and crazy idea comes. Why not blow up the military Denkmals as a way of freeing Germany from the war bug? The Allies are stupidly making women and children suffer, while the military class and militarism flourish. What is wanted is a bomb for each Bismarckian and royal Denkmal.

Finds Café Crowded

From the Denkmal we go to the residential quarter. We try to get a taxi, but there is none. I saw just three during that day. It has grown to be tea-time. After a short walk, we enter a popular café. Here at last is a large group of people. There are many well-dressed women, retired officers or officers home on leave, and some slightly wounded soldiers.

The tables in the big building or scattered about on the side walk are all occupied. A band is playing gay music. On the surface all looks well. But a line of Whitman flashes through my mind:

> *Smartly attired, countenance smiling, form upright, death under the breast-bones, hell under the skull-bones.*

There is no chatter and no laughter. The faces are lined with sadness. Except among the women, there is no youth. All are shrunken, listless, distraught. Coffee "Ersatz" (coffee mixed with a substitute), and tea "Ersatz" is being served. There is no milk and no sugar. The few cakes are made of an unknown substance. I try one, but cannot swallow it. Only the music is cheerful. There is a revival of band-playing in Germany. It is needed to hide the lack of laughter and talk.

Mind and Body Starve

There are but two topics of conversation—war and food shortage. There is nothing else to discuss, for there is little business, no trade, no reforms, no scientific discoveries, no creative work. Life has become mere existence—a prison existence. Mind and bodies are shrinking from a shortage of intellectual and physical nourishment.

This first day in Germany is the worst. Fresh from war-free countries, the impression is vivid. After a little I become adjusted. All who live in Germany get adjusted. The changes have come gradually. One month sugar stops. When this is an old story, then one must learn to do without milk. Herr Smyth fails one week, and Herr Bauer weeks later. This slow decline blinds Germany to what is really occurring. But the total, seen by a stranger, is appalling.

Across the street from the café is a little circular space with benches. On a bench is seated a tragic, well-dressed mother in deep mourning. Her child plays beside her, innocently happy. He climbs up and down, and finally knocks a paper bag from the bench. A roll tumbles into the dust and darts under the bench, covering itself with dirt. The mother picks it up, carefully brushes it, and gives it to the child, who eats eagerly. Everywhere are similar pathetic incidents.

Go to City's Best Hotel

My spirits sink lower and lower. "Look here," I say firmly to my companion, "I've got to have a square meal. We are going to the best and most expensive hotel in town."

That evening we dine at the Atlantic, and have a meal that is satisfying. By a skillful use of wine, salt, and some stray scraps of fat, the table d'hôte dinner is equal to that of a second rate American hotel. The slice of meat served is no bigger than my hand, brown and juiceless, but the soup, fish, vegetables, and dessert would pass muster anywhere.

It seems cruel to eat of Germany's best, but henceforth I decided to live at the most expensive hotels.

That night a picture flashed before me. It is the vision of a big unoccupied building. In large black letters upon its front is the inscription: "English Reform Church," and in its gaping windows are plastered, printed signs reading: *"Zu vermieten"* (To Let). No wonder God's buildings are to let. God, the Spirit of Love, must have difficulty finding any place to rest these days.

Starts for Berlin

Next morning my companion and I separate. She starts for Switzerland, and I for Berlin. My inability to speak German is disconcerting. I manage to get on the train, but in the dining car

I am helpless. I content myself with tea, bread, and cheese, the only words I know.

In the compartment with me is an attractive young woman and her husband. They offer me magazines and papers. I summon up courage to say: "*Ich kann nicht Deutsch sprechen*," and show them my credentials. The young woman is immediately interested. She speaks to me in excellent English.

In May, 1915, I spent ten days in Berlin. Then English could not be spoken with comfort. Flushed faces and angry looks were the result. To-day English is tolerated. Occasionally, eyes follow me questioningly; the official class resent it, but the people are always friendly.

A year ago there was bitter hatred of America. "American bullets"[17] were flung in one's face everywhere. To-day the average person is pathetically eager to be friends. Slowly the people are awakening. For months the newspapers have fed them on the triumphs of Germany and the perfidy of other nations. But these stories of glorious German victories have resulted in—what? A lean and barren country, under-nourishment, death, the hatred of other nations. The people begin to doubt their leaders.

To call these people "barbarians" is an outrage. They are like ourselves, just folks, kindly and generous; deceived and browbeaten by a ruthless military group.

The young woman in the railway carriage belongs to the well-to-do bourgeoisie. She is eager to talk. "Why," she asks, "does the world think we're beaten when we have soldiers in Belgium and France?" Often this question is asked. Boasting no longer exists. Instead comes the plaintive query: "Why are we beaten, and why must we suffer?"

We gaze out of the window as the train speeds on. We pass great stretches of desolate, barren, juiceless land. It is sandy and difficult to cultivate. It is the worst portion of Germany. A tear is in my companion's eye. "We have got to have food," she avers, and then a moment later: "Oh! why can't we have peace?"

Throng About Monument

It is early afternoon when we reach Berlin. I leave the train slowly. When I reach the station entrance the taxis and carriages are

---

17. A reference to German resentment that a neutral America was providing munitions to the enemies of Germany

all taken. An aged porter with a push-cart volunteers to conduct me to the Adlon.[18]

It is Sunday. I follow the push-cart through the silent streets, but as we pass the Tiergarten[19] a great throng of people is visible. They flow in and out about the Hindenburg[20] Denkmal. That figure is made of wood and covered with nails. You pay a small sum, and hammer in a nail. In this manner patriotism and Hindenburg devotion are inculcated, and the Government army gets the money.

If ever there were a systematic smashing of Denkmals, it would create a busy day for Berlin. There are so many of them. The Tiergarten strasse is lined with ugly monstrosities of royalty. Many figures are portraits of English nobility who intermarried with Germans. Evidently, whatever comes to Germany becomes German, for all are decorated with wreaths and flowers.

Crowd Not Happy

But the Sunday crowd that moves about the Tiergarten is not happy. As in Hamburg and elsewhere, the men are old or very young, except for the sprinkling of lean, pale, nerve-racked soldiers.

But Berlin has more life than Hamburg.

It is the busiest spot in Germany. It and the munition districts are the centers of activity. Berlin is more active than it was a year ago. Then action seemed suspended. The city was crowded, but idle. The populace was too tense, excited, and grim to work. It moved restlessly upon the streets, waiting a glorious victory. The future was ignored. A long war was not dreamt of.

There was a shortage of fodder, so thousands of cows were killed. This lack of foresight meant in time a shortage of milk and butter.

But Germany was too sure of triumph to think in terms of years. But now conditions have changed. The assurance and arrogance have vanished. In their place is a dull resignation. All life is centered on mere existence.

18. The Adlon Hotel, a luxury hotel
19. A large park
20. General Paul von Hindenburg commanded the Imperial German Army during World War I.

The wounded who have come back have gone to work. Wagons carrying supplies and old patched taxis returned from the front move upon the streets. The necessities of life must be had. Berlin, the seat of government, must secure them.

Little to be Bought

So on the surface there is bustle and action, and life somewhat resembles the normal. But it is a queer, limited, down-at-the-heel activity. People are upon the streets, but the stores are nearly empty. There is a shortage of things to buy. The very rich still purchase, but cheap things are only to be had with Government cards.

That is the tragedy of Germany—the sore spot that festers. The pinch has come, and the rich protect themselves at the expense of the poor.

At the Adlon and other great hotels one suffers little. There is no sugar, but saccharine is served, saccharine which ordinarily can only be had by a doctor's order. It is true the allowance of meat, bread, and butter per person is the same. At the Adlon, butter is furnished on Tuesday and Friday, the two meatless days. For breakfast one received a pat no larger than a big straw berry, and that is all.

Fowls Feed the Rich

But the meat problem hardly touches the rich. Chickens, ducks, and birds are not called meat. They are to be had at high prices. On meatless days they are always served at the Adlon. The fat from these birds to an extent makes up for the lack of butter. Moreover, the poor frequently have no money for meat or butter, and their allowance is purchased by the rich.

It is marvelous with what ingenuity the big hotels conceal deficiencies. That is why visitors and reporters fail to see the underlying truth.

Duck is served the night of my arrival. The table d'hôte dinner is $1.75. I eat every scrap. It is not enough for a hungry man, but for me it is satisfying. As I rise from the table I say to the waiter: "That is as good a dinner as I ever ate." He smiles broadly, greatly pleased.

But I go to bed tormented by the lean and shrunken people I have seen. It is foolish to starve out Germany.[21] This procedure does not hurt the governing classes and the rich. They will not suffer until the rest of Germany is dead.

Starvation kills off the poor, but leaves the militarists intact. This is not the way to crush militarism. It cannot be done by pressure from the outside. Regeneration always comes from within. Revolution or evolution—not smashing—is what is needed.

---

21. A reference to the British naval blockade that prevented Germany from any maritime commerce, including the importation of food

Chapter 5

✦

✦

✦

✦

✦

Pacifists

Forty-four American women traveled to The Hague in April 1915 to attend the International Congress of Women, which would become better known as the Women's Peace Congress. The gathering came in response to a building international movement of women and women's organizations intent on stopping this war and preventing future wars.

For three days, twelve hundred delegates from twelve countries shared their war stories, including many "black-clad wives" and "sorrowing mothers." Their final action was to pass resolutions that called for peace, no transfer of territory, democratic control of foreign policy, and universal women's suffrage. The congress created two committees to carry their resolutions to leaders in each of the capitals of the warring and neutral nations. One committee set off for the Scandinavian countries and Russia. The other, headed by American social reformer Jane Addams, went to England, Germany, France, Italy, and the United States.

Two of the articles included here document the experience of journalists who attended the congress. For them the most remarkable thing about the congress was that it was happening at all. That women, whose countries were at war with each other, whose armies were slaughtering each other's husbands and sons, could sit next to each other and share their distress. "These glimpses of tragedy wrung our hearts," Madeleine Doty explained. "We ceased to be enemies or friends. We were just women."

After the congress, Mary Chamberlain sat with three other journalists to share impressions. They were tired of meetings, notetaking, and straining to understand foreign languages. They wanted to clear their vision and find the real spirit of the event they had just witnessed. Chamberlain's article offers a more objective after-action report of the congress, with background on how it came about and its achievements.

Drafting high-minded resolutions was one thing; conveying them to the warring governments quite another. Mary Hamilton accompanied the delegation headed by Jane Addams as it visited Berlin. The group arrived in Germany only days after a German submarine sank the British passenger liner *Lusitania*. That event charged their visit with heated conversations about the U.S. sale of munitions to Britain and France. Hamilton describes circumstances in Germany and their meetings regarding peace.

Later that same year, another peace effort unfolded, when wealthy industrialist Henry Ford chartered an ocean liner for a private peace mission to war-torn Europe. He hoped to draw so much publicity to the cause of peace to force action by the warring countries. Composed of an odd mix of peace advocates, the group was beset with internal disagreements, a power struggle, and an outbreak of influenza during the voyage. Ford himself abandoned the project, and the press and world opinion came to ridicule the effort.

Helen Ring Robinson, a suffragist and Colorado state senator, joined the Ford peace mission, sailing on the chartered liner *Oscar II* when it took its message of peace to Europe in December 1915. In "Confessions of a Peace Pilgrim," she explains the discord that occurred on the voyage and her ultimate disillusionment with the mission.

Madeleine Zabriskie Doty (1877–1963)

Black-clad wives had made speeches. Sorrowing mothers
had shown their agony. The battle-field became a reality,
covering with dead and dying sons and husbands.
These glimpses of tragedy wrung our hearts. We ceased to
be enemies or friends. We were just women.

"At The Hague"
Madeleine Zabriskie Doty
Short Rations: Experiences of an American Woman in Germany,
1917

It was six P. M. when we left our boat. For several hours she had
been steaming up the narrow waterway to Rotterdam, while the
peace and quiet of Holland descended upon us. On passing barges
Dutch families gazed at us wonderingly. The man of the family,
pipe in mouth, sprawled on deck, and the kiddies dangled their
feet in the water. The song of birds filled the air and buds were
bursting on every tree. The sky was the softest blue. New York,
with its bustle and roar, seemed nearer war than this lazy land of
fresh spring sweetness.

But we had no time for loitering. We dashed from the ship to
the railroad station. There was just two hours before the conference at eight.

When we reached The Hague we found wild confusion. The city
was full of Belgian refugees. There were few vacancies at hotels.
At every street corner one encountered cabs filled with women
delegates madly driving from one hotel to another. Eventually
we all found shelter, but there was no time for dinner. We set off
immediately for the great meeting hall. When we arrived an important looking official waved us sternly back. We had n't stopped for
tickets. But we stood our ground and shouted to a Dutch woman
beyond the entrance, "We are the Americans."

Instantly she was upon us. "Oh," she cried, as she grasped our
hands. "I'm so glad you're alive and not blown up, or at the bottom
of the sea. We did n't know what had happened." Then she led us
triumphantly inside.

It was a gay, if hungry, American delegation that burst upon
the meeting. As Jane Addams mounted the platform and the audience realized we had come, they broke into tumultuous applause.
The place was crowded. People stood everywhere. Seventeen women
sat on the platform, representing different nations. The opening
address was made by a Hollander, and the first speech delivered by
a German.

From the beginning the object of the congress was made
plain. It was not to stop war, but to protest against war and to
lay plans for future peace. For the first time in history, a band

Members of the American delegation to the Women's Peace Congress, held in The Hague in April 1915. Several of the delegates/journalists reported on the congress and on their subsequent visits to Germany in the wake of the *Lusitania* sinking. *Source:* George Grantham Bain Collection, Prints and Photographs Division, Library of Congress, LC-B2- 3443-11.

of women from belligerent and neutral nations had organized. They had risen above war's hatred and grasped hands, as women and mothers.

We went back that night to our scattered dwellings full of fine courage. The moon shown down upon us. The canals shimmered in the moonlight. The Hague seemed a haven of rest and strength. But next morning we saw a sight that made war a reality. On the green plain in front of the assembly hall thousands of young men were being drilled. All Holland was mobilizing. While a thousand women in a big hall were discussing ways to save life, across the street thousands of men were learning how to take life.

It was a mixed company who attended the conference. The diversity was not in ideas, but in careers and temperaments. There were rich and poor, the cold reserved people of the North, and the fiery passionate people of the South. There were women lawyers and women dressmakers, artists and stenographers, reformers and journalists, and many just plain mothers. These women had come together in spite of difficulties over mine-strewn seas and past frontier searches.

Perhaps the Belgian delegates made the most dramatic group. Their path had bristled with difficulties. They had had to get passports from the enemy. The first German appealed to was obdurate, but an official higher up was sought. The sturdy, determined, and energetic Mademoiselle Hammer would not be denied. "We wish to attend a women's congress. It is important; you must let us pass," is what she said. Her courage won the day. But the difficulties were not over. The Belgian train service was inadequate. The first of the journey had to be made in a borrowed automobile. After a while this was stopped, then the women descended and marched two hours with heavy suitcases. Finally the frontier was reached. Then came a search. At last after weary hours of waiting and travel the Belgians arrived triumphant. The word that they were in the hall spread like wild fire. They were invited to the platform. Up they went to fill the vacant chairs next to the German delegation. The house rose in excitement. Then it broke into frantic applause. Handkerchiefs and hats were waved madly and the air was filled with cries of "Bravo." For in spite of our diversity, one bond held all together— the belief in the sacredness of life.

Under the inspiration of the great ideal, under Miss Addams's gentle and wise guidance, under the soft beauty of Holland, our differing personalities and nationalities intermingled. Each morning we worked together; each afternoon we talked and walked and played together and each evening we heard one another speak.

And every day incidents occurred which were pregnant with meaning. On one occasion Mr. and Mrs. Pethick Lawrence of England invited Dr Augsburg and Fräulein Heyman of Germany to dine. A gasp went 'round the dining-room as this little group entered. I was one of the party and heard what was said. "We ought, of course, to get out of Belgium," said the Germans, "but then when you judge us, remember that England is in many places she ought not to be."

"Yes," said the Englishman and woman, "there is, for instance, the Rock of Gibraltar. We have no right there. Some day that rock must go back to its rightful owners." For hours those amazing people talked in great friendliness. They readjusted the world. They did it on the basis of justice, instead of diplomacy. At the close of the evening the Englishman escorted the German ladies to their car and gaily waved his hat in farewell. Such examples had their effect. Soon each was trying to outdo the other in tolerance.

This did not mean a lack of sympathy for the Allies—on the contrary. For instance, Holland's position was thus stated by a little Dutch woman: "When the war broke out, our hearts were with Germany. We have German blood in our veins. The Queen's husband is a German, and the mouth of the Rhine lies in our land. But after a while a change came. Belgian refugees poured into our land. My town of six thousand inhabitants had four hundred to care for. I had five of them in my house. They told tales. We came to dread German autocracy and militarism. We are a free people. We believe in democracy. Before the war three hundred thousand men and women signed a petition for woman suffrage. That's a big number for this little land. Gradually the Queen's attitude has changed in spite of her German husband. Her ministers have made her fear Germany. If Holland went to war to-day it would be with the Allies. We would rather risk English domination than endure German militarism." So spoke this gray-haired, middle-aged Dutchwoman. Then she added, gazing dreamily at her peaceful land: "Of course, if trouble came, we could open our dikes. But we don't want war. Recently there was a call for a hundred thousand additional volunteers. Only ninety men from the big city of Amsterdam responded. No—Holland does n't want war."

Such personal talks were as illuminating as the congress, and as the days glided by we grew ever closer together. The beauty of Holland made us mellow. Overhead the sky was always blue; gay tulips filled the land with color; the air was fragrant with the smell of flowers. Outer dissimilarities merged in the universal. The ties of love, motherhood, and future welfare held.

Only once was a note of nationalism struck as against internationalism. The program from the beginning had centered on plans for future peace. All had agreed the small nations must be insured their integrity, there must be freedom of the seas, that trade must be free to all, that future disputes must be settled by some kind of international cooperation and agreement. On these matters there was perfect accord—accord in spite of difference in language, for every speech had to be put into three tongues—French, English, and German. It was not until the war itself was discussed that there came a rift. That the war should be discussed was inevitable. Day by day, as we sat side by side, we had learned of the suffering in the war-ridden lands. Black-clad wives had made speeches. Sorrowing mothers had shown their agony. The battle-field became a reality, covered with dead and dying sons and husbands. These glimpses of tragedy wrung our hearts. We ceased to be enemies or friends. We were just women. All preconceived plans vanished. There grew an urgent need to do something. It was then the following motion was presented: "Be it resolved that this congress urge the governments of the world to put an end to bloodshed and begin negotiations for peace." On the instant came the note of national-ism. The Belgian delegation rose to its feet. What did peace mean? Surely not the Belgians would be a subject race. Out from their tortured hearts came the cry, *Je suis Belge avant tout.*"[1] Sympathy throbbed in our hearts. Eagerly we explained. A peace founded on justice was our dream. "Would we," they asked, "insert the word just before 'peace'?" Gladly the suggestion was accepted. Both England and Germany voted for the amendment.

Such were the women who made up the congress. Such were the things they said. But as the days came for departure, a rest-lessness grew visible. The suffering of war had laid its hold on the delegates. They wanted something more than mere resolutions—they wanted immediate action. To go quietly home had become impossible. Then a member rose to her feet, "We can't stop here," she begged. "We have demonstrated our solidarity, but there is something greater. We must demonstrate that moral courage to call for the end of war now. Courage to think of no one but the dying men on the battlefield, who turn their glazed eyes to us seeking help. Courage to say not one more shall be killed. Courage to say we can't wait—we must have peace now. Courage to carry this demand personally from nation to nation." This was her plea. Sobs broke from grief-stricken mothers. Tears streamed down faces. Women were stirred past utterance. No vote was needed to carry the motion. The audience rose as one.

So ended the congress, but these meetings were but the prelim-inary steps. In a few days Jane Addams with two other women

---

1. I'm Belgian first and foremost.

started on her pilgrimage. She was to bear the women's message from nation to nation.

What effect this meeting of women will have, who can tell? Idealistic, impractical, it may have been, but little it was not while war rages, force reigns on earth and we forget it is ideas that made that force possible. But ideas can also create good-will. No thought sent out into the world dies. The future lies in our hands. It is for us to mold it.

Mary Chamberlain

"Everybody talks about victory," said Rosika Schwimmer in one of her stirring speeches, "but we women know; that every victory means the death of thousands of sons of other mothers."

"The Women at The Hague"
Mary Chamberlain
The Survey, June 5, 1915

The four of us sat over coffee in the cafe of the Hotel Central in The Hague.

Soldiers in peaked caps, loitering with their sweethearts, passed the window; bicyclists zigzagged dangerously through the crowd: and once in a while, the last bit of Dutch picturesqueness—the wooden shoes, flaring white head-dress and gold hair-pins of a peasant woman, kept us aware that this black-coated orthodox stream of passers-by was not the ebb and flow of Broadway. Inside, the vermilion trimmings and gold braid of smart uniforms gave color to the stodgy gathering of Dutch folk, and a jolly American rag time, though bereft of the American cafe dance-floor, lightened the heavy menu of fish and meats and compotes.

The International Congress of Women was over. The four of us were journalists—tired with taking notes, seeking interviews, hurrying to meetings, straining our ears to foreign languages. We were in danger of losing sight of the spirit of the congress in our zeal to "get a story" from some delegate, in our efforts to straighten out names and numbers and speeches. Now for the first time we were trying to touch this spirit and to clear our vision by an exchange of impressions.

"It was bourgeois," said the Socialist, "a gathering of senti-mentalists. The real people who want the war stopped are the working people and they would have nothing to do with this congress. To me it seemed barren and cold. Why. I've heard a little East Side striker rouse a meeting to a pitch of enthusi-asm that was never touched by those clubwomen and suffrage leaders."

"Self-control, you mean, not lack of feeling," objected the short-story writer. "I felt a great swell of emotion under the reserve of those women from warring nations. Constraint was necessary or it would have burst on the meeting like a shower of shrapnel."

"And as for the delegates from neutral countries," added the newspaper woman, "I'm sure the minds of many of those women were poisoned for the first time with the fear of war. For the first time I believe that hundreds of Dutch women in that audience real-ized that war would mean the flowers of Holland soaked with the blood of the recruits drilling there in front of the Dierentium where the congress met."

From the press-table of the congress back to America, to England, to Germany, to Scandinavia. I knew criticisms had gone as diverse as these. With them had gone others less honest, less intel-ligent, more partisan. The newspapers of the countries from which the delegates came denounced the congress as "pro-German," as traitorous, as hysterical, as base and silly. Some people claimed an influence for the congress far wider than it can attain for years, others decried it as futile.

Bewildered by this wrangle and confusion. I left my friends in the cafe and went to Jane Addams to ask her opinion of the congress. For three days Miss Addams had, as president, steered the business of the congress through a sea of resolutions, amend-ments and suggestions given her in French, German, English and Dutch. She was thoroughly acquainted with the hitches and obstacles that clog every international conference and had been most closely in touch with the members of the congress.

"The great achievement of this congress," said Miss Addams thoughtfully, "is to my mind the getting together of these women from all parts of Europe, when their men-folks are shooting each other from opposite trenches. When in every warring country there is such a wonderful awakening of national consciousness flowing from heart to heart. it is a supreme effort of heroism to rise to the feeling of internationalism, without losing patriotism."

With a rush of tenderness and sympathy I remembered some of the women who sat beside Miss Addams on the platform at the congress—frail little Miss Courtney and Chrystal Macmillan. British to the fiber yet offering a hearty second to many resolutions proposed by German delegates; Lida Gustava Heymann, whose honest straightforward ways made one smile at the insinuation of a congress packed with German spies; valiant Eugenie Hamer, who pushed through from Belgium with five companions; warm-hearted Rosika Schwimmer from Hungary; and Frau Leopoldine Kulka of Austria, with her quiet blue eyes and patient face.

Nearly everyone of those women who sat there side by side so dignified and courteous, had brothers, husbands or friends facing each other in maddened fury or even now mown down by each other's bullets. It was a great test of courage for these women to risk the bitterness of their families, the ridicule of their friends and the censure of their governments to come to this international woman's congress. In the midst of the war tumult which is making all Europe shake, it meant a far sweep of imagination to realize that the feelings of mothers, sisters and wives are the same in all countries and it took the finest generosity for these women to associate themselves in a discussion of means to restore international good will.

The congress that bore this fruit was planned with doubt and misgivings. When the International Alliance for Women Suffrage held its last congress at Budapest in June, 1913, it was decided to hold the next convention at Berlin in June, 1915. Meanwhile the war broke out, kindling its hatred between nations and burning away all thought of an international suffrage gathering. However, a few broadminded women still held fast to their ideals in the midst of these rough realities. Among them, the Dutch National Committee for International Interests, a sub-division of the Alliance for Women Suffrage, ventured to lift up its voice. It proposed that the congress which it was impossible to hold at Berlin should be convoked instead in the Netherlands.

The twenty-six separate countries affiliated with the international alliance were approached, but the answers received were on the whole discouraging. The idea itself met with general favor but it was considered advisable to refrain from holding official assemblies. Therefore, the only chance of success lay in separately consulting the prominent women of the different countries, both belligerent and neutral.

This consultation took place with the result that a meeting was held on February 12-13 in Amsterdam, attended by a number of British, German, Dutch and Belgian women. Here the plans for the International Congress of Women were laid, the preliminary program was drawn, invitations were sent out, committees appointed and the emphasis of the congress turned from political equality to peace.

The next difficulty in the path of the congress confronted, not the central committee at The Hague but those who desired to take part in the conference. It was one thing for these women to accept the invitation to the congress; it was another for them to reach Holland. Of 180 British women accepting the invitation to the congress, two only arrived—Kathleen Courtney and Chrystal Macmillan, English suffragists and members of the International Committee on Resolutions, who reached The Hague a week before the congress opened. The other 178 were first pared down to 24 by the secretary for Foreign Affairs, who advised the Home Office to limit the issuance of passports. Reginald McKenna, British secretary of state for Home Affairs, has explained this action by stating that his colleague in the Department for Foreign Affairs believed that so large a number of English women in a city near to the scene of war and infested with the enemy's spies would constitute a danger for the country. Therefore 24 delegates were sorted out, representing the most important organizations and seeming most prudent in giving out information. In doing this Mr. McKenna, was careful to make it understood that these delegates had received no official character.

The reason for the non-appearance of these twenty-four picked delegates is not quite so clear and must be explained as the "fortunes of war." When a member of parliament who objected to the participation of English women in the congress, asked Mr. McKenna if any of the twenty-four had actually reached The Hague, the secretary replied: "No, indeed. You know that all communication between England and Holland was interrupted after the delegates received their passports."

But while these twenty-four women were waiting at Folkstone for any sort of boat to convey them to Holland, Miss Courtney and Miss Macmillan were making up in quality of membership what England lacked in quantity. It was the hard work and perseverance of these two women that made one almost forget the small proportion of delegates from this allied nation in the membership of the congress. One Canadian delegate, Laura Hughes of Toronto, crossed the Atlantic to represent the colonies.

The action of the British government in suspending traffic between England and Holland was also responsible for nearly cutting off the American contingent from the congress. For four days the steamship Noordam, loaded with ammunition for the Dutch government in the hold, and with forty-two peace delegates to the Dutch capital in the first cabin, lay at anchor off Diel. The delegates sent telegrams to the American ambassador at London and the American consul at Dover; they held meetings to devise ways and means to investigate the halt; finally, they settled down to face the fact that they were as nothing compared to the transference of troops to France or the movements of the British fleet. Then just as mysteriously as she had been delayed, the Noordam was ordered to proceed, and we reached Rotterdam without meeting mines or further mishaps, the very day the congress opened.

Much has been said by the press and critics of the congress of the "Germanizing" of this peace meeting. The thirty German delegates and the fifteen Austrians and Hungarians present have been called the "Kaiser's cat's-paws," German spies and many other names. It has been suggested that the German and Austro-Hungarian governments were only too glad to be represented at a peace meeting; it has even been hinted that the expenses of the congress were met by German government funds. Strangely enough, the newspapers of a country from which a large number of delegates were excluded by government orders—Great Britain,—were loudest in proclaiming that the congress was steamrollered by the Germans!

As a matter of fact, the way of the German, Austrian and Hungarian delegates was not altogether paved with ease and cordiality. Although they finally received their passports without trouble, they were at first suspected by their governments and at all times they have been the butt of ridicule and calumny of the press and the general public. The union of German women, for example, has almost unanimously denounced the participation of German women in the congress.

All the delegates openly declared that they did not represent the sentiment of the majority of women in their fatherlands, but only small, radical groups. Among them are women whose names are well known to the international Suffrage Alliance and in social work. Anita Augspurg and Lida G. Heymann of Munich, are founders of the suffrage movement in Germany; Helene Stöcker and Fraülein Rotten of Berlin are, respectively, president of the League for the Protection of Mothers, and an officer of the League for the Care of Prisoners; Rosika Schwimmer of Hungary, represented the Association of Agricultural Woman Laborers, a suffrage organization of peasant women; Vilma G. Gücklich and Paula Pogány, are the president and secretary of the Hungarian Feminist Alliance; Anna Zipemowsky is a member of the Hungarian Peace Association; Leopoldine Kulka and Olga Misar came as delegates of the Austrian Women's Union (suffrage); Bertha Frölich, as delegate of the Society of Temperance women; and Darynska Golinska came from Austrian Poland with a memorial from the suffering Polish women demanding the rebuilding of an independent Poland as an "indispensable reservation" in a lasting peace.

Likewise Rosa Genoni of Milan, lecturer, writer, and the sole delegate from Italy, did not claim to represent the widespread feeling of her country-women. "The other women in Italy," said Madame Genoni, "were frightened to cross Germany to Holland, for they fear in Italy that war may break out any minute. Alas! in Italy they do not think only of peace. Everybody desires it perhaps, but first of all they think of national interest. Even the peace associations in Italy are drawn into the mesh of war."

From the Scandinavian countries came large delegations to the congress, representing in most instances the committees formed in these northern nations for the international congress. Among them stood out such names as Anna Lindhagen of Sweden, inspector of children's institutions and one of the seven women members of the town council of Stockholm; and Thora Daugaard of Denmark, representing 15,000 suffragists.

No Russian or French woman attended the congress. Whereas the European press overlooked much that was of real and lasting importance in the Congress, few papers failed to publish in full the manifesto of the Conseil National des Femmes Françaises and L'Union pour le Suffrage des Femmes. organizations representing more than 150,000 French women. The manifesto is addressed "to the women of neutral and allied countries." It is a touching document courteously declining for French women a share in the congress and proudly declaring that "in order that future generations may reap the fruit of this magnificent display of self-sacrifice and death, French women will bear the conflict as long as it will be necessary. At this time united with those who battle and die, they do not know how to talk of peace."

The manifesto further proposes that French women can talk of peace only when justice has been triumphantly vindicated by the heroic defenders of the French nation.

In spite of this manifesto many letters were received from individual French women telling their desire to reach the congress and of the impossibility of traveling so far. Among them was a telegram of sympathy from Jules Siegfried, president of the Conseil National des Femmes Françaises, and a letter signed by Mme. Duchene, Chairman of the Section du Travail du Conseil National and by some fifteen working women, which offered to "the women of other nations good wishes and assurance that we are ready to work with them more ardently than ever to prepare the 'peace of tomorrow.'"

Russian women sent a letter expressing much the same sentiment as did the French manifesto, but the very feeling which kept these French and Russian women from the congress drove five valiant little Belgian women across the border into Holland from devastated Belgium. Eugene Hamer and Mlle. Sarton, vice-president and treasurer of L'Alliance Belge des Femmes pour la Paix par l'Education, decided that no peace congress attended by German and Austrian delegates should pass resolutions without a hearing before Belgian women. They determined not to vote but to protest against any measure, such as the calling of an armistice, which they deemed unjust to their country.

With three companions they obtained permission from the German authorities to go. They went by automobile to Esschen, where they were searched to the skin; thence they walked for two hours to Rosendahl across the Dutch border, and from there they traveled to The Hague by train. Then, when Mlle. Hamer and her friends at last reached the congress, it was Dr. Augspurg of Munich who welcomed them to a seat on the platform.

So, over seas and mountains, pushing aside dangers and obstacles, more than three hundred women "got together" with the Dutch delegates and visitors who crowded the meetings night after night. However any might criticize the proceedings of the congress, none could fail to admire the magnificent spirit of these women who dared clasp hands with women from an enemy country. Even if this international Congress wields little influence, it was, as Miss Addams said, a lasting achievement in thus uniting from every corner of Europe different sympathies and beliefs in one great yearning for peace.

But as I talked with Miss Addams, another thought came into my mind. Was it not, I asked her, a higher test of courage than "getting together" when the trenches were bleeding with wounded comrades, to "stick together" until out of their common suffering these women evolved a charter of common aspiration? Someone in the café had spoken of a mutual distrust that seemed to constrain the delegates. Now, talking with Miss Addams, I realized how this mistrust had gradually melted. Like my Socialist friend, I missed the flare of passion which kindles a meeting held to score a specific wrong; I revolted sometimes at dodging realities and floating in a cloud of theories: I, too, missed the vigorous robust solidarity of a congress bound together by the sense of the inter-dependence of labor. But more and more I was feeling that strong, sober solidarity based on universal mourning.

"Everybody talks about victory," said Rosika Schwimmer in one of her stirring speeches, "but we women know; that every victory means the death of thousands of sons of other mothers."

It was grief and sympathy that welded us together.

At the first session of the congress, without a dissenting voice a motion was carried making the basis of membership in the congress the acceptance of two resolutions—that women shall be granted equal political rights with men and that future international disputes shall be subject to conciliation and arbitration.

With the meeting-ground of the congress thus defined, the way was left open for debate and discussion on any other resolution to be considered. But so great was the unity of feeling that day after day of conferences slid by with no or little friction. Indeed, the monotony of perfect accord caused us at the press table to snatch and overemphasize the faintest spark of sensationalism—the harangue, for instance, of the militant suffragette who vowed that for every woman in England wishing to attend the peace congress 1,000 wished to fight: or the excitement of a Belgian lady who thought that the phrase "backward nations" referred to Belgium. Many resolutions were passed unanimously such as those protesting against women's sufferings in war. Demanding democratic control of foreign policy, urging that the education of children be directed toward peace and that women be represented in the conference of powers after the war. Even the radical resolutions introduced by the American contingent went through without protest. Among these were resolutions calling for open seas and free trade routes, for the acceptance of the principle that investments in a foreign country be made at the risk of the investor, for mediation without armistice and for the establishment of a permanent international conference which shall deal with practical proposals for future international co-operation and shall appoint a permanent council of conciliation for the settlement of differences arising from social and economic causes.

From the German delegates came a resolution of even greater import which repudiates the right of conquest. This resolution affirms that there shall be no transference of territory without the consent of the residents and urges that autonomy and a democratic parliament shall not be refused to any people.

When the resolution came up for vote advocating universal disarmament and urging all countries to take over the manufacture of arms and munitions of war and to control international traffic in the same, a stir was created by a delegate from the United States who moved an amendment that "traffic in arms from neutral countries be prohibited." Miss Addams ruled the amendment out of order as bearing upon present conditions, but added that she herself as an American citizen favored it.

Aside from the delay and slight confusion caused by tedious translation, there was but one hitch in the proceedings of the congress. It came after Madame Schwimmer's appeal for women to "call a thunderous halt *tomorrow* that shall overthrow the thunder of the trenches." By a rising vote the congress had voted to accept without debate this resolution urging the governments of the world to put an end to bloodshed and to begin peace negotiations. Then Mlle. Hamer, burning with the spirit of the French manifesto, pleaded for a peace based on justice "which would return to Belgium her liberty, independence, richness and prosperity." Unanimously the congress voted to insert in this most important of resolutions:

"The congress demands that the peace which follows shall be permanent and therefore based on principles of justice."

Thus "arbitration" bridged the one division of feeling in the congress which threatened a serious split.

What will come of it all?

That is what the world of practical people, who demand immediate results, is asking. When I questioned my Socialist friend, she scoffed a little bitterly, "A lot of talk that will blow away with the delegates." But the newspaper woman reflected that it would leave its stamp on the woman movement in every country, and the magazine writer declared that its end was already attained in dispelling the idea of implacable hatred between women of warring countries.

The one immediate step of the congress was to delegate envoys, women from both neutral and belligerent nations, to carry the message expressed in the congress resolutions to combatants and non-combatant countries. Already Jane Addams, Aletta H. Jacobs, chairman of the executive committee of the congress, and Rosa Genoni of Italy, have been received by the court of Holland, have presented the resolutions to the prime minister of England and have come back to the continent in a tour which includes the capitals of Germany, Belgium, France and Austria. They will later be joined by Kathleen Courtney of England and Anita Augspurg of Germany, and will visit the neutral countries of Switzerland, Spain and United States. The entrance of Italy into the war will prevent these delegates visiting Rome as planned.

Meanwhile another group has been appointed to go to Denmark, Sweden, Norway, and Russia.

To students of diplomacy and to the "practical" people of the world the expeditions will seem, like the congress itself, the action of visionaries. They will laugh at a "parcel of women" bearing resolutions to prime ministers who are vexed with the burdens of war. They will sneer at its futility and assail its temerity. But to others, and especially to us who attended the congress, the mission of these women will mean that the spirit of the congress will not be girded by the canals of Holland but will reach across trenches smoking with war.

Alice Hamilton (1869–1970)

The Lusitania was still in everyone's mind and the first note from America had just been received. I talked to many people who accepted the sinking of the vessel without questioning. She was carrying ammunition; she was armed; the passengers had been warned, and had no more reason to complain....

"At the War Capitals"
Alice Hamilton, M.D.
The Survey, August 7, 1915

The Survey has asked me to write the narrative of Miss Addams' journey to present the resolutions of what is now usually called the Woman's Peace Congress at The Hague to the governments of the warring and of some of the neutral countries. The delegation consisted only of Miss Addams and Dr. Aletta Jacobs of Amsterdam: but Dr. Jacobs took with her a friend Frau Wollf ten Palthe of The Hague, and Miss Addams took me. We two were not official members of the delegation and usually took no part in the formal interviews with ministers of foreign affairs or chancellors; so that my account of our wanderings must be confined to the unofficial parts, to the people we met informally and the impressions we gained as we passed through the countries, and stopped in the capitals and the life there.

There were absolutely no hardships encountered anywhere, not even real discomforts. Inconveniences there were in the shape of tiresome waiting in consular offices for passports,— a formality which had to be repeated in between each two countries; but aside from that, travel was easy and comfortable. The first government visited by the delegation was the Dutch,

since the congress was held at The Hague, and after that came
Great Britain where the delegation saw Mr. Asquith[2] and Sir
Edward Grey.[3] I did not accompany Miss Addams to London, for
just then I had an unexpected opportunity to go into Belgium
and chose that instead, so that her experiences there I did
not share in and cannot describe. The beginning of our joint
pilgrimage was on May 19, when with the two Dutch women we
left Amsterdam for the day's journey to Berlin.

Germany looked far more natural than we had been led to expect;
indeed, the only unusual feature to my eyes was the absence of
young and middle-aged men in the fields where the work was being
carried on almost entirely by women, children and old men.

We reached Berlin at night and the next morning, as we
drank our coffee, Dr. Sudekum's card was brought up. Readers
of The Survey will probably remember him as a prominent Socialist,
a member of the Reichstag and an authority on city planning,
who visited this country some two years ago and spoke in many of
our large cities. We went down to meet him but seeing no one in
the room except a few officers, thought there was some mistake:
when, to our surprise, a tall, blond soldier came up and saluted
and we recognized that this was actually Dr. Sudekum. We had
never supposed that he would actually be in the army though we
knew that he was one of the military Socialists,—indeed, one of
those selected by the Kaiser to go on a mission to Italy and try to
persuade the Italian Socialists that Italy should remain loyal to the
Triple Alliance.

We talked together and he told us of Italy's probable entrance
into the war, insisting that it would be a matter of no military importance, but an act of unforgivable treachery. He had been up all the
night before at the foreign office and his eyes had that dull hunted
look that goes with sleeplessness and intense emotion. He was the
first one to attack us on the subject of America's sale of munitions of war to the allies, an attack to which we became wearily
accustomed before we left Germany and Austria. Dr. Sudekum was
just back from nine days at the front and claimed that every shell
which had fallen in that part of the line while he was there was
an American shell. Nevertheless, he was most friendly and readily

2. Herbert Henry Asquith, British Prime Minister, 1908–1916
3. Sir Edward Grey, British Foreign Secretary, 1905–1916

Alice Hamilton, MD, reported on the Women's Peace Congress and on the committee from the congress that delivered the call for immediate peace to the leaders of
the warring and neutral nations. *Source:* George Grantham Bain Collection, Prints
and Photographs Division, Library of Congress, LC-B2- 5118-815.

promised to do what he could to secure an interview for the delegation with Count von Jagow of the Foreign Office.

After he left, I went out on a few errands and got my first impression of Berlin. The city, of course, was in perfect order, yet the war
met me on all sides. The walls were placarded and the windows full
of appeals for money for all sorts of objects: for blinded soldiers,
for the relief of the widows of the heroes of a certain battleship,
for a woman's fund to be made up of pennies and presented to the

Kaiser, and—much the most terrible of all—long lists of the latest casualties. But there were no wounded soldiers to be seen and no evidence of poverty and suffering, the relief work is apparently well done. Later on, when we were taken around by Dr. Alice Salomon, we saw how work has been provided for those who need it, for the women especially. I had a curious sensation on that expedition of having seen and heard it all before; and then I remembered that just a little while ago in Brussels I had seen gentle Belgian ladies organizing work for the Belgian poor in exactly the same way as these gentle German ladies were doing it for the German poor. And in Paris, and in London, it was the same.

We had been told before we went to Germany that the people were absolutely united in a determination to fight until Germany was victorious, that there were not a dozen men the length and breadth of the land who were even thinking, much less talking, of peace.

Of course, such unanimity is inconceivable in a nation of sixty-five million thinking people, and it was easy enough for us to convince ourselves that it did not exist. From the first we met men and women who were pacifists. The one who stands out most prominently in my mind, is the clergymen [sic: clergyman], Sigmundt-Schultze, who is fortunately too lame to serve in the army. He has gathered around him a group of people, free from bitterness and from ultra-patriotism, fair-minded, and deeply sorrowful over the war. Many of them belong also to a group that calls itself *Das Bund Neues Vaterland*, which stands for very much the same things as the Union of Democratic Control in England,—that is, for a peace without injustice or humiliating terms to any people, no matter who is victor.

Of course, we also met people who held the point of view which we in America have been led to think, universal in Germany. The Lusitania[4] was still in everyone's mind and the first note from America[5] had just been received. I talked to many people who accepted the sinking of the vessel without questioning. She was carrying ammunition; she was armed; the passengers had been warned, and had no more reason to complain than if they had

---

4. The British passenger liner *Lusitania* was sunk by a German submarine on May 7, 1915, with the loss of 1,198 lives, including 128 Americans.

5. In the wake of the *Lusitania* sinking, President Woodrow Wilson sent several diplomatic notes to Germany protesting their submarine policy.

deliberately entered a city that was being besieged. These people were absolutely sure that Germany was fighting in self-defense only, and their respect for the military was so great that they looked upon the acts of the Belgian *franc-tireurs*[6] as horrible crimes.

Toward the invasion of Belgium most of them held the belief that it had been a military necessity, but that there must be no permanent occupation. No one believed in the tales of atrocities. "If, you knew our good German soldiers, you'd see how impossible all that is."

As for our selling munitions of war to the allies, the resentment it arouses is almost incredible. Many of them seem to suppose that all the ammunition used by the allies comes from America. The American wife of a German noble man told Miss Addams that a widowed friend had come to see her, with a bit of shell which some soldier had sent her from the front, saying it was the shell that had killed her husband. And the woman had shown her the ghastly thing, and said: "Look at it and tell me if it is an American shell."

We stood up stoutly for our country, arguing that it was Germany which had prevented both Hague congresses from pronouncing against this very practice, that Germany had herself invariably taken every opportunity to sell munitions to warring countries, that for us to change international law and custom in the middle of the present war in favor of Germany and to the detriment of the allies would be an unneutral act, but it was mostly useless. I think we convinced, perhaps, two or three men. Most of them did not even listen to our explanations.

There was no difficulty in securing an interview for Miss Addams and Dr. Jacobs with Count von Jagow and although Dr. Bethmann-Hollweg[7] did not consent to see the delegation, he granted Miss Addams an interview. I waited for her in a spacious room in the chancellery on the Wilhelm Strasse, looking out on a great shady garden right in the heart of Berlin. From there we went to pay some calls on men who we thought might throw some light on the question of the possibility of neutral nations acting as negotiators

---

6. Civilian soldiers, guerilla fighters. Remembering the effectiveness of French civilian fighters during the Franco-Prussian War (1870–71), Germany took harsh reprisal against civilian combatants in WWI.

7. Theobald von Bethmann-Hollweg served a Chancellor of the German Empire from 1909–1917.

between the warring countries. It was very easy to secure the introductions we wanted, partly through Sigmundt-Schultze and partly through some friendly American newspaper men.

We called first on Prof. Hans Delbrueck who lives next door to Harnack, his brother-in-law. Miss Addams was greatly tempted to call on the latter, for she has always had a great admiration for his book, *Das Wescn des Christenthums*.[8] But Sigmundt-Schultze who was with us advised her not to, saying she would only be disappointed, he had gone in heart and soul for the war.

The interview with Delbrueck was not enlightening. He did not seem to me wise or just, and his idea of the sort of intervention which would be of value in this crisis was so utterly un-American that we thought it hardly worth listening to. Briefly, he advised that President Wilson should use threats to the two chief belligerents and thus bring them to terms. "Let him," he said, "tell England that he will place an embargo on munitions of war, unless she will accept reasonable terms for ending the war, and let him tell Germany that this embargo will be lifted unless Germany does the same."

Miss Addams told him that such a move would be impossible, even if it were of any value; that for the President to use threats would be to lose his moral force, and that he would not have the country behind him. But Delbrueck waved aside as absurd both these objections. "Moral influence is nothing," he said, "what is needed is armed mediation. Your President has the right under your constitution to do this, he need not consult the country."

He went on to say much that he had already said in his article in the Atlantic, that Germany desires no new territory in Europe, but what she requires is colonies, and that he would be in favor of her evacuating Belgium on condition of her being given concessions in the Belgian Congo. He was one of the Germans who could see no argument in defense of our sale of munitions and who considered the sinking of the Lusitania absolutely justified.

I found Maximilian Harden much more interesting. He is a little man with a big head, almost all of it forehead and hair, his eyes tired and burnt-out and his general aspect full of weary depression. People had warned us against him, calling him a fire-eater, one of the men who had done most to encourage the war. To us he seemed

8. *The Essence of Christianity*

quite the contrary; he seemed to regard it as a terrible tragedy. He was very fair to our country, saying that Germany had no right to criticize our sale of ammunition to the allies. He said he had always told the Germans that since they had a great advantage in their enormous factories at Essen, England naturally must strive to offset it by an equal advantage, and this she had in her navy which enabled her to buy the supplies she could not manufacture. He said it was poor sportsmanship for Germany to protest. As for help from the neutral nations in this crisis, he seemed to think it the only hope, and yet not an immediate hope.

Miss Addams was entertained by the large women's organization, the Lyceum Club, which has a beautiful building of its own. We dined there with some of the leaders and afterwards there was a reception and Miss Addams spoke, but they did not wish her to speak of the peace congress or of her mission. As everywhere, excepting in Hungary, the women's suffrage organizations and the International Council of Women had pronounced against the meeting at The Hague and made it difficult for their members to attend. Nevertheless when we talked to these women individually, we found them much more moderate than we had been led to expect. Indeed, as I look back on our German visit, I can remember but two persons who spoke to me with the sort of bitterness that I have heard from German-Americans over here, even though the war is so very close to them. I suspect that that is the real reason: that the tragedy is too great for rancor and uncharitableness. One woman said to me, when I quoted something from this side of the water, "I am far past all that now. At first I was bitter, but that is gone now. I have almost forgotten it."

One must always remember that the Germans read nothing and hear nothing from the outside. I talked with an old friend, the wife of a professor under whom I worked years ago when I was studying bacteriology in Germany. She and her husband are people with cosmopolitan connections, they read three languages besides their own, and have always been as far removed as possible from narrow provincialism, but since last July they have known nothing except what their government has decided that they shall know. I did not argue with my friend, but, of course, we talked much together and after she had been with us for three days she told me that she had never known before that there were people in England who did not wish to crush Germany, who wished for a just settlement, and even some who were opposed to the war.

Then she said, "I want you to believe this. We Germans think that the Fatherland was attacked without provocation, that our war is one of self-defense only. That is what we have been told. I begin to think it may not be true, but you must believe that we were sincere in our conviction."

Helen Ring Robinson (1878–1923)

Ours was the first great peace advertising expedition in history. And the peace we advertised was not a mere negation, a cessation of strife. It was a deep, abiding constructive force.

"Confessions of a Peace Pilgrim"
Helen Ring Robinson
The Independent, February 14, 1916

Some of the members of the Henry Ford Peace Expedition that sailed to Europe last December believed the "miracle" might happen. I was one of them. The miracle—that somehow, thru God's providence, we might hasten the establishment of a righteous peace for blood-soaked Europe. There might be only one chance in a million, but, with a world aflame I was even willing to gamble on miracles.

Moreover, there were those documents in the keeping of Mme. Rosika Schwimmer! Documents duly authenticated, we were assured, which showed that the belligerents were all eagerly awaiting the "miracle," too. And the fact that most of us on the Peace Ship were people of no importance could count as nothing against the expedition, whose strength must lie in the compelling power of a big, unselfish, courageous idea—not on "Who's Who in America."

But the "miracle" did not happen.

Mme. Schwimmer, a brilliant Hungarian woman, was from the beginning of the adventure to its close the controlling force of the expedition. By the time we reached Norway every member of the party who was not absorbed into her remarkable personality realized that this was a heavy handicap.

Mme. Schwimmer was on fire with zeal for the success of the expedition. But the very fact of her race, in a certain sense the fact of her sex, also, with the years of her life set against a background of suspicion and intrigue and autocracy, made her peculiarly unfitted for the leadership of some 170 Americans, many of them given to large language on the subject of "democracy."

And yet, as her devotees would indignantly protest, if ever a daring soul questioned the infallibility of her leadership or her right to dictate the very thoughts of the Peace Pilgrims, "there never would have been a Henry Ford Peace Expedition if it had not been for Rosika Schwimmer."

That is quite true.

So much the finer, then, would have been her renunciation if she had been great enough to renounce. If, after formulating the big idea, after enlisting Henry Ford for the adventure, by the force of her vibrant earnestness, after placing her knowledge and her documents at the disposal of the expedition, she had shown the still greater devotion of effacing herself from it, who knows but the "miracle" might have waited on the renunciation?

As these are my confessions, I am willing to admit that I do not carry my pacifism to the point of belligerency. But a super-pacifist is different. It was the super-pacifists who gave the Peace Pilgrims the "third degree" on a stormy December night in mid-ocean.

There were, of course, some self-seekers and grafters in the expedition. It could hardly be otherwise with a company of nearly two hundred Americans, gathered together in great haste, to travel what was, after all, a rainbow route—with a multimillionaire and unlimited pots of gold at the end of it.

Most of the Peace Pilgrims, however, were devoted lovers of humanity, so moved by the horrors of the war which is making a desert of civilization that they had left their homes and their business, had endured inconvenience and ridicule and financial loss, had dared the wintry gales of the North Atlantic and the perils of mine-strewn waters to follow a vision of peace and good will.

It would seem that they could read their titles clear to honorable standing on the Peace Ship.

But some of the self-elected elect among the super-pacifists thought otherwise. They believed the time had come for a sifting of souls.

Colorado state senator Helen Ring Robinson on board the Ford Peace Expedition ship, the *Oscar II*. *Source:* George Grantham Bain Collection, Prints and Photographs Division, Library of Congress, LC-B2- 3694-13.

Somebody-Or-Other appointed a committee and this committee, in collaboration with Mme. Schwimmer, prepared a platform with three planks. The first two planks dealt, in placid, platonic terms, with world peace and international disarmament. Then came the third plank, better known as the "third degree," which pledged the unyielding opposition of all members of the Ford Peace Expedition to any increase whatever, under any circumstances whatever, of the naval or military forces of the United States, and called upon all good Americans everywhere to oppose the recommendations of President Wilson's message on preparedness, lately delivered to Congress.

Now only one member of the company, Mr. S. S. McClure, had read the President's message. There were some, therefore, who felt incompetent to pass judgment upon it. There were others who thought themselves unequal to fixing the policy of America amid whatever flux of circumstances in a war-tossed world. There were those whose indignation at the manner of presenting the platform left them little concern with its matter.

"If we must sign such a document in order to be welcome guests at this 'house party,' surely, in common courtesy, a copy of it should have been sent us with the invitation," protested one of these, a woman from the West who had sacrificed much to join the expedition.

But there was no escaping the "third degree." The platform committee were determined. There could be no discussion. No comma in the document could be altered. The oracle had spoken. The tripod was unshaken. Only those who were willing to sign the platform could remain "full members" of the Henry Ford Peace Expedition. The souls of the expedition must be sifted.

They were.

It is an interesting fact that the name of every self-seeker in the party is written large after that famous platform, with the names, I gladly grant, of many sincere and earnest men and women who believed in the declaration and lost sight of the other issues involved.

It was about this time that, for all my knack of hoping, I lost hope of the "miracle."

But my belief in the good to be accomplished by the expedition never faded. And even assuming, as I am willing to do, that the "Unofficial Neutral Conference" which we left behind us may accomplish little or nothing, the results of the expedition justify that belief.

It is unfortunate that our Eastern press has created so different and false an impression. But here again I blame the incompetency of the Peace Party administration for much of the cynicism of the newspaper people attached to the expedition.

Most of the newspaper men and women came with open minds. That was their business. Some of them thrilled to the same hope that inspired Henry Ford. One of them, the representative of a great news gathering agency, a hater of war and injustice, an incurable idealist, told me on the first day of our outward journey that he also believed in the possibility of the "miracle." Yet before we reached Christiania his wireless reports bit like acid, and others of the press people grew increasingly antagonistic.

Much of this was mere contagiousness. But for some of it Mme. Schwimmer and her subordinates were plainly responsible. Newspaper men mistrust the oracle and the tripod. And even a reporter is human, after all. You rarely melt him to tenderness and praise by calling him a liar and a brute—even if he is one.

Doubtless it is all very different in Hungary.

There are "war millionaires" in Norway as in America, twenty-five newly made ones in the small city of Bergen alone. Perhaps that was one reason why, when we reached the capital of Norway, we found the press not apathetic but hostile. Moreover our expedition had been tagged as "pro-German"—and Christiania sympathizes with the Allies.

Yet in Christiania, from the beginning of our stay there, the big idea of the Peace Ship justified itself.

Remember that this "big idea" was not the "miracle" of which a few of us mild-minded voyagers dreamed. While Jenkin Lloyd Jones[9] was swathing the idea in metaphors and things like that, Henry Ford stripped it of all its trappings and observed casually, "It pays to advertise."

To advertise, to mobilize the forces of peace as the forces of war have been advertised for ten thousand years—that was the true purpose of the Henry Ford Peace Expedition.

Ours was the first great peace advertising expedition in history. And the peace we advertised was not a mere negation, a cessation of strife. It was a deep, abiding constructive force. It was the soul of an individual, the soul of a nation. We advertised that the soul of America was peace. And Norway answered that her soul was peace also. The science and the scholarship of Norway as represented in the famous organization rather ineptly styled "The Student Body" welcomed us and joined in our campaign. The ministerial alliance arranged a great mass meeting for us. The Social Democrats arranged another. And when we left Norway a representative group of men and women accompanied us as members of the party.

In Stockholm the story was repeated with emphasis. The waves of war are breaking very close to those Scandinavian countries, cruel waves and high. And only war was talked of when we reached Stockholm; when we left the city a week later everyone was talking peace.

9. A Unitarian minister, well known for his opposition to war. A member of the Ford Peace Expedition.

The orators of our party feared our mission might prove fruit-less in Denmark, for that little nation, in the grip of monstrous fear, passed some months ago a law forbidding all public meetings to discuss public questions. Yet a score of private receptions and club meetings gave ample opportunity for explaining the purpose of the expedition, while at a banquet given by *The Politiken*, the greatest newspaper of all Scandinavia, the speakers were assured an audi-ence of a million readers.

The last stopping place before the disbanding of our party was at The Hague.

Now The Hague is a little blasé about peace, tho she thinks she invented it. Yet it was in that city I had my most inspiring experience.

I was riding with two other members of the expedition in an open taxi. Our car stopped for a moment just as a middle aged Hollander, an artizan, plainly, was passing. He looked at us, then stopped, and lifting his hat said just two words. "America! Peace!" while his voice had a tone and his eyes had a light as if he were before a shrine.

We had all, no doubt, fallen far short of what we meant, we Peace Pilgrims who had left our own country with the gibes of newspaper paragraphists ringing in our ears. But for all our failures we had at least done this for our native land:

People had reproached us with being a buzzard nation when first we landed. They accused us of feeding too noisily on war profits. From the beginning we had told them another story, of the millions on millions of plain Americans like ourselves who shared in Europe's agony and ardently longed for peace.

They had listened to us. Sometimes we could feel that our words carried conviction. And here was a man who had learned the truth—that the real soul of America is peace.

I recalled how various militant Americans, including a former President of the United States,[10] had been distrest last December lest our expedition should make America appear ridiculous. I am glad to record now how the expedition helped to make the name of the United States once more respectable.

S. S. Rotterdam

10. The reference here is to Theodore Roosevelt, who was a vocal advocate for Preparedness and U.S. entry into the war.

Chapter 6

❖

❖

❖

❖

Wartime Adventures

S ome dangers of the war zone were consciously accepted, while others sprang from ambush. When danger pounced journalists often became part of the story rather than detached observers, thrusting them into harrowing adventures. Such occasions illustrated one fundamental rule of war correspondence: that a journalist's personal adventure in pursuit of a war story was itself a war story. Everything they experienced, every detail they shared, every outrageous twist in the action, illustrated the dramatic changes wrought by war. For readers in the early twentieth century, the drama was compounded if a woman had such experiences. In the articles in this chapter, three women war correspondents relate a first-person, wartime adventure.

Chicago Tribune reporter Mildred Farwell found herself in an unexpected confrontation with the Bulgarian army in the winter of 1915. Detained by the Bulgarians in a Red Cross compound in Serbia, Farwell became the focus of a rescue effort and was featured in numerous stories from other war reporters. Upon her release, she wrote a series of stories for the *Tribune* detailing her experiences. Her two articles included in this chapter explain the dramatic stand-off between Red Cross officials and a Bulgarian army commander.

No woman journalist had a better résumé as a war correspondent than Eleanor Franklin Egan, having covered the Russo-Japanese

War of 1904–05 and the 1905 Russian Revolution for *Leslie's Weekly*. Her reporting during WWI for *The Saturday Evening Post* was notable for the number of locations from which she reported, including difficult and dangerous locales such as Serbia, Turkey, Mesopotamia, and Armenia. However, the greatest danger found Egan as she traveled on a Greek tramp steamer from Greece to Egypt.

One of the most dangerous fronts throughout the war was not on land but on water. German submarines, U-boats, relentlessly attacked shipping in the coastal waters around England and France and in the Mediterranean. In this article, Egan paints in vivid detail her harrowing and deadly encounter with an Austrian U-boat. The article appeared in April 1917, the same month the United States entered the war.

In late January 1917, when Germany announced that it would resume unrestricted submarine warfare, attacking any and all ships in the Atlantic, including those from neutral America, Mary Boyle O'Reilly received an urgent telegram from her editor. Boyle had been covering the war for the Newspaper Enterprise Association (NEA) since its opening days. Now NEA asked if she would consider running the German submarine blockade and reporting on her adventure. She took the assignment, sailing on the "last ship for home."

Lifeboat drills and a relentless vigil by passengers for submarines kept tensions high throughout the voyage. But they escalated on February 3, when the ship received news off the wireless that the United States had taken a fateful step toward war by severing diplomatic relations with Germany. In the article "Star Woman Runs Blockade," O'Reilly captures a snapshot of Americans on the cusp of entering the war.

Even the relatively safe circumstances of a French army guided tour for journalists had the potential to turn dangerous. On a press tour to a "safe" battlefield, Elizabeth Shepley Sergeant had the misfortune of standing too close to another reporter who picked up a souvenir of the battlefield. The souvenir happened to be a hand grenade. It exploded, killing that reporter and seriously wounding Sergeant. She spent seven months recuperating in the American hospital in Paris and from that experience wrote a war memoir, *Shadow-Shapes: The Journal of a Wounded*

Woman. The memoir excerpt included here gives an impression-istic account of the accident.

Mildred Farwell (1880–1941)

We had decided before hand if they broke in to take a picture as evidence, and I had already snapped one when the officer saw me. He gave a bellow of rage and the next thing I knew 200 pounds of fat Bulgarian and I were wrestling for the kodak.

"Americans Try a Big Bluff to Save Serb Food"
Chicago Tribune, May 7, 1916

"Bulgars Seize Serb Food Left with Americans"
Chicago Tribune, May 8, 1916
Mildred Farwell

The second Bulgarian army came into Monastir on Dec. 5.[1] Line after line of stolid, chunky soldiers. Their faces distinctly oriental, heavy and rusé at the same time—marching as well as Europeans (a thing I've never seen since).

The officer, decorated with flowers by the girls who made eyes at them from the windows and balconies, were only too delighted to be photographed and posed as they passed my camera. Like a brown wave the army flowed through and over the narrow, twisted streets.

We had been trying all day unsuccessfully to see the authorities about Serbian stores. Miss Mitchell and I held up the cavalry as it progressed in state down the main street to force into an officer's hand one of Dr. Forbes'[2] precious stock of four visiting cards, to be given with his compliments to the Bulgarian general. That evening we were commanded, not requested, to go to the division.

Interview with Bulgar

A neutral consul beforehand had seen the paper the Serbians had given us, and told it was en regle,[3] but I for one confess that my

---

1. Bulgaria entered the war on the side of the Central Powers by invading Serbia on October 11, 1915.
2. Dr. Harry Forbes of Boston, worked for the American Red Cross in Serbia.
3. According to the rules

knees shook as we three filed into headquarters. Our dignified progress was slightly impeded by chilblains. We found Col. Popoff, the general's aid[e], with an air of military severity, ensconced behind a huge desk. Throughout the rather heated interview he leaned on his sword as if it were to be the instrument of our instant execution.

Col. Popoff gave us a message from the commandant. That as all stores in Monastir now belonged to his government we were immediately to hand ours over to the authorities, that we might have twenty-four hours' respite in which he would telegraph Sofia for further orders, but if the answer was unfavorable, they would be taken by force.

Play Game of Bluff

I am afraid we were guilty of eagle-screaming—a bad habit. We told him to come and take them. Then we asked permission to communicate with our consul or a safe conduct for one of us either to Sofia or Salonika. Regretfully both requests were refused.

For the next week we and the military played a Balkan game of poker. (Give a Bulgarian two days' practice and he would outbluff the most hardened shark.)

We locked and barred the ambulance gates and the general posted guards outside. Many of them had been in America and were a little dubious about such behavior to her citizens.

Try Entreaties, Threats

We had visits from the commander, from the doctors of the Bulgarian Red Cross, from officers of varying rank. We unlocked the gates, ushered them in, and heard what they had to say, ushered them out, and locked the gates again. They offered to buy the supplies to return them later. They tried entreaties, they tried threats.

Dr. Forbes had only one answer—the stores are for the hungry civil population. We did not feel it right to sell or give to a hostile government to be used for military advantage, what the Serbs, though they had plenty of time to either transport or destroy, had at our earnest entreaties left for another purpose.

Dr. Forbes finally wrote to the general that out of courtesy he had delayed the distribution several days, but as the people were literally starving, he could do so no longer. The answer to this was that the general's representative would take the stores next day. In the morning the usual miserable creatures were hanging around the gates.

We went outside and in fear and trembling began to distribute hard-tack with one eye fixed on our guard, a small Bulgarian soldier in an overcoat much too long and too large. He made a motion with his bayonet, surprisingly not at us but at the crowd. With the greatest importance he hustled and poked them into line, then turned to us for approval.

O, delightful Balkans, our jailer was helping us. He kept the people back while we gave out the hard-tack, and until another soldier sauntered reluctantly through the crowd. He was trying to look fierce, as he came over to Dr. Forbes and laid one hand feebly on his shoulder. The doctor gave away another piece of hard-tack, just to see if he meant it or not, and the soldier, obviously frightened but obeying orders, took hold of his shoulder again.

Officially we were stopped. We took our bag of hard-tack and retired inside the fortress, locking the gate again.

One morning the clinic was crowded with patients and in full swing when I heard little Miss Troyan, our Macedonian interpreter, calling: "They've come and they've got the doctor." I was out of the door in three leaps to find Dr. Forbes at the gate, struggling with an officer and some soldiers, while several others threatened him with fixed bayonets.

We had decided before hand if they broke in to take a picture as evidence, and I had already snapped one when the officer saw me. He gave a bellow of rage and the next thing I knew 200 pounds of fat Bulgarian and I were wrestling for the kodak. Two soldiers had hold of my arm so he got it away from me, broke and jammed it into his pocket.

In the meantime Dr. Forbes had run to the door of the house where the supplies were kept; he tried to get the key out of the lock, but it stuck, and he could only pretend to put it in his pocket. It fooled the soldiers, however, and a few of them jumped him at once.

Peril Doctor with Bayonet

I saw a confused mass of struggling arms and legs. The officer, purple in the face, hopping around the edge yelling directions.

Several soldiers held their bayonets within six inches of Dr. Forbes and only too obviously were aching to reduce the distance.

It takes a lot of force in the Balkans, evidently, to subdue any one, but numbers after all are numbers, and by the time the soldier had discovered the key in the lock and dropped Dr. Forbes, there was nothing we could do, though panting with rage, but give up and sit helplessly watching the removal of what we then thought was our property.

In the middle of the excitement the civil government of Monastir made a theatrical entrance. A small man in a sort of "hunting-the-chamois" costume stalked in between the soldiers, one hand in the breast of his coat, one behind him (the classic state[s]man's attitude). He raised his hat, a fur shako, with great stiffness to Dr. Forbes.

"I have come to you," he said, "you ought to have come to me." "But who on earth are you?" Dr. Forbes asked. "I am the governor or Monastir," he replied.

Governor Shows Authority

We ought to have known it. Some are marked at birth for greatness. Even in the most intimate moments of domestic life he would have looked every inch a governor.

"You should have asked me about this affair. It was my business, not the military authories, and," his voice raising all the time, "my brother is the American consul in Sofia, and he'll tell Mr. Vope-e-e-ka that you make trouble with the Bulgarians. As for that gentleman," pointing at Dr. Forbes, "he is not American, I know well Americans, they sit quiet, they smoke their pipes."

He stopped, looked fiercely at us, and feeling he had crushed us by his arguments, turned on his heel and stalked out. Later I heard some of this remarkable individual's history. His brother had never been American counsul in Sofia, but one of the minor clerks in our office there. He had been sent first to Skopje as governor, but Lady Paget[4] had found him so intolerable that at her request he had been removed.

---

4. Dame Louise Margaret Leila Wemyss Paget, Lady Paget, established a hospital in Serbia prior to WWI to fight epidemic disease. After the war began, it treated wounded Serbian soldiers.

Flees with 6,000 Francs

Finally, after stirring up all sorts of trouble and lording it over every one, he left Monastir hurriedly with 6,000 francs in gold. The Bulgarians have tried to disown him; they say they are looking for him, and wish to execute on him summary martial law (before he has spent the 6,000 francs).

They are still looking. They'll never find him; he is much too clever; the cleverest man I met in the Balkans. Some day he will emigrate to America and become one of our leading politicians. He should be a great success in the United States.

Twenty thousand Bulgarian troops waxed and grew fat for a week on our Serbian supplies. The only excuse offered was they needed it. We never saw a receipt for anything that was taken, and though a written protest was accepted by the commandant to be forwarded to our consul, it evidently traveled only as far as the headquarters waste basket. Although there was a wireless in the field near the ambulance, we heard no word at all from the outside world for two months.

Americans Closely Watched

I understand now how the third degree will break the nerve of even an honest man. Until the arrival of the first Bulgarian army staff and the Germans we had to stand all sorts of petty annoyances. Back in America the remembrance of a certain spectacled officer with the appearance of a studious fish, hunting like a sleuth hound in the ambulance outhouses for hidden bags of flour, is an amusing one. At the time it was not at all funny.

The military authorities ordered us to deliver to their tender mercies our most intelligent interpreter, an American citizen. Though a Macedonian by birth, on the trumped up charge, entirely false, of having defrauded two Bulgarian soldiers eight years ago in America of $40.

Interpreters Make Escape

The soldiers offered to settle for $30, but a written guarantee of his safety if he did give himself up was refused, knowing of what little use was their American citizenship in the Balkans. He and the other interpreter, also an naturalized American, preferred to escape over the border. They hid for a day or so in a house by the river, that, like most of the Turkish houses, had a secret door (you could pass by these hidden ways from courtyard to courtyard in Monastir without going out in the street), evaded the city guards in disguise, and went with a smuggler over the mountains into Greece.

A Greek, looking gigantic in his peasant's clothes of white wool, came into the clinic two days later. It was the smuggler. He made signs he wanted his neck doctored; when he got Dr. Forbes alone there was nothing the matter with it, but he produced a dirty scrap of paper; on it written in pencil as well as I can remember was: "Dear Friends: Hope you never have soch experience—cloths— burn up on montin; no shoes—snow over ancles.

"Two Sisters"

From it we gathered our interpreters were safely across the border. Their messenger pleaded for sugar as his reward. I had hidden one precious loaf under my bed, and he came to my room for it. My land-lady, strongly disapproving, chaperoned from the door. He was a formidable looking visitor as he stood with the loaf under one arm.

"O, Amer-ika, Amer-ika," he whined yearningly.

Our beloved country was at least well thought of by the smuggler.

Eleanor Franklin Egan (1879–1925)

I would, if I could, make you hear the feeble wails of the little Arab baby I picked up and tucked away under my wet coat, and feel the weight of the dead woman they dragged in and threw across my knees.

"In the Danger Zone"
Eleanor Franklin Egan
The Saturday Evening Post, April 28, 1917

I was leaving Greece. The war I had run from in Serbia, in Bulgaria and in Turkey snarled at my heels in Athens. Greece was mobilizing; everything was in the utmost confusion, and I knew I must get away, my objective then being my own homeland, where there was no war. Sailings of the Italian ships to Brindisi had not been suspended;

but in that direction the greatest danger lay. There were rumors of Austrian submarines, and one was made to believe that to the westward they were as thick as fishes in an aquarium. Very well; I would go down to Egypt, and from Egypt I would go to Malta, from Malta to Palermo, and thence across to Naples. There was a promise of British and Italian convoy on this route, and the sensible idea is always to seek the safest possible avenue.

When the war is over I am going back to Greece for the sole purpose of inquiring into the subject of Greek shipping facilities and seamanship. They really ought to be better than they are, even though they are Greek. I had crossed the Atlantic on a Greek ship and had made several trips between Athens and Saloniki—to say nothing of running in and out and up and down the islands of Greece; and I thought I knew the worst. But the Borulos! That was the name of the ship I took to get from Athens to Alexandria. It was not a matter of choice, else I think one look would have been enough. She was what is known as "about a two thousand tonner"—dirty beyond belief, and packed to her rails with a motley throng of Greeks and Arabs, men, women and children. She was owned by an English company, but she was run by Greeks. And at that time, because Greece was mobilizing, any beachcomber or human derelict alive, if he had two hands and a pair of legs to stand on, could ship in a Greek crew as a first-class sailor.

English Castaways

It was the Borulos or nothing, everything else afloat being engaged in service connected with either Greek mobilization and the transportation of troops to Macedonia, or with the battle of Gallipoli, which was then wallowing along to its end.

The Borulos it had to be. But what difference did it make? Goodness me! It was only about forty hours to Alexandria; it was October; the Mediterranean was in a mood to do nothing but lie lazily still; and the softness of the air was like a benediction. One could make the trip on anything that would keep afloat and have no need to worry about accommodations if there just happened to be a corner of the deck unoccupied. It was with such feelings of entire unconcern that I went aboard.

I can never think of that part of the world in any terms but terms of color. Even now, when I remember the drowned, with their black heads bobbing on the surface of sea, I remember, too, the silver light that lay all round them. I may be fanciful, but it was as though the sea refused to look menacing and rather sought to express a profound pity for its unhappy victims.

The first day began with the mauve dawn of the East; and I lay in my deck chair all through a flaming sunrise and the glinting brilliance of a long morning, looking back at the receding shores of many-islanded Greece. Then came another soft October night and another perfect sunrise. Could anyone remember war in the midst of such peace? I think not. No vision of danger could creep even into the outer most edges of one's thought. That was how it was.

Eleanor Franklin Egan was one of the most prolific journalists of the war. She never hesitated to travel to the most isolated and dangerous locales and had an uncanny ability to be on the spot of a breaking news story. *Source:* Arnold Genthe Collection, Prints and Photographs Division, Library of Congress, LC-G432- 2468-A.

I was the only English-speaking passenger aboard. I think there were probably thirty or thirty-five persons on the first-class deck; but they were all Greeks or Egyptians or near-East half-castes of some kind. There was a brother of the Sultan of Egypt, who took up more room than anybody else. His wife, the Princess, was with him, and there was a retinue of giant black eunuchs and Nubian maids, who kept coming and going, swiftly and silently attending to the wants of the exalted ones, and making themselves very generally and picturesquely entertaining to the likes of me. For the rest, they were quite commonplace when one got used to their violent manners and their explosive conversational peculiarities.

The three hundred-odd other passengers suggested nothing but nomadic tribes. Where they spread their padded quilts and unpacked their food baskets, there they were at home. And they covered every foot of space on the well decks and on the super structures fore and aft. And babies—well, in a crowd like that there would be babies everywhere, of course; shrill-voiced babies with dirty faces and nearly naked little plump brown bodies. It was horrible to see them drown.

It was along about three o'clock in the afternoon when we picked up the Englishmen. By that time we were far out of sight of land and were steaming along through a smooth sea south of Crete. We caught sight of the lifeboats away off on the horizon; and when we had come up close to them we stopped, while their men rowed alongside, where sailors were lowering a gang way. Excitement? Yes, naturally; but at that time an excitement of interest only, not of fear.

They were twenty-seven Englishmen whose ship had been sunk by a submarine about two hours before. They had been set adrift and were rowing north, with a determination to reach the shores of Crete, about one hundred miles away.

They should have gone on; it would have been much better for them if they had. But who is to resist the temptation of a ship under such circumstances? We were bound for Alexandria, and nothing suited them better than to get to Alexandria, where they would be taken care of by British authorities and could get immediate passage home to England. They were needed by England, and that seemed to be the only thing they were thinking of; though the fourteen-year-old "boy" of the crew did confide in me later that he thought he would try for a "berth ashore."

He had an imagination, that boy; and had suffered in his own way when he saw his ship go down. He didn't just blubber everything right out. He had his dignity and self-control as well as anybody. But I was a sort of blood sister, speaking his own language; he had been a long time away from his own kind of women folks. After all, he was only fourteen; and it was not long before he was talking to me quite freely and telling me lots of things.

He had left all his little treasures aboard and he could not bear to think of them. Then there was a man in Cyprus whose mother lived in his hometown in Scotland, and this man had given him a letter to deliver—a letter with money in it. He had tucked it away for safe-keeping in the little locked box under his berth, and when the submarine came he forgot all about it.

"I know he'll think I took the money!" That thought troubled him more than anything.

I gathered that the sea was his home and his ship the dearest thing in the world to him. The submarine had stood off and "planted nine shots along her water line." That was the way he told me about it; and he said that as she was going under her masts looked to him like arms outstretched, and he had to shut his eyes tight. He tried not to, he said, but he: "cried like a kid!"

The Submarine Appears

We pulled their two lifeboats up and suspended them amidships, even with the first class deck rail. And there they hung, ready for instant use. We had four lifeboats of our own—only four—but they were roped in and canvased in and nailed in and rusted in and painted in, and were apparently about as useful as the ornaments on the woodwork.

I thought maybe I could write about this now; but it is not so easy. Who is to describe the sullen, murmurous quiver that went through that crowd the minute they understood the full significance of the Englishman's situation? A submarine! A ship sunk two hours before! And everybody knew we were low in the sea, with a heavy cargo for the base that was supplying Gallipoli![5]

---

5. This occurred while the Allies were fighting in Turkey at Gallipoli.

I think the British captain was sorry he had brought his men aboard when he found what our ship was like. He told me afterward that if he had only had a gun on his ship he could have saved himself and consequently us; but that was before the British had abandoned the idea that peaceful voyages were possible and that no British ship must carry guns into a neutral port. The Sailor Prince—that was the name of the English ship—had carried a gun on her outward voyage as far as Gibraltar; but there they took it away from her.

"It was a twelve-pounder,[6] like the ones on the submarine," said the captain; "and if I had had it—well, I saw 'em in plenty of time and I'd 'a got 'em, as sure as anything!"

After he had made a few calculations with regard to our situation he went to the Greek captain and—if an Englishman can implore—implored him either to turn back to Greece with his human freight, or make a big detour to the eastward, off the regular course of traffic. But the Greek shrugged his very fat shoulders and kept right on. I went timidly to the engineer, with whom I could communicate in a mixture of French and English, and asked him whether it would not be wise to swing out our lifeboats, provide our passengers with life preservers and go quietly among them with instructions as to what they should do in case of emergency. He just laughed at me. That is what he did—he laughed! But he rather explained himself later by saying that if he touched the lifeboats or suggested precaution there would be a panic at once in that awful mob. And he may have been right. He knew his people.

I was standing by the rail when the submarine came up—all by myself. We'd steamed along for quite a distance by that time and, everybody became very quiet. We were longing for darkness. That was it; we knew we must hurry silently into the shelter of night. I got up and walked to the rail to look westward into the evening sun colors. It was one of the most beautiful sunsets I ever saw. But I was not so interested in it, really, if the truth must be told. I was restless, and I was tremendously interested in the surface of the sea. I always shall be after this. Never again shall I be able to sweep a bright horizon from a ship's deck without seeing that black hulk rising like a whale come up to "blow."

___

6. A commonly used, three-inch caliber naval gun.

The Earthquake

Your mind at such a moment is like a film in a camera. It catches and fixes every minutest detail. I remember the white wash of the sea off the submarine decks, though it rose halfway between us and the sky line. I remember the instantaneousness of the flash of fire and the reverberating boom which caught up just in time to mingle with the crack of an exploding shell and the loud swish of a geyser that it threw into the air. It was the explosion of that shell that settled our fate. If the submarine could have used some other kind of signal the panic would not have been so instantaneous and complete. But the concussion shook the ship; and all those buried in the bowels of the ship—firemen, engineers, sailors, steerage passengers, everybody—thought just one thing, and that thing was "Torpedoed!"

A good many years ago I was on a ship in the China Sea, bound from Nagasaki to Manila.[7] We were off the shore of Formosa, and steaming along in a bright midday calm. We were at luncheon in the big saloon and everybody was as calm as the sea was calm. Suddenly we struck something. Or did we? Everybody started up and there was that quick catch of terror which makes for an immediate rush for safety. The Empress of China had been piled up on a rock in that vicinity a short time before, and I am sure everybody thought at once of the Empress of China. I know I did. The American skipper, a fine specimen of the big bluff sea-dog type, was at the head of his table; and, before anybody could really make a move, he was on his feet, shouting above the high murmur and laughing in a way to arrest general attention.

"Say," he said, "don't you know earthquake when you feel one! What did you think we had struck? Bottom? Not yet! Maybe you think seawater is a liquid. Well, it ain't; it's a solid—and that was an earthquake. It was a terror, too! Something happened somewhere!"

By that time everybody had settled down again and the good ship went sedately along. I thought of that when the shell exploded. It had the same kind of "feel," and I had to clutch the rail to steady myself.

Goodness knows how long I stood there. I don't. Moreover, I have no idea how the first impulse of the crowd expressed itself. I suppose

---

7. Egan and her husband, Martin Egan, co-edited the *Manila Times* in the years before WWI, during which time she traveled widely in Asia.

there must have been a momentary hesitation of unbelief before a scream was uttered; but when the sobbing sounds of fear did penetrate my daze they curdled my blood—and that I know.

I turned finally and started aimlessly for the gangway that led below to the cabins. I think I had some idea of acting with great poise and deliberation. That would be the first thing, naturally, to occur to an Anglo-Saxon mind. Though *Kultur*[8] has done much for us by way of steeling our nerves to the shock of horror, our instinct to conceal fear and to meet the great crises of our lives with decent decorum is not a product of *Kultur*. It is a matter of age-long pride of blood; of age-old boast and precept. Besides, I had been enjoying the steadying effect of much talk with those almost ludicrously cool British sailors. I remember that a terror-stricken child ran into me first, and that I took him firmly by the shoulders, and was whispering something to him when his even worse terror-stricken mother clutched him away from me.

Then I got caught in the crush at the gangway, I being seriously bent on going down when everybody else was in frantic haste to come up. I remember blackened firemen and uniformed officers and sailors fighting women and children and other men in a way that chilled my heart and closed the very shutters of my mind. In a dim, far-away kind of illumination I now see fear-maddened eyes and faces, and feel the tight grasp of hands that thrust me here and there, and back at last against the deck rail.

It was toward the Englishmen's life boats that the crowd stampeded. They were the only lifeboats instantly available, and more than three hundred persons had gone insane with a determination to get into them. More than three hundred? Yes; I should think there must have been. There were that many passengers, and all my most vivid memories are of men of a stampeding crew.

There was a Greek sailor standing in the bow of the boat toward which I had been rushed by the mob, and I turned in time to see him cutting away like a madman at the ropes that held it. I had just sense enough left to observe instantly that nobody was doing anything at all to the ropes at the other end; and then it was, I think, that I lost my reason too. The boat was already overloaded and people were still crowding into it, and I got a swift, terrible

8. A cultural attitude associated with Germany which emphasized individual subordination to the state

vision of its being loosed at one end only, and of the whole struggling, screaming lot of them plunged into the sea. I reached out and
caught the sailor's arms; but—

I think I went over just as that boat fell. How? I wish I knew.
There was a clutch of hands behind me, a sudden lift, a long
sickening drop—and I was looking wide-eyed through the blue
seethe of the sea. Some noble soul, of course, had tried to lift me
into the lifeboat and had caught me off my balance as I struggled
with the sailor. When I came up and caught my breath in the
air, and began mechanically to keep my head above water, I was
still thinking that I must go to my cabin and get a life belt. I had
been thinking this subconsciously all the time; and that shows
how quickly it all happened.

The Austrian Commander

By the time I had adjusted myself and had stroked my way out
into a space by myself—away from the clutching hands and the
struggling others—our submarine had come up and was lying
under our bows, with two twelve-pound guns trained on our
water line. It was the English captain who told me afterward that
they were twelve-pounders, else I should not have known. Here-
after, though, I think I shall always know a twelve-pounder when
I see one, because I looked straight into their muzzles from where
I floated in the sea.

My eyes ran down the gleam of them, seeing photographically
their every detail, including the folding apparatus that held them
up. Behind them stood two gunners, as straight and still as statues
of men. They were awaiting the order to fire, and I had a sort of
frantic feeling that I was exactly in range and was likely to be blown
to bits. Such a story needs no lugubrious trimmings; but in telling
it I am convinced that I am detailing the experience of hundreds
of others, and I experience in my thoughts of these others a deep
horror which clamors to express itself.

The commander of our submarine was an Austrian; and if the
German idea is right he should have been court-martialed and shot
for being weak—and merely human. I wish I knew who he was,
because he ought to be known and noted as an astonishing and
admirable exception. And he may be alive yet, though in his occupation the chances were all against him. I imagine that he was once

just a proud, upstanding navy man, with swashbuckling thoughts, perhaps, and dreams of brave fights with fighting ships. But he was not fitted to command a submarine under orders to be ruthless. He wept!

After all, my experience has its differences, has it not? When I say it is like the experience of hundreds of others I mean only that drowning is drowning, and the utmost in terror is the utmost. But we had our advantages. The water of the Mediterranean was warm and so buoyant that even our drowned kept afloat. But the North Atlantic, where American and British ships pass and pass— treading softly these days—the North Atlantic is cold, bitter and its waves are crested with strangling spray.

They got me. I was picked up by one of the lifeboats. And I could go on for fourteen pages telling about my absorbing thankfulness for that little craft when I sank into it, exhausted. But that is not important except that I always think of it when I read about lifeboats being shelled. This is the supreme crime in which I cannot believe; yet I know—if I know anything— that people who have been through such a thing cannot lie about it.

In the Lifeboat

Do you realize how difficult it is to launch a lifeboat in the first place? Do you know anything at all about the blessed feel of one when it is the only thing between you and the illimitable awfulness of black sea depths? Frail-seeming safety at best, it is the very absolute in defenselessness. I cannot by any effort of imagination conceive what my feeling would have been like had the guns of that submarine been turned upon us. Yet even that has been included in the experience of some.

I am going to skip all the particulars about how my lifeboat was filled with sailors and firemen mostly; how we rowed round afterward and picked up others, until the big chief steward, who was in command, decided we had all we could take care of; how three lifeboats were stampeded as they were launched and swamped as soon as they touched the water; how one woman after another threw her children into the sea, screaming to God to let them be saved by someone, somehow; and how the long swells caught little bodies and swept them far out beyond reach of rescue.

Yet I would, if I could, make you see the pitiful ship drifting aimlessly and dejectedly there under the guns; and I would, if I could, make you see how the sunset bathed all the horrors in a marvelous light. I would, if I could, make you hear the feeble wails of the little Arab baby I picked up and tucked away under my wet coat, and feel the weight of the dead woman they dragged in and threw across my knees. I would, if I could, call up before you all the twenty-five drowned—fourteen of them children, and only three of them men—and have you listen to their stories. But these are details, only details.

When I read the other day about a woman from the destroyed Laconia wrapping her long hair about the neck and shoulders of a freezing, dying man, I thought to myself: "Details!" If details could really be grasped; if we had not been made incapable of regarding details; if we could think in anything but figures and values—so many dead and so much lost—just one such incident would be enough to rouse the whole civilized world to rebellion.

Suddenly, above the clamor and crash of disaster, I heard a sound of English; and it came from the submarine. Everybody in my boat was talking—shrieking—in Greek or Arabic; and the big chief steward, who was sitting just in front of me, was making more noise than anybody. I pounded him on his round fat shoulders with my fists and managed to top his pitch in an effort to quiet him. Then suddenly, though only for an instant, everybody was quiet and the sound of English came to us again. It was a curious coincidence that at that moment the steward caught sight of a red flag, hanging limp from a staff on the submarine, and exclaimed:

"Mon Dieu, c'est Anglais!"

But just then a light breeze spread the flag out before us and showed us the star and crescent. Turkish? No; Austrian, without a doubt. But they used different flags on different occasions to make it appear that they were numerous.

We pulled over as fast as we could and came up under the hull of the submarine, I insisting and insisting that we must hear what the commander was saying. And it was then that I observed his extraordinary weakness. I have said he wept, and that is what he actually did, while his eighteen boys were in a state of intolerable excitement—all but the two at the guns. They stood like graven images—waiting.

Nearly every man on the deck of the submarine was engaged in trying to resuscitate someone, and the drowned or half drowned were nearly all children. The submarine had launched a collapsible boat, and the only thought then in any of their minds seemed to be a thought of rescue. They were almost frantic about it. The commander had a little unconscious Greek boy by the belt of his knickerbockers; and in a mechanical kind of way he was pounding him on the back and, at the same time, calling out at the top of his voice, over and over again:

"Are there any more people aboard?"

I suppose if someone had just then said to him, "No, sir; all off!" he would have given the command to fire. But nobody did. I have no idea what other kind of response he got; but I, at least, put every ounce of myself into an insistent and reiterated "No!" And I added: "Can't you see? Can't you see?"—together with some wild cries, on my own account, about women and children. It was the only sound of English he heard. I suppose he had tried both German and French, without results, but I assure you he spoke English with a perfect Anglo-Saxon accent. He turned and looked down into my face and, with a kind of sobbing effort, said:

"Well, go on back to your ship. We are not murderers!"

So? So? Could it be true?

I want to draw a long dash here to indicate that after this came a dazed, unthinking submission to demands as they presented themselves—for hours on hours. There was a busy, hysterical rush of rescue and resuscitation, but all the details in my mind are connected with individual cases: some saved and brought back to life, others given up for dead after everything possible had been done for them. And all the time we were drifting, drifting there, with the submarine lying by, not knowing in the least what should be done. It must have been three or four hours later when I met the English captain on the deck and asked him, quite casually, whether or not we were going to be sunk after all.

And he said:

"I don't know. What is it you Americans say? Oh, yes—'Search me!' They are still down there and I rather fancy they are in a nasty kind of mess. They don't know what to do. They 'ave betrayed themselves, you see; and if they let us go we can run faster into the arms of the British Navy than they can run to safety. But that captain can't murder us! 'E ain't the murderin' kind, else 'e would 'ave 'ad the job over with by this time. 'E bit off more'n 'e could chew—poor chap! I feel a bit sorry for 'im. 'E ain't used to pickin' up ships loaded to the rails with lunatics and babies, and without a lifeboat to bless 'emselves with. But don't you worry— and, for Gawd's sake, go and get some dry clothes on! You'll be ill, first thing you know!"

Mary Boyle O'Reilly (1873–1939)

"Fellow citizens, the United States has severed diplomatic relations with Germany."
The flag under which we sail is no longer protection.

"Star Woman Runs Blockade"
Mary Boyle O'Reilly
Seattle Star, February 17, 1917

NEW YORK, Feb 17.—With the Stars and Stripes at the taffrail, but no barber pole stripes on the sides or checkerboard flags on the mastheads, I have just passed thru the submarine zone of frightfulness on the American liner New York, THE LAST SHIP FOR HOME.

A vast landing shed held by soldiers; one table at which Britishers sit to be questioned, another at which Yankees stand for the same ordeal. A final interrogation, a grudging stamping of departure cards, a swift passage along the gauntlet, and I and 200 other American citizens are "safe" on the last boat home.

No parting cheer to the towering ship, no final greeting to the empty dock, as the first blockade runner slipped into the stream. Such are my last impressions of Liverpool.

Passengers are carefully cabined near the gangway stairs and life belts are laid open beside every berth.

I take my orders for the trip from a clam-eyed stewardess from the lost Titanic.

"Madam will dress warmly with fur coat and sea rugs laid ready," she tells me. "There is a handbag for money and jewels, the stateroom will be hooked open and you will have one night's sleep fully dressed lying upon the couch," she added.

Obviously, the orders come from the captain on the bridge—the comprehensive non-committal rule of the sea.

There is no mention of raiders[9] or submarines.

Gray, murky and fogbound sea shrouding the graves of the Arabic and Lusitania.[10] Gaudily painted ships shrieking their nationality from waterline to topmast. The Philadelphia limping into port with a smashed screw. Two slim, black torpedo boat destroyers sneaking to sea thru the deepening gloom. That is the picture the harbor presents.

Then a zone of broken water, a course inside the fastnet to avoid vast mine fields, a glimpse of the guardian ring of trawler patrols—indefatigable, unhonored and unsung, fishers, and fighters, too.

Here, if anywhere, pirate submarines lie waiting. If we get thru, other American ships can follow in safety.

Tie Children in Life Belts

Women glance at each other in silence; men's faces grow grim; children are tied into life belts. No one mentions either the Germans or the English. War weary and war protesting, we are Americans going home.

Then, of a sudden, the ship's long lean hull lunges thru hills of water. The blockade breaker is convoyed thru the first danger zone by the God of storms.

A wild night. On deck, the tiresome tramp of a double watch, thru the dark; from the sea-swept bow, the lookout's "All's well," lonely as a curlew call.

From the silent chamber where the whispering wireless drops the world's news, a messenger speeds to the captain. He rises, tired-eyed, and confident.

News of Diplomatic Break

"Fellow citizen, the United States has severed diplomatic relations with Germany."[11]

The flag under which we sail is no longer protection.

9. German surface warships used to sink commercial vessels
10. Passenger ships that had been sunk by German submarines
11. On February 3, 1917, President Woodrow Wilson severed diplomatic relations with Germany, moving the United States a step closer toward entering the war.

An elderly lady slips to the piano. Her cameo face, flushing faintly, she begins to sing. Not "Columbia," nor "My Country," but that nobler clarion call, "The Battle Hymn of the Republic." "As He died to make men holy, let us die to make men free." It is the creed of Americans facing Fate on the last boat home.

The ship heads into a new course, southwest of Hatteras, along a lane shipless to its dimmest horizon. The ocean, green and sullen, is a vast loneliness.

"This charting evades the lurking German raider," comments a New York banker. "Where escape is almost easy, threats of attack prove the folly of frightfulness."

"And the futility," add the dozen disciples of destruction, American engineers returning from exploding Rumanian oil wells for the British government.

Shuffleboard and quoits have lost their interest. The latest pastime is searching for undersea cruisers. The newest pastime is finding those significant holes in the deck planking which mark the position of a scoutship's quick firers.

"The old warship is racing home to cast off civilian gear," comments a bearded boatswain. "Eighteen years ago this month somebody mined our battleship Maine. Before you could lay a course from the Narrows to Nantucket, this 'greyhound' New York was a scout cruiser.

"That's what frightfulness does, quick as a flash, and meant to spread panic. We may be 'too proud to fight'[12] until some furriners offer us insult."

The children aboard have a new romp, a splendid, exciting game, which only good children may play, with certain funmaking sailors.

Three toots of a boatswain's whistle. Shrill cries, "To the boats, to the boats," and all dash off shouting and scrambling, dragging cork floats and blankets.

Next minute the fearless kiddies line up solemnly for expert inspection. Woe betide that child who fumbles when adjusting its life belt. That "survivor" is "dead." The "saved" continue the game.

Cry at Sight of Land

And the patient, sad-eyed mothers, who sit watching, whisper to each other: Should the youngsters here live to be very old, these

12. A reference to a speech given by President Woodrow Wilson after the sinking of the *Lusitania*, in which he refers to America as a nation too proud to fight

things will be remembered. So the threat of a sea tiger's spring will poison men's minds for a generation."

And so it went for seven days.

And on the eighth, Fire Island. It rises out of the sea bank, gilded by sun rays. As one person, passengers swarm to the plunging rail. The man in the checkered cap starts to whistle and fails.

The old lady whose ancestors poured at the Boston tea party dries her tears, quite unashamed.

The average American speaks out frankly, despite a catch in his throat: "Back there," his lean arm semaphores toward Europe, "back there, while the people pray for peace, the rulers decree war at any price—God knows why."

Elizabeth Shepley Sergeant (1881–1965)

"Put that on the ground, please," he says curtly.
"I am not sure what it is."

Shadow-Shapes: The Journal of a Wounded Woman, October 1918–May 1919
Elizabeth Shepley Sergeant

Four American women, with a Frenchwoman in nurse's uniform, their guide, are descending from the train at Épernay, where they are met by a French officer. Plump, pink, smiling, the officer. They have come for an afternoon's drive to Rheims and the American battle-fields of the Marne, and will return to Paris *via* Château-Thierry in the evening.[13]

Ravaged fields, shapeless villages…. Soon the Lieutenant has stopped the motor by a steep hillside. The battle-field of Mont-Bligny, very important in the defence of Rheims. He warns us that it has not been "cleaned up"; that we must touch nothing unless we are sure of its nature.

The ladies stream up and across the field, littered indeed with all sorts of obscene rubbish. Someone finds a German prayer-book. Someone else an Italian helmet. There may be a skull in it, warns the Lieutenant; but hangs a French one on his own arm for me. Mademoiselle has a queer-looking object—a series of perpendicular

13. Shepley was on a French army guided tour that had been arranged for several women journalists.

tubes set in a half-circle, with a white string hanging down at either end. The inside of a German gas mask, she says. We all walk across the hilltop as far as the holes dug in the ground by the forward French sentries; we look toward the German lines beyond—then turn back along the crest of the hill, where it drops off sheer to a wide valley. The Lieutenant, Mademoiselle, and I are ahead, the others some fifteen yards behind. Suddenly the officer notes what Mademoiselle is carrying:

"Put that on the ground, please," he says curtly. "I am not sure what it is."

A stunning report, a blinding flash, and I am precipitated down the bank, hearing, it seems, as I go the Lieutenant's shriek of horror:

"My arm, my arm has been carried away!"

I lift my head at once: two women cowering with pale faces, then running toward the road; the third standing quiet by a stark, swollen figure—the Frenchwoman, stretched on her back, with her blue veils tossed about her. Great gashes of red in the blue.

"*Macabre* of the movies" ... and aloud I hear a voice, which is mine, add:

"She is dead."

"Yes ... Terrible."

I seem oddly unable to get up. Ringing in my ears. Faintness. The effect of the explosion. Very tiresome, not to be able to help. I crawl farther down the hill to get away from blood. But something warm is running down my own face. Blood! I sit up and take out of the handbag still on my arm a pocket-mirror. Half a dozen small wounds in my left cheek. Unimportant. But my eyes fall casually on my feet, extended before me. Blood! Thick and purplish, oozing slowly out of jagged holes in my heavy English shoes and gaiters. I seem to be wounded. Queer, because no pain. I call to one of the women. She makes a meteoric appearance, tells me I am splashed with blood from the dead; is gone again. I must, I think, lie down. The chauffeurs seem to be above me on the hill now, carrying the officer away. A long interval. They are bending over me.

"Can you walk?"

"I'll try."

It does n't work. So they make a chair with their arms. One of them is grumbling that the other women aren't on hand.

"*Les blessés sont plus intéressants que les morts*—the wounded are more interesting than the dead," he remarks.

From my "chair" I note more objects, innumerable objects similar to the one that exploded, straggling like octopi in different parts of the field. The soldiers grin when, in a voice of warning, I point them out. Hand-grenades, they say. Now we have reached the first limousine. The officer is propped on the right half of the back seat, his bloody sleeve (not empty yet) hanging at his side. I am lifted in beside him, my shoes removed, my feet placed on the folding seat. Those nice, expensive brown wool stockings from "Old England" ruined....

The chauffeurs refuse to wait for the other ladies. Must find hospital at once. Unpleasant sensation of severing all connections with the friendly world. Inhuman country. Badly rutted roads. The officer, quite conscious, desperately worried:

"I did tell them not to touch anything, did n't I, Mademoiselle? They'll break me for this." Repeated again and again. Also the reply, "It was n't your fault, Monsieur."

A bleak barrack at last. An amazed "*major*," who sticks his head into the bloody car. But can do nothing for us. Gas hospital, this. Surgeons eight kilometres farther on. I feel pain at last and the Lieutenant is suffering. But we talk a little—about his wife, and his profession of teacher. Will I write to his wife to-night for him? Say he is not so badly hurt....

Dusk already. Two more dreary barracks in a plain, lean and grey. Another French doctor, black-bearded and dour. Very displeased to see both of us, especially the woman. Two stretchers. The Lieutenant disappears in one direction while I am carried into the triage and dumped on the ground. To be tagged, I suppose, like the wounded I have seen in the attacks of the last year. At least twenty Frenchmen lounging in this barn-like place. Orderlies, stretcher-bearers, wounded soldiers, all pleasantly thrilled.

"We must cut off your clothes, Madame."

"*Bien, monsieur.*"

I can be dry too. But if there were the least kindness in his grim eyes, I should tell him how desolated I feel to be giving so much trouble in a place where—I know it as well as he—women are superfluous.

Compound fracture of both ankles. Flesh wounds from *éclats*.[14]
A little soldier writes out a *fiche* in a deliberate hand while I am
being bandaged, and given ante-tetanus serum. The *fiche* goes in a
brown envelope, pinned on my breast as I lie on the stretcher.

"Is it serious, Monsieur?"

"The left foot, yes, very."

"Can I not make connections with the rest of my party, so as to
send a message to Paris?"

No, the chauffeurs had gone already. I am to be sent to a hospital
near Fismes. And the stretcher proceeds to the door. Stygian darkness now. As the men slide me into the lower regions of the ambulance I look up and see, peering down from the top layer, the very
white, rolling eye balls of two very black Senegalian negroes.

"You thought you'd be alone?" remarks the dry surgical voice.
"No ... *Bon voyage, madame.*"

The ambulance door seems hermetically closed. How the engine
groans on the hills.... How heavily the black men breathe above
me.... How my foot thumps.... How the hammering on the wheels
pounds in my head when we break down.

Another lighted triage. I am lying on another mud floor,
surrounded again by men, men. Perhaps I am the only woman
in the world.... But the atmosphere is more friendly. An orderly
approaches:

"You have three compatriots here."

"American soldiers?"

"American nurses."

Were ever such blessed words? And the tall, sure, white-veiled
woman who comes in to take my hand, and not reproach me for
my sex, seems to divine just how I feel. *Croix de Guerre*,[15] with
palm—Mayo graduate—can this be the nurse who lived so long
in a cellar at Soissons, nursing American soldiers? I put her in
a Red Cross article months ago! A presence to inspire instant
confidence.

"Only a bed in a *poilu*[16] tent," she apologizes. "Impossible to
make a woman comfortable."

* * *

14. Shrapnel
15. A French medal for bravery
16. Nickname for French soldiers

After treatment for her injuries from an accidental grenade explosion, Elizabeth Shepley Sergeant spent a long period of recovery in the American hospital in Paris. She is pictured here with nurses in the garden of the hospital. *Source:* Elizabeth Shepley Sergeant Papers, American Literature Collection, Beinecke Rare Book and Manuscript Library, Yale University.

The bed is grateful. Long, long wait. Finally a surgeon with a woman assistant materialize beside me. Surgeon with red face and shabby uniform, and, as bandages unroll, a troubled look. He says immediate operation is necessary.

Miss Bullard confides me to an orderly, Mercier. She cannot see me again to-night. Must prepare two hundred new arrivals, *blessés*[17] of yesterday's attack, for operation. Mercier seems kind. To be brought out of ether by an ex-*coiffeur*[18] is normal, after all this. When the stretcher-bearers come he helps them lift me; wraps blankets about my bloody and exiguous clothing. He says he ought not to leave his ward, but he comes along beside the stretcher, snubbing the *brancardiers*,[19] who are lower in the hospital hierarchy than *infirmiers*,[20] as I have already discovered. The movement of the stretcher on these human shoulders is soothing, though. And the rain that falls on my face from the black night. Too bad to leave it for the lighted X-ray room, so narrow and stuffy, and full of perspiring men. They can't even find the *éclats*. I point out where they must be. Long wait on the floor. At last the summons to the operating-room.

The surgeon is ready. In a white blouse, with a large black pipe in his mouth. He removes it to caution the men who are lifting me on to the table:

"Voyons, voyons! Don't you see it is a woman?"

A true Gaul. Unable not to point the ruthless fact. I turn my eyes to the green-painted ceiling. It is spotted with black, black like the surgeon's pipe. Flies. The assistant ties my hands to the table. (In peace-time, I reflect, they wait till one is unconscious.) The surgeon is bending over my wounds now, shaking his head, and his next phrase has no double meaning, and his voice no irony:

"All because a foolish woman wanted a little souvenir of this great, great war. ..."

I am getting ether in large quantities. Sensation of vibration—of waves beating, and through it voices very clear:

"Who is she?"

"A journalist." ...

* * *

The tent again. Blackness, clammy chill, penetrating pain. Mercier's hands smell strong of cigarettes. Kind Mercier, washing my face very tenderly ...

17. Wounded soldiers
18. Hairdresser
19. Stretcher bearers
20. Male nurses

Chapter 7

✦

✦

✦

✦

Russian Revolution

It was hard to push war headlines off the front page of newspapers in the spring of 1917, especially since America had
just entered the war. But Russia managed to do that. By cast-
ing off a three-hundred-year-old imperial dynasty and embracing
democracy, Russia won the sympathies of many in the west and
attracted reporters. Among the many American journalists who
traveled to Russia in the summer of 1917 were some half-dozen
women. They quickly discovered that Russia's new democracy
faced mounting resistance from a faction known as the Bolsheviks.
Throughout the summer and fall, tensions mounted as counterrev-
olutionary forces gained strength and threatened Russia's Provisional Government.

Like other journalists drawn to Russia in 1917, Louise Bryant
arrived in that tumultuous summer, between the revolution that
deposed the Czar and the revolution that brought the Bolsheviks
to power. The Bell Syndicate, Bryant's employer, had assigned
her to report on the war "from a woman's point of view." That
meant covering conditions on the home front. How was the civilian
population—largely women and children—adapting to the priva-
tions of war?

Many thought that a newly democratic Russia would be a more
effective ally in the war. However, Bryant realized on her arrival in

Russia that the war was very quickly being overshadowed by the continuing forces of revolution. The excerpt from Bryant's war memoir included in this chapter describes her arrival in Russia and captures the bewildering landscape of a country in the midst of war, revolution, and counterrevolution. As her story dramatically indicates, it was difficult to determine exactly what was happening, who was in control or attempting to seize control, where factional loyalties aligned, and how much longer Russia would remain in the war.

One of the biggest news stories from that Russian summer involved women enlisting for combat. With Bolsheviks actively encouraging soldiers to desert the army and military revolutionary councils subverting discipline, the Russian army was on the verge of collapse. But a unit of female soldiers emerged—the Women's Battalion of Death—that pledged to die protecting Russia. They would go where the men would not, they boasted. They would shame the men into returning to the trenches.

Every woman journalist in Russia got a piece of that story, including suffragist, political activist, journalist Rheta Childe Dorr. Dorr befriended the battalion commander Maria Botchkareva, followed the unit through training, and accompanied them on their journey to the front lines. Her story included here reveals the numerous fault lines jeopardizing Russia's continuing involvement in the war.

San Francisco Bulletin reporter Bessie Beatty was on hand for the ultimate triumph of the Bolsheviks in the October Revolution. (According to the Julian calendar then used in Russia, the revolution occurred on October 25; according to the modern Gregorian calendar, the date was November 7.) By associating with socialist reporters John Reed and his wife Louise Bryant, Beatty gained privileged access to many revolutionary events. In her article included here, she describes the dramatic events of October 25, 1917, the day the Bolshevik Revolution seized power.

Louise Bryant (1885–1936)

As our names were called we submitted our passports, answered questions, wrote down our nationality, our religion, our purpose in Russia, and hurried to unlock our trunks for the impatient soldiers.

"From the Frontier to Petrograd"
Louise Bryant
Six Red Months in Russia, 1918

Nobody believed that our train would ever really reach Petrograd. In case it was stopped I had made up my mind to walk, so I was extremely grateful for every mile that we covered. It was a ridiculous journey, more like something out of an extravagant play than anything in real life.

Next to my compartment was a General, super-refined, painfully neat, with waxed moustachios. There were several monarchists, a diplomatic courier, three aviators of uncertain political opinion and, further along, a number of political exiles who had been held up in Sweden for a month and were the last to return at the expense of the new government. Rough, almost ragged soldiers climbed aboard continually, looked us over and departed. Often they hesitated before the General's door and regarded him suspiciously, never at any time did they honour him with the slightest military courtesy. He sat rigid in his seat and stared back at them coldly. Everyone was too agitated to be silent or even discreet. At every station we all dashed out to enquire the news and buy papers.

At one place we were informed that the Cossacks were all with Korniloff[1] as well as the artillery; the people were helpless. At this alarming news the monarchists began to assert themselves. They confided to me in just what manner they thought the revolutionary leaders ought to be publicly tortured and finally given death sentences.

The next rumour had it that Kerensky[2] had been murdered and all Russia was in a panic; in Petrograd the streets were running blood. The returning exiles looked pale and wretched. So this then was their joyful home-coming! They sighed but they were exceedingly brave. "Ah, well, we will fight it all over again!" they said with marvelous determination. I made no comments. I was conscious of an odd sense of loneliness; I was an alien in a strange land.

1. Cossack general Lavr Kornilov. Bryant arrived in Russia in September 1917, during Kornilov's unsuccessful attempt to strengthen Alexander Kerensky's Provisional Government against the building strength of the Bolsheviks.
2. Alexandr Kerensky, Prime Minister of the Provisional Government that had been put in place following the February Revolution and the removal of the Czar.

Louise Bryant's name is rarely mentioned without being associated with her more famous husband, the war correspondent John Reed. However, Bryant established her own journalistic reputation with her coverage of Russia's Bolshevik Revolution. *Source:* Louise Bryant papers (MS 1840), Manuscripts and Archives, Yale University Library.

At all the stations soldiers were gathered in little knots of six and seven; talking, arguing, gesticulating. Once a big, bewhiskered mujik[3] thrust his head in at a car window, pointed menacingly at a well-dressed passenger and bellowed interrogatively, *"Burzhouee!"* (Bourgeoise). He looked very comical, yet no one laughed....

3. Peasant

We had become so excited we could scarcely keep our seats. We crowded into the narrow corridor, peering out at the desolate country, reading our papers and conjecturing ...

All this confusion seemed to whet our appetites. At Helsingfors we saw heaping dishes of food in the railway restaurant. A boy at the door explained the procedure: first we must buy little tickets and then we could eat as much as we pleased. To our astonishment the cashier refused the Russian money which we had so carefully obtained before leaving Sweden.

"But this is ridiculous!" I told the cashier. "Finland is part of Russia! Why shouldn't you take this money?"

Flames shot up in her eyes. "It will not long be a part of Russia!" she snapped. "Finland shall be a republic!" Here was a brand new situation. How fast they came now, these complications.

Feeling utterly at a loss, we strolled up and down, complaining bitterly. Once we found we could not buy food, our hunger grew alarmingly. We were saved by a passenger from another car who had plenty of Finnish marks and was willing to take our rubles.

At Wiborg we felt the tension was deep and ominous. We were suddenly afraid to enquire the news of the crowds on the platform. There were literally hundreds of soldiers, their faces haggard, in the half light of late afternoon. The scraps of conversation we caught sent shivers over us.

"All the generals ought to be killed!" "We must rid ourselves of the bourgeoisie!" "No, that is not right." "I am not in favour of that!" "All killing is wrong ..."

A pale, slight youth, standing close beside me, unexpectedly blurted out in a sort of stage whisper, "It was terrible.... I heard them screaming!"

I questioned him anxiously. "Heard who? Heard who?"

"The officers! The bright, pretty officers! They stamped on their faces with heavy boots, dragged them through the mud ... threw them in the canal." He looked up and down fearfully, his words coming in jerks. "They have just finished it now," he said, still whispering, "they have killed fifty, and I have heard them screaming."

Once the train moved again we pieced together our fragments of news and made out the following story:

Early the day before had arrived messages from Kerensky, ordering the troops to Petrograd to defend the city. The officers

had received the messages but remained silent and gave no orders.
The soldiers had grown suspicious. They mumbled together and
their mumblings had become a roar. At some one's suggestion, they
marched in a body and searched for the messages. The messages
were found. Their worst suspicions were confirmed. Rage and
revenge swept them away. They did not stop to separate innocent
from guilty. The officers were sympathisers of Korniloff, they were
aristocrats, they were enemies of the revolution! In quick, wild
anger they dealt out terrible punishment.

The details of the massacre were exceedingly ugly, but no
description of mine is necessary. Every Russian writer who has
ever written about mob violence has described the swift terrible-
ness of these scenes with amazing frankness. Realising that the
most serious of all dissolution and revolt is military mutiny, our
hearts fluttered at the unutterable possibilities....

We were interrupted in our reflections by a wail from the
Russian courier who found himself in a curious dilemma. "What
shall I do?" he asked of us dismally. "I have been nearly a month at
sea and God knows what has happened to my unfortunate country
in that time. God knows what is happening now. If I deliver my
papers to the wrong faction it will be fatal!"

It was past midnight when we stopped at Beeloostrov. It was the
last station. We were so certain all along that we would never get
to Petrograd that we were not surprised now when soldiers came
on board and ordered us all out. We soon found, however, that it
was just another tiresome examination. Crowded into a great bare
room, we stood shivering nervously while our baggage was hurled
pell-mell into another. As our names were called we submitted our
passports, answered questions, wrote down our nationality, our
religion, our purpose in Russia, and hurried to unlock our trunks
for the impatient soldiers.

The officers startled us by beginning to confiscate all sorts of
ordinary things. We protested as much as we dared. In explanation
they replied that a new order had just come in prohibiting medi-
cines, cosmetics and what-not. Next to me in line was an indignant
princess whose luggage contained many precious "aids to beauty,"
all of which had already been passed hurriedly by bashful censors
and custom officials many times before. But that unreasonable
new order upset everything; rouge-sticks followed rare perfumes,

French powder, brilliantine, hair-dye—all were thrown roughly into a great unpainted box, a box whose contents grew rapidly higher and higher, a box that had the magic power to change what was art in one's hand-bag into rubbish in its insatiable maw.

The princess pleaded with the soldiers, used feminine wiles, burst into hysterical weeping. Poor, unhappy princess, forty, with a flirtatious husband, handsome and twenty-three! The situation was far too subtle for these crude defenders of the revolution! Only an old monarchist dared to be sympathetic, but I noted that he took care to be sympathetic in English, a language few of his countrymen understand. "Madame," he remarked testily, "there is a strong hint of stupid morality in all this. You must remember that to the uncultured all implements of refinement are considered immoral!"

The husband offered tardy consolation. "Be calm, my darling, you shall have all these things again." Unfortunately he would never be able to make good his promise, for in these rough days of the new order cosmetics are not considered important and Russian ladies are forced to go "au natural."

We arrived in Petrograd at three in the morning prepared for anything but the apparent order and the deep enveloping stillness that comes before dawn. My friends of the train soon scattered and were lost in the night, and I stood there in the great station confused, with what was left of my baggage.

Presently a young soldier came running. "*Aftmobile?*" he enquired in a honeyed voice. "*Aftmobile?*" I nodded assent, not knowing what else to do and in a moment we were outside before a big grey car. In the car was another soldier, also young and pleasant. I gave them the name of a hotel some one had told me about—the Angleterre.

So we were off whirling through the deserted streets. Here and there we encountered sentries who called out sharply, received the proper word, and allowed us to pass. I was consumed with curiosity. These soldiers wore neither arm-bands nor bits of ribbon. I had no way of knowing who or what they were…One of them wanted to be entertaining, so he began to tell me about the first days of the revolution and how wonderful it was.

"The crowd raised a man on their shoulders," he said, "when they saw the Cossacks coming. And the man shouted, 'If you have come to destroy the revolution, shoot me first,' and the Cossacks replied, 'We do not shoot our brothers.' Some of the old people who remembered how long the Cossacks had been our enemies almost went mad with joy."

He ceased speaking. Mysteriously out of the darkness the bells in all the churches began to boom over the sleeping city, a sort of wild barbaric tango of bells, like nothing else I had ever heard....

Rheta Childe Dorr (1866–1948)

Some quite terrible-looking men appeared at some of the stations, stuck their unkempt heads in the car windows and shouted: "Why are you going to fight for the dirty capitalists? We won't give our lives for the English bloodsuckers."

"Women Soldiers of Russia May Rescue the Republic"
Rheta Childe Dorr
The Sunday Star (Washington, DC), October 21, 1917

The women soldiers of Russia, the most amazing development of the revolution if not the world war itself, I confidently believe, will, with the Cossacks, prove to be the element needed to lead, if it can be led, the disorganized and demoralized Russian army back to its duty on the firing line.

It was with the object, the hope, of leading them back that the women took up arms. Whatever else you may have heard about them this is the truth.

I know these women soldiers very well. I know them in three regiments, one in Moscow and two in Petrograd, and I went with one regiment as near the fighting line as I was permitted. I traveled from Petrograd to a military position "somewhere in Poland" with the famous Botchkareva Battalion of Death.

I left Petrograd in the troop train with the women. I marched with them when they left the train. I lived with them for nine days in their barracks, around which thousands of man soldiers were encamped. I shared Botchkareva's soup and cassia, and drank hot tea out of her other tin cup. I slept beside her on the plank bed.

Rheta Childe Dorr in 1913, when she served as editor of *The Suffragist*. *Source:* Harris & Ewing Collection, Prints and Photographs Division, Library of Congress, LC-DIG-hec-03403.

I saw her and her women off to the firing line, and after the battle into which they led reluctant men I sat beside their hospital beds and heard their own stories of the fight. I want to say right here that a country that can produce such women cannot possibly be crushed forever.

It may take time for it to recover [from] its present debauch of anarchism, but recover it surely will. And when it does it will know how to honor the women who went to fight when the men ran home.

The Battalion of Death is not the name of one regiment, nor is it used exclusively to designate the women's battalions. It is a sort of order which has spread through many regiments since the demoralization began, and signifies that its members are loyal and mean to fight to the death for Russia. Sometimes an entire regiment assumes the red and black ribbon arrowhead which, sewed on the right sleeve of the blouse, marks the order.

Battalion of Death

Regiments have been made up of volunteers who are ready to wear the insignia. Such a regiment is the Battalion of Death commanded by Mareea Botchkareva (the spelling is phonetic), the extraordinary peasant woman who has risen to be a commissioned officer in the Russian army.

Maria Leontievna Botchkareva (1889-1920) the Russian woman who formed the Women's Battalion of Death. *Source:* George Grantham Bain Collection, Prints and Photographs Division, Library of Congress, LC-B2- 4600-7.

Botchkareva comes from a village near the Siberian border and is, I judge, about thirty years old. She was one of a large family of children, and the family was very poor. Mareea married young, fortunately a man with whom she was very happy. He was the village butcher and she helped him in the shop, as they had no children.

When the war broke out in July 1914, Mareea's husband marched away with the rest of the quota from their village, and she never saw him again. He was killed in one of the first battles of the war, and the only time I ever saw Botchkareva break down was when she told me how she waited long months for the letter he had promised to write her, and how at last a wounded comrade hobbled back to the village and told her that the letter would never come.

"The soldiers have it hard," she said, when her brief storm of tears was over, "but not so hard as the women at home. The soldier has a gun to fight death with. The women have nothing."

For months Mareea Botchkareva watched the sufferings of the women and children of her village grow worse and worse. She decided that she could not endure it to sit in her empty hut and wait for death. She would go out and meet it in the easier fashion permitted to men. That is the way she explained to me why she joined the regiment of Siberian troops encamped near her village. The men did not want her, but she sought and got permission, and when the regiment went to the front she went along.

Earns Cross of St. George

She fought in campaigns on several fronts, earned medals and finally the coveted cross of St. George[4] for valor under fire. She was three times wounded, the last time in the autumn of 1916, so badly that she lay in a hospital for four months. She got back to her regiment, where she was now popular, and I imagine something of a leader, just before the revolution of February 1917.

Botchkareva was an ardent revolutionist, and her regiment was one of the first to go over to the people's side. Her consternation and despair were great when, shortly after the emancipation from czardom, great masses of the people, and especially the soldiers at

4. The Order of St. George is the highest Russian military medal.

the front, began to demonstrate by riots and desertions how little they were ready for freedom.

The men of her regiment deserted in numbers, and she went to members of the duma who were going up and down the front trying to stay the tide, and said to them, "Give me leave to raise a regiment of women. We will go wherever men refuse to go. We will fight when they run. The women will lead the men back to the trenches."

This is the history of Botchkareva's Battalion of Death, or rather of how it came to be organized. The Russian war ministry gave her leave to recruit.

The woman soldiers are not school girls, and Botchkareva's battalion has no man officers. Three drill sergeants, St. George Cross men all of them, did assist in the training of the battalion while it remained in Petrograd. Other men drilled it behind the lines, but Botchkareva and another remarkable woman, Marie Skridlova, her adjutant commanded and led it in battle.

Daughter of an Admiral

Marie Skridlova is the daughter of Admiral Skridloff, one of the most distinguished men of the Russian navy. She is about twenty, very attractive if not actually beautiful, and is an accomplished musician. Her life up to the outbreak of the war was that of an ordinary girl of the Russian aristocracy. She was educated abroad, taught several languages and expected to have a career no more exciting or adventurous than that of any other woman of her class.

When the war broke out she went into the Red Cross, took the nurses' training and served in hospitals both at the front and in Petrograd. Then came the revolution. She was working in a marine hospital in the capital. She saw many of the horrors of those February days. She saw her own father set upon by soldiers in the streets, and rescued from death only because some of his own marines who loved him insisted that this one officer was not to be killed.

She saw her hospital ward invaded by a mob, and wounded officers murdered in their beds. Her own life, when she vainly tried to defend one of her patients, was threatened. She heard men she had nursed back to life curse her for an aristocrat unfriendly to the revolution, which happens not to be a fact. She saw women and children killed in their homes by wild bullets from the street. She saw what was coming in Russia, and went home and took off her Red Cross uniform.

"Women will need to do something more for Russia than bind up wounds," she told her father. And when the announcement was made that a woman's battalion was forming she went to him and told him she was going to enlist. He took her, his only daughter, to Botchkareva, and himself wrote her name on the regimental roll book.

Every woman in the battalion has some such history.

Did the world ever witness a more sublime heroism than that? Women, in the long years which history has recorded, have done everything for men that they were called upon to do. It remained for Russian men, in the twentieth century, to call upon women to fight and die for them. And the women did it.

Women Rush to Enlist

Women of all ranks rushed to enlist in the Butchkareva Battalion. There were many peasant women, factory workers, servants and also a number of women of education and social prominence. Six Red Cross nurses were among the number, one doctor, a lawyer, several clerks and stenographers and a few like Marie Skridlova, who had never done any except war work. If the workingwomen predominated I believe it was because they were the stronger physcially. Botchkarova would accept only the sturdiest, and all her soldiers, even when they were slight of figure, were all fine physical specimens.

The women were outfitted and equipped exactly like the man soldiers. They wore the same kind of khaki trousers, loose-belted blouse and high peaked cap. They wore the same big boots, carried the same arms and the same camp equipment, including gas masks, trench spades and other paraphernalia. In spite of their tightly shaved heads they presented a very attractive appearance, like nice, clean, upstanding boys. They were very strictly drilled and disciplined and there was no omission of saluting officers in that regiment.

The battalion left Petrodgrad for an unkown destination July 6 in our calendar. In the afternoon the women marched to the

Kazan Cathedral, where a touching ceremony of farewell and blessing took place. A cold, fine rain was falling, but the great half-circle before the cathedral, as well as the long curved porches, was filled with people. Thousands of women were there carrying flowers, and nurses moved through the crowds collecting money for the regiment.

Even though the woman soldiers were under the protection of the church during the ceremony, the situation was rather tense. The Bolcheviki[5] well knowing the moral effect of women offering themselves for death in battle, had sworn that they should not be allowed to reach the trenches. "We'll kill you first!" declared these chivalrous gentry.

One Girl Turns Traitor

They had done everything in their power to breed dissension in the ranks, and had actually succeeded in enlisting one of their own women, a girl from Cronstadt, who created a great deal of mischief before she was unmasked and turned out of the regiment. The women were so outraged by the discovery of a traitor in their midst that for an hour or so it looked as though they could not be restrained from doing her violence. But sober heads prevailed and the girl from Cronstadt was allowed to go unharmed.

I passed a very uneasy day that July 6. I was afraid of what might happen to some of the women through the malignancy of the Bolcheviki, and I was mortally afraid that I was not going to be allowed to get on their troop train. I had the usual application to the war ministry to be allowed to visit the front, but my application seeemd to be lost in a mountain of red tape. Perhaps they are acting on it now, I don't know. I went to the front without my permit.

The Bolcheviki did not attack the women at any time during the day, but a crowd of them was at the station and did their best to break up the line of marchers. The women literally had to fight their way to the train platform.

Our train consisted of one second-class and five fourth-class carriages. I had a place in the second-class compartment with the

---

5. An alternative spelling of Bolsheviki / Bolshevik

nachalnik, or commander; the adjutant, Botchkareva, Skridlova, and a big peasant girl named Orlova, who was the battalion standard bearer. We had cushioned seats, without bedding or blankets, to sleep on, but the rank and file slept on hard wooden bunks.

We had picnic food of every variety, more than I dreamed was in Petrograd, for people brought forth all sorts of private stores and loaded the train with white bread, cake, chocolate, canned fruit and all sorts of delicacies. We had tea and sugar also, and every soldier carried a tea kettle.

Urged Men to Go Home

Friday night, all day Saturday and until late Sunday afternoon we traveled southward. At every station great crowds, principally of idle soldiers, waited for the train. Some were friendly, others were not. Some quite terrible-looking men appeared at some of the stations, stuck their unkempt heads in the car windows and shouted: "Why are you going to fight for the dirty capitalists? We won't give our lives for the English bloodsuckers."

And the women retorted, shrilly eloquent: "Go home then, you cowards, and let women die for holy Russia."

There was something indescribably strange about going on a journey to a destination absolutely unknown, except to the one in command of the expedition. Yet everyone was happy, and the only fear expressed was lest the battalion should not be sent at once to the trenches. As for me, when we arrived at our destination, some two miles from the barracks prepared for us, I had a moment of longing for the comparative safety of the trenches. For what looked to me like the whole Russian army had come out to meet the women's battalion, and was solidly massed on both sides of the railroad track as far as I could see.

I looked at the nachalnik calmly buckling on her sword and revolver. She had a satisfied little smile on her lips.

"You may have to fight those men out there before you fight the Germans," I said.

"We are ready to begin fighting any time," she replied.

She was the first one out of the train and the others rapidly followed her.

Bessie Beatty (1886–1947)

On my way back I walked through the Dvortsovaya Square.
Four armored cars were drawn up under the shadow of the
mighty granite shaft in front of the Winter Palace, their guns
pointing significantly at the Palace windows. Flaming red
flags were freshly painted on their gray sides, and on one in
large letters was the word "Proletariat."

"The Rise of the Proletariat"
Bessie Beatty
Asia: Journal of the American Asiatic Association, 1918

Winter and the Bolsheviki came to Russia on the same chill breeze,
and each brought a strange new world.

Late one afternoon in early November I walked through the
gray streets of Petrograd, and shivered. It was not cold as the thermometer speaks, but cold as a room where death awaits a tardy
undertaker—desolate, ugly, forbidding. Autumn was already dead,
and the burial long overdue. The last copper-colored leaf had been
stripped from the trees and trampled in the dust some days since.
The gray trunks of the birches were nude and conscious of it.
The city was wrapped in a futile cloak of fog, too thin to hide its
nakedness, every barren shrub and battered cornice pleaded with
delayed winter to cover its shame.

I turned my face away from the Summer Garden and walked
quickly past. A million years had gone since that spring day six
months before when the sparrows occupied themselves with house
building in the green leaves, and Vera and Ivan on the benches
below devoted themselves to castle building. At that moment
I hated the city, which I had come to love as one loves a naughty
child for all its faults and virtues, its hopes, passions, and potenti-
alities, and failures; for the sum of its stormy, troubled self.

I hurried back to my blue and white room in the War Hotel,
drew the curtains, turned on all the lights, and curled up on the
couch to bury myself in a book of verse and shut it out.

The next afternoon at three o'clock I reached for the desk telephone to call the American Consul. There was no answer. I pushed
the hook up and down, tempting fate in the shape of an irate opera-
tor, but it produced no response.

"Has it come?" I asked myself, and laughed at the question. It had been the current one in Petrograd for weeks. Every time the electric light failed, the water turned off, or some one banged a door, Petrograd jumped automatically to the same conclusion: it has come!

I put down the receiver, straightened the papers on my desk, and started for the censor's office. A new sentry was pacing up and down outside the hotel. On the Morskaya, in the block below, the armored car in the courtyard of the Telephone Exchange had moved nearer the sidewalk, and was flaunting the guns ominously at the passing throng. I hurried on, bent on getting my letters ready for the weekly express. Mr. Novometzky, the kindly censor, who softened one's heart to the whole tribe of blue pencilers, shook his head despairingly when I entered.

"Well, it has come," he said. "There is trouble again. These are bad times for poor Russia."

I left him and walked briskly toward the Nevsky on the trail of a possible courier who would carry my mail across the world to San Francisco. At the Moika[6] a crowd had gathered around a big limousine. Three soldiers held a brief parley with the chauffeur, and one of them climbed into the vacant seat beside him. Further down the street another car was stopped, then another, and another. In my eagerness to see what was going on, I almost bumped someone off the sidewalk. I looked up to apologize, and found Arthur Bullard standing beside me.

"What's happened?" I asked.

"I guess it's come," he answered.

"But are they Government or Bolsheviki?"

He shrugged his shoulders. "Who can tell."

The street cars began to pile up on the Nevsky. Word passed down the street that the bridges had been swung open across the Neva, and trouble had already commenced.

It was dark when we walked back to the hotel, where excited groups were gathered in the dimly lighted lobby, "Orchadie" hurried across to meet me. Her pretty little oval face was pale above the collar of a sealskin coat, and the hand she slipped into mine was cold and trembling.

6. The Moika Palace, where some government offices were located

"It has come!" she said. "You must not stay here. It is not safe. There will be much bloodshed. We are going away at once to the home of a friend. You must go with us."

I shook my head, laughingly reminding her of the many wild rumors through which we had both lived safely, and went upstairs to wash for dinner. I dined that night with a French aviator, and afterward we stood in the lobby, and watched a Battalion of Death file through the whirling door and encamp on the marble floor. At ten o'clock we wandered into the black streets. The Nevsky was quiet. The Palace Square was almost deserted. Along the Neva, at the entrance to each of the bridges, a group of soldiers crowded around a log fire. Here and there in the centre of the circle was a small boy, thrilling like small boys the world over at the lateness of hour, the bigness of his companions, and the adventure of the moment. A few stops removed from each of these groups was a wagon filled with ammunition.

Back in the hotel I met Baron B., whose title, estates, and sympathies were all bound up in the hope of a return of the monarchy.

"Well, we have got them on the run this time," he said.

Only a week before I had sat next [to] him at a dinner, where before my amazed eyes they toasted the Czar, and sang the old tabooed national anthem. Our host, an Englishman, had introduced him as a great officer and an absolutely fearless human being.

"He helped to stop the retreat from Tarnople on the southwestern front after the July offensive," he said. "You ought to have seen him lining up those deserters before the firing squad. He made quick work of the bloody cowards."

I urged the Baron to tell me of his experiences, and shuddered as I listened. He had nothing but contempt for Kerensky, his Commander-in-Chief, and was eager for his downfall. His only fear was that the Soviet would not take over the government.

"Two weeks of the Bolsheviki, and we will be able to lick these people into shape," he said. "The worse things get, the sooner they will be willing to listen to reason. You don't know the Russians."

We've got them on the run this time—what could it mean? No good to Kerensky, I was sure; no ultimate good to the masses of the Russian people, if Baron B. could have his way.

There was nothing in the situation that night that augured well for Kerensky's government. He was like a man poised on a tight-rope.

The cry, "All power to the Soviet!" grew louder and more insistent with every passing hour. The Russian workers, the youngest proletarian group in the world, were the most class-conscious and determined, and—they had guns. The fleet was Bolshevist. I had no doubt of that. The Petrograd garrison was Bolshevist. Every report from the front indicated that the men in the trenches had swung further and further to the left. The land and peace hunger clamored for immediate satisfaction.

Kerensky, trying like the true Democrat he was to please everyone, succeeded in pleasing no one. He had lost touch with the masses. Attacked from above and below, from within and without, there seemed little hope for him. Those who should have been behind him with every energy and influence they possessed, were secretly willing his downfall, and some of them plotting to bring it about. Individual members of the Allied military missions, still clinging to the old belief that Russia could be saved by a man on horseback, in spite of the Korniloff fiasco, which should have taught them better, were meeting behind closed doors where they discussed not the way to save Kerensky, but a way to put a dictator in his place. The names of Korniloff and Savinkoff[7] were again bandied about wherever two or three military men were gathered together.

Poor Kerensky—too big, and not big enough! Any one of his problems was a man-sized job. He was packing the load of a broken industrial and economic machine, inherited from the régime of the Czar, a corrupt, inefficient and disloyal bureaucracy, and a betrayed and disillusioned army. His uncomprehending military partners, the Allies, were urging the impossible, and refusing to grant the demand of the Russian masses for a statement of war aims and a publication of the secret treaties, without which Kerensky could no longer hold the faith of his followers. Dark forces of the old order were working with German intriguers to augment the chaos, and above and beyond and beneath everything was the honest cry of the people for "Peace to the world!" and "Land to the Peasants!"

The Bolsheviki promised peace and land. They promised more. They promised that the workers should "arise and put a stop to war and capitalist exploitation forever."

7. Boris Savinkov, a long-time member of the Socialist Revolutionary Party, served as Deputy War Minister in the Provisional Government.

They were dreaming big dreams in Russia that night; scheming big schemes; and they were not unaware that the dreams and schemes would be used in the future by the rest of the world, perhaps as patterns by which to model, perhaps only as horrible examples and tragic warnings. It was an hour in which one needed all of one's faith to believe that the human march is forward, no matter how many members of the family are lost on the way.

At daybreak, a company of Red Guards from the Viborg factory district—men whose only equipment was a rifle slung over the shoulder, and the conviction that the hour of the proletariat had come and that they were the defenders of the cause of the workers of the world—came to a halt on the north bank of the Neva. The bridges were guarded by cadets from the Engineer's School, placed there the night before, when Kerensky had ordered them opened. At the point of their guns, the factory workers ordered the officers to close them again. The engineers obeyed and the street cars started blithely on their way back and forth across the river, just as though nothing had happened. At the same moment two detachments of Bolshevist soldiers and sailors, acting under orders from the military Revolutionary Committee, took possession of the Telephone Exchange and the General Staff. It was all done so swiftly and quietly that the Bolsheviki battle was half won before Petrograd awoke to the knowledge that civil war was on.

It was nine o'clock when Petrov brought me tea and word that the Bolsheviki had that moment taken possession of the hotel. Petrov's astounding news sent me hurriedly into the hall, and into the arms of a squad of soldiers. The young officer in command detained me.

"*Amerikanka Korrespondent*," I explained, and indicated a desire to go down stairs. "*Pazhal'sta, pazhal'sta!*"[8] he said, bowing low, and motioning his men to let me pass.

At the head of the winding staircase groups of frightened women were gathered, searching the marble lobby below with troubled eyes. Nobody seemed to know what had happened. The Battalion of Death had walked out in the night, without firing so much as a single shot. Each floor was crowded with soldiers and Red Guardsmen, who went from room to room searching for arms, and arresting officers suspected of anti-Bolshevik sympathies. The landings

8. Please, please

were guarded by sentries, and the lobby was swarming with men in faded uniforms. Two husky, bearded, peasant soldiers were stationed behind the counter, and one in the cashier's office kept watch over the safe. Two machine guns poked their ominous muzzles through the entry way. My letter of credit was inside the safe, and the only other money I had was an uncashed check for eight hundred rubles. I started for the National City Bank on the slender chance of finding it open, and was just in time. Within the hour the Bolsheviki captured the State Bank, and all the others promptly closed their doors.

On my way back I walked through the Dvortsovaya Square. Four armored cars were drawn up under the shadow of the mighty granite shaft in front of the Winter Palace, their guns pointing significantly at the Palace windows. Flaming red flags were freshly painted on their gray sides, and on one in large letters was the word "Proletariat." A crowd of perhaps twenty mechanics and chauffeurs tinkered with guns and engines, making ready for instant action. Occasionally a man looked up from the nut he was tightening to offer some comment on the situation. The whereabouts of Kerensky was the chief topic of the moment.

"He is not there now," said one of them, pointing with his wrench in the direction of the Palace. "He ran away to Finland in the night."

"He is not in Finland," said another scornfully. "He went away to get troops. He is coming back to fight us."

"They say he escaped to the front disguised as a Red Cross nurse," said a third, with a sneer that produced a loud burst of laughter from his companions.

Inside the Palace, seated around the mahogany table in the great Council Chamber, where the Czar of all the Russias spoke the commands that made an Empire tremble, fifteen members of the Provisional Government grimly waited. In the hall outside the door ten military school cadets kept watch. These, the Woman's Regiment, and a company of cadets encamped on the lower floor, were all that stood between them and the rising army of the workers. To them the whereabouts of Kerensky was no secret. He had gone in search of loyal troops who would rise to the protection of the Provisional Government, and upon his success or failure they must stand or fall.

It was noon when I returned to St. Isaac's Square. The Marinsky Palace, where the Council of the Republic was meeting—once the home of the Council of the Empire, mouthpiece of absolutism in old Russia—was surrounded by sailors, soldiers, and Red Guardsmen. The Palace guards offered no resistance when a crowd of sailors demanded admission. They swarmed through the entrances, and appeared simultaneously in various parts of the hall. A sailor, a tam o'shanter on the back of his head, long ribbon streamers flying out behind, stepped up to President Avksentieff.

"Stop talking. Go home," he said. "There is no Council of the Republic!"

Avksentieff and his followers demurred for a moment; then, looking around the room at the men in blue, adjourned and filed into the square. The Council of the Republic, hope of Tseretelli, Cheidze, and those other moderate socialists who were trying so desperately to stave off the final break, was at an end. The more radical socialist members went to Smolney Institute where the delegates from all parts of Russia were flocking to the second All Russian Congress of Soviets.

At three o'clock I started for Smolney, Daddy R., full of misgivings, trotting beside me. We walked down the Morskaya toward the Telephone Exchange. Just opposite we halted. Coming toward us in regular marching formation was a company of military cadets, strapping, handsome fellows from the officers' school. Before they reached the building the commander halted them. Half of the number walked deliberately past the armored car, turned and approached from the other side. A volley of rifle fire broke the stillness, and the crowd scurried to the cover of doorways and side streets. A gray-bearded, benevolent looking *dvornik*[9] dragged me inside a courtyard where a dozen other people sought shelter, and clanged the great iron door shut behind us. A beggar, with legs cut off at the knees, hobbled beside me.

Crack! Crack! went the rifles again—then a moment of breathless silence. The *dvornik* cautiously opened the door a few inches, and I put my head out. The street was deserted. The cadets were crouched in kneeling positions on the sidewalks against the wall, guns pointing at the Telephone Office. The *dvornik* pushed the door shut again, and this time he locked it and motioned us to follow.

9. Doorkeeper, caretaker

We crossed a courtyard, and turned into a dark, narrow tunnel, through which we picked our way over piles of debris and up and down stone steps till we came into the open a block below.

By another route, Daddy R. and I made our way back to the Morskaya. I stepped to the middle of the street to see what was happening, but a Russian officer motioned me away.

"They will fire again in a minute," he said. "They are trying to take the Telephone Exchange from the Bolsheviki."

He had no sooner finished speaking than the front of the building commenced to belch lead in a shower that sent the cadets hurrying in search of shelter. An armored car hove in sight from the opposite direction, opened fire, and completed the rout of the attacking force.

We hurried toward the Nevsky. The bridge across the Moika was bristling with guns. Four armored cars barred the way, and a crowd of soldiers and sailors worked rapidly throwing up a barricade across the street. One man stretched flat on the wooden pavement, prepared to fire a machine gun from the protection of a telegraph pole. The Red Guards waved the passengers back from the bridge, but the tracks were left open, and the cars went back and forth unhindered. We tried to make our way through the old France Hotel, which wanders all over the block between the Morskaya and the Moika, and out onto the canal by another entrance. Again we were turned back. Another volley of gunshot sent us scurrying to the shelter of a basement shop.

When things were once more quiet we emerged and jumped on a street car, already packed to the limit with men, women and children eager to get out of the danger zone. Crowded in among them was a boy who sat placidly reading a paper-backed novel. It was nearly five when we reached the entrance of Smolney. The great building, until a few months before a private seminary where the feminine flower of feminine aristocracy was cultivated in seclusion, had suddenly become an arsenal, bristling with guns and swarming with armed men. Soldiers in dun-colored coats, grimy and unshaven, sailors, spic and span in trim blue uniforms, and workers in worn and shoddy suits, flowed through the doors in an endless stream.

Upstairs the Workmen's and Soldiers' Deputies were gathering for the Congress of Soviets. They were coming together to decide whether the Bolsheviki demand of "All power to the Soviets" should be granted. It was a question already being answered by the voice of the guns.

The meeting was to open at five. At nine the crowd in the great chaste white Assembly Room was still waiting for action. Outside in the dimly lighted corridors, hundreds of men with muddy boots tramped back and forth, in and out of committee rooms. Soon after nine, a delegate from the Bolsheviki group announced that his party was still in caucus, unable to come to an agreement, and asked for another hour's delay. A murmur of disapproval ran through the room. Nerves were at trigger-tension. For once Russian patience seemed to be about to reach its limit.

Another hour passed. Suddenly through the windows opening on the Neva came a steady boom! boom! boom!

"What's that? What's that?" asked the sailor of the soldier, and the soldier of the workman.

A man with pale face and blazing eyes fought his way through the crowd onto the platform.

"The cruiser 'Aurora' is shelling our comrades in the Winter Palace. We demand that this bloodshed be stopped instantly!" he shouted.

"It's a lie!" said one of them.

"It's just another trick of the bourgeois to divide our forces!" said a second.

A few men hurried from the hall, but the crowd had received too many startling rumors that day to be much disturbed by another one.

Again came the boom! boom! boom! from the direction of the Neva. Again the murmur of questions.

"It's a motor lorry cranking up in the courtyard below," some-one ventured.

That moment the attention of the crowd was diverted by the arrival of a man of medium height, square shouldered, lean, dark and tense-looking. His face was white, and his black hair brushed back from a wide forehead, black moustache and small black beard, his black jacket and flowing black tie, still further emphasized the alabaster whiteness of his skin. He stood within a few feet of me, one hand in his pocket, and with sharp, quick glances took in the measure of that strange sea of faces.

"Here's Trotzky!"[10] whispered the man beside me. "Come, I want you to meet him."

Before I had time to acquiesce or protest I found a lean hand grasping mine in a strong characteristic handshake. We stood there for a few moments talking of inconsequential things, but all of us charged with the tensity of the hour. There was keen intelligence here, nerve, a certain uncompromising streak of iron, a sense of power, yet I little suspected I was talking to the man whose name was within a few brief weeks to be a familiar word on every tongue—momentarily the most talked of human being in an age of spectacular figures.

At twenty minutes to eleven our conversation was abruptly cut short by the appearance of Dan, who opened the meeting. It was Dan's swan-song. Only a few weeks before in this gathering his voice would have been law, but with the swing of the workers to the left his power was gone. The mass had broken with its leaders, and every comment from the crowd indicated more definitely the irrevocability of that break. Dan announced he would not make a speech, declaring that the hour in which his comrades were being shelled in the Winter Palace, and self-sacrificingly sticking to their posts, was not the hour for oratory. He said that 513 delegates had been seated, and the new presidium of 25 members would contain 14 Bolsheviki. With this, the spokesman of the various parties pronounced the names of their representatives. Leaders of the social patriotic groups, of the Mensheviki[11] and Socialist Revolutionists, refused to take their place in the presidium, and the Menshevik Internationalists declared they would delay joining the presidium until certain questions were settled.

The Bolsheviki, with Nicolai Lenine[12] and Zenovieff[13] at their head, climbed to the platform. A great cheer went up from the Bolshevik supporters. Lenine and Zenovieff, who had been in hiding since the July riots, had that day come out of their holes to take an historic part in this new revolution. When the ovation

10. Leon Trotsky, an influential leader of the Bolsheviks. He would later become one of the seven members of the first Politburo, founded in 1917 to manage the Bolshevik Revolution.

11. A moderate wing of the Russian Social Democratic Workers' Party, opposed to the Bolsheviks.

12. "Lenin" and "Nikolai Lenin" were pseudonyms sometimes used by Vladimir Ilyich Ulyanov, the head of the Bolsheviks. Various transliteration spellings also appeared in print.

13. Grigory Zinovyev, another Bolshevik leader.

had died down, Dan briefly stated the object of the meeting before relinquishing his place to Trotzky.

"The business of the Convention," said he, "divides itself into three heads. A governmental crisis, the question of war and peace, and the Constituent Assembly."

"Take up the question of peace first," shouted a soldier in the crowd.

It was all that was needed to set the indignation of the Mensheviki flaming.

"Tavarischi, forty minutes have passed since we announced that our comrades were being shelled in the Winter Palace, and the cruiser 'Aurora' is still firing. We demand that this bloodshed be stopped immediately."

"A committee has already been sent out," someone else declared.

Martoff, perhaps the ablest of the Menshevik Internationalists, took the platform, and in a voice ringing with indignation demanded immediate settlement of the governmental crisis.

"If this Convention wants to be the voice of revolutionary democracy, it must not sit idly by before the rapidly developing civil war which may result in a disastrous explosion of the counter-revolution," he said. "When the question of the organization of the government is being settled by the conspiracy of a single one of the revolutionary parties, we are challenged by only one problem; the immediate warding off of this impending civil war."

He proposed the appointment of a committee for negotiating with other socialist parties and organizations to stop the rapidly developing clash.

The resolution was passed, but instead of immediately appointing a committee, Trotzky permitted the Convention to listen to the opinions of delegate after delegate on a number of subjects not pertaining to the question. It was a critical moment in the history of the Russian Revolution. Perhaps it was some bitter memory of insults he had suffered at the hands of these other leaders, perhaps it was simply the natural inability of the Russian to compromise, or a combination of these and other motives, that made Trotzky delay action, and thereby toss away his opportunity for compromise. Probably even he himself could not say.

Meanwhile the guns on the Neva continued their eloquent boom! boom! boom! Kharash, a delegate from the Twelfth Army, got the floor.

"While a proposition for peaceful settlement is being introduced here, a battle goes on in the streets of Petrograd," he said. "The Winter Palace is being shelled. The spectre of civil war is rising. The Mensheviki and Socialist Revolutionists repudiate all that is going on here and stubbornly resist all attempts to seize the government."

"He does not represent the Twelfth Army," cried a soldier from the ranks. "The army demands all power to the Soviets."

Twenty others were on their feet the same instant.

"Staff! Staff! He comes from the Staff! He is not a soldier," they shouted angrily, shaking their fists at the delegate from the Twelfth.

Pandemonium broke loose. The shouts of the men inside the building drowned the boom of the guns outside. In the midst of it a man demanded and got the floor.

"We are leaving the Convention," he said. "We can stand no more! We are going unarmed to die with our comrades in the Winter Palace."

A hush fell over the crowd. It was broken only by the sound of shuffling feet as the speaker led the way to the door, followed by a hundred or more of the conservative revolutionists, who filed quietly out.

At midnight, with three fellow-correspondents, I left the atmosphere of that memorable meeting, gray with smoke and charged with battle, and headed for the Winter Palace.

Chapter 8

❖
❖
❖
❖
❖

Americans in France

T he entry of the United States into the war in April 1917 changed the way journalists covered the conflict. For one, the number of American reporters in Europe increased dramatically, including many women journalists. Many women's magazines, such as *Pictorial Review, Delineator, Woman's Home Companion, Good Housekeeping*, and *Ladies' Home Journal*, posted their own correspondents to Europe. Since American wives and mothers were now sending their husbands and sons to fight, they had an intense interest in hearing about their activities. During the roughly one-year period between U.S. entry into the war and its introduction into combat operations, women journalists chronicled the experience of Americans in France and how the French and Americans adjusted to each other.

Dorothy Canfield Fisher was in Paris on July 4, 1917, when the first units of American troops paraded through the French capital. Her eyewitness account captures snapshots of onlookers overcome with emotion, seeing their new ally as a welcome savior in France's long struggle with Germany.

In "America Meets France," Elizabeth Shepley Sergeant visits the same subject later in 1917, when France and America were adjusting to their new alliance. She introduces another phase of American involvement, the thousands of representatives of the aid organizations that arrived in France to support U.S. troops and the long-suffering French population. She traveled to France with "three hundred and fifty strenuous idealists," volunteers from the YMCA and the Quakers, full of determination and excitement. Sergeant styles the moment as the transition between America's abstract "spiritual communion" with France in the early years of the war and its concrete presence in France now that the United States has entered the conflict. One Frenchman cautions Sergeant that Americans "still imagine war to be a noble adventure," whereas in France the sacrifices and restrictions had become a way of life, a grim new reality.

Veteran journalist Rheta Childe Dorr had a son serving in France. To her nothing mattered as much as learning about his wellbeing. Knowing that hundreds of thousands of other American women felt the same, Dorr began the widely syndicated column "A Soldier's Mother in France." In the column included here, Dorr reassures mothers and wives that the army's military police prevent soldiers from getting into trouble.

By the summer of 1918, Americans soldiers had made their long-awaited entry into combat. By this point in the war, some quarter million American soldiers were arriving in France every month. It was at that juncture that *Good Housekeeping* magazine sent its editor Clara Savage to France. *Good Housekeeping* had already run articles about the women in France, but now Savage would serve as its own war correspondent to cover American involvement. She began her assignment with a first-impressions article about her ocean voyage and settling into wartime Paris. "The French love us," she assured her readers, and they love the American soldiers who are so visible around the city.

Dorothy Canfield Fisher (1879–1958)

In that part of Paris all the children had been let out of school and stood in lines on the curbstones, little pathetic, rather pale and pinched, city-poor-quarter children, each with a tiny American flag and a tiny flower.

"The Sammies in Paris"
Dorothy Canfield Fisher
Everybody's Magazine, September 1917

This is July 5th now, and I don't want to send this letter off without telling you about our part in the Fourth of July celebrations. We had succeeded in getting a room with a balcony on the Rue de Rivoli, where the American troops were to pass, and we were there at half-past nine, expecting the troops about ten. There was a very large crowd, the usual prosperous, bourgeois, holiday Paris crowd in that quarter of the city, women with folding chairs, well-dressed elderly men and lively, well-turned-out children.

Just before the procession was announced, an aeroplane gave an exhibition of fancy flying not more than a hundred and fifty feet above the heads of the crowd. I have seen a great deal of air gymnastics since I have been in France this time, but never anything approaching the dizzy wildness of those swoops and dives. We were all carried away with enthusiasm over the Airman's extraordinary mastery of his machine, and the roar of applause drowned out the noise of his motors. But I would be surprised if others there didn't have the same idea that I did—that it was a very foolhardy business to do all that over the heads of an immense crowd.

With one final double bow-knot, he dashed off as the music was heard, and the worn blue uniforms of a band of old Territorials[1] appeared in front of the long column of American khaki. The enthusiasm was very great, everybody shouting, waving flags, and throwing flowers. The men looked very much better turned-out and marched much more smartly than they had the day before, on leaving the station. Everybody comments on their long, loose-jointed, rolling stride, which is very different from the French quickstep.

The moment they had gone by, John, Sally and I rushed across the street and down into the Metro, because I was very anxious to see the reception in one of the poor quarters of Paris. We made a short cut to a place near the end of their march and reached there three-quarters of an hour before they did. The contrast between the crowd we had seen on the Rue de Rivoli and the crowd there, was astonishing and dramatic. On the Avenue Dumesnil people were five and six deep as far as the eye could see up and down the long street, and hardly a person who did not evidently belong to the working classes. In that part of Paris all the children had been let out of school and stood in lines on the curbstones, little pathetic,

1. Territorials were reserve units in both the French and British armies.

An enormously accomplished woman, a Ph.D. in French, an education reformer, fiction writer, and founder in France of a children's hospital and a Braille Press for blinded veterans. Dorothy Canfield Fisher's war articles appeared in numerous magazines. Her war fiction and sketches appeared as the book *Home Fires in France* in 1918. *Source:* Author's collection.

rather pale and pinched, city-poor-quarter children, each with a tiny American flag and a tiny flower. The working girls were there from the factories, still in their work aprons, with their sleeves rolled up, and mothers with numerous families, who had brought the entire brood out to welcome the Americans.

We walked for a long distance back of and through this crowd, stopping from time to time to listen to what they were saying.

When American troops arrived in Paris on July 4, 1917, enthusiastic crowds showered them with flowers. These doughboys paused for ceremonies at the tomb of the Marquis de Lafayette, the French aristocrat who fought in the American Revolution. *Source:* American National Red Cross photograph collection, Prints and Photographs Division, Library of Congress, LC-A6196-1702-Ax.

One woman, jumping up and down with excitement, said: "Oh, I am so glad I am going to see them; I never saw any Americans in my life." I gathered from her accent that she expected them to wear feathers and paint their faces with war paint. I can not begin to tell you the atmosphere of genuine friendliness and evident good feeling which permeated this enormous crowd. I never felt anything like it in my life. We stopped finally just before the turn into the little Rue de Picpus, where Lafayette's tomb is situated, and waited for the troops to come. When they arrived, they were walking bouquets, having been showered with flowers all along the way. Every button had a flower stem twisted around it, their hats were all wreathed, and every rifle barrel had a bouquet on it. The officers in front had their saddles banked with flowers, and what was even more significant of the warmth of the welcome given to them was that their Anglo-Saxon self-consciousness and stiffness had entirely disappeared, and the men whom we had seen on the Rue de Rivoli, slouching along with a rapid, powerful American gait, without a glance to right or left, were now flushed and smiling, nodding and exchanging inarticulate greetings of friendliness with the people who rushed out from the side to give them more flowers and to shake their hands and to touch the big American flag which they carried.

We were swept along by this crowd, and were not at all sorry to find ourselves, all three of us, marching rapidly beside the soldiers in the midst of the dense crowd of working people who accompanied them, filling the street solidly from the houses on the one side to the houses on the other side.

I listened with all my ears, as you can imagine, to the comments that were made, and as everybody was talking at the top of his voice, to be heard above the din, I caught a good many, some of them amusing. A great many times they said: "Oh, ils sont fameux"—they're fine. I heard several times: "How tall and thin they are!" Once or twice, with a hearty emphasis, almost of admiration: "Heavens, how ugly they are." (And this was really true. I didn't realize, until I saw a mass of them together, how the Lincoln type of powerful, raw-boned, sincere ugliness has persisted in many Americans); and of course a thousand times "Vive les poilus d'Amérique."[2]

One working woman walking in front of me, carrying a baby, kept saying: "It makes me want to cry when I see their flag here," and an old man said: "I hope there is a German spy on every street corner."

But what pleased me most of all was what a middle-aged, middle-class woman on the street-car going home said to me after she noticed John's uniform. She said: "Every time I see the American flag it makes me think: 'No the Germans were wrong. Ideals are the realest things there are.'"

The flowers were still showering down just like something you read about. I never saw it before. The soldiers were really walking on flowers and had their arms full besides. A big rose fell into Sally's hands, and I called to her, above the roar of the cheering, to give it to the American soldier by whose side she was trotting and to tell him she was a little American girl. She handed it to him but

2. "Poilu" was a nickname for French soldiers. Here the phrase would mean "Long live the American soldiers."

was too shy to say anything, so I called out to him: "It is an American child." I saw his lips moving as he called the attention of the other men in his line, and as they marched they all leaned forward with a very friendly look of surprise and pleasure at Sally. I suppose in that utterly foreign crowd it must have seemed very strange to them to see a child of their own nationality.

There were almost no policemen in that quarter of the city and very little effort was made to restrain the crowd from doing as it pleased; and what it pleased was to rush into the streets as the flag went by and join itself to the procession. It was an awful crush and I never heard such a noise in all my life; but I never was in a more orderly crowd than that very poor and very excited one. I won't say that the three Americans who were in the midst of it weren't almost as excited as the French.

It was impossible, of course, to get into the Cimetière de Picpus, although, as an American Ambulance family, we had a right to. But I didn't want to hear any speeches anyhow. To have heard a professional politician orate after having heard for over an hour that great, continuous roar of deep popular emotion, would have been too great an anti-climax. So we profited by being in an eddy near a side street, slipped out and took the Metro over to the nearest restaurant. We were very tired, but really very happy, as we sat there watching the American flag in with the other Allied flags fluttering over the restaurant door.

Elizabeth Shepley Sergeant (1881–1965)

The fact is that France and America are exactly in the position of two people who have become engaged by correspondence and are meeting for the first time in the flesh.

"America Meets France"
Elizabeth Shepley Sergeant
The New Republic, December 29, 1917

The other day I met an American naval lieutenant in a Paris tram, enquiring of the puzzled woman conductor the way to Notre Dame. As we went over the Pont-Neuf together we paused to look at the

curving Seine with its noble chain of bridges, and the gray-blue pile
of the Louvre against the misty October sky.

"Paris is a beautiful city all right," he said earnestly, "but I don't
think much of the people."

"What's the matter with them?"

Well, he had been cheated by cabdrivers and had been refused
admittance to the Opéra and the Louvre. When I remarked that
the monuments were closed to visitors because of the scarcity of
labor, he insisted:

"But I told them I was an American! Usually if you say that you
get anything you want."

American stock in France began at the top of the market, and
we have received so many special privileges and so much spontaneous gratitude that we are only just waking up to the fact that
we must take our place among all the other hordes of foreigners,
friendly and inimical, who have invaded the soil of France in the
last three and a half years. I was waiting in the sad little room
where permits are given out for the *Zone des Armées*[3] when a boy
in khaki strode in demanding immediate attention. The sergeant,
after asking his business, offered him a wooden chair and a dirty
number like the rest of us; the French widow of twenty, who wanted
to visit her husband's grave; the broken old farmer, who had to
study the remains of his beet sugar refinery; the Red Cross engineer who must reach the village he was rebuilding; the French
Captain, who had a sick mother near Compiègne.

"But it's 4:30 and if I'm not at the Prefecture by 5:00 I can't get
off tomorrow!"—and to the sergeant's irritating smile:

"Look here, don't you know we come over here to help you?
And this is the way you treat us."

The difference between France in the abstract—the France
with which we have been in intimate spiritual communion since
1914—and France in the concrete begins to make itself felt on any
Bordeaux liner before she has cleared New York harbor. We had, for
instance, as descendants of Lafayette and Rochambeau,[4] a much
be-medalled aviator, a solemn munitions expert, a flip journalist, an
elderly professor, and several nondescript commercial gentlemen.

---

3. Areas near the front lines where military activities were taking place. Access to these
areas was restricted.
4. French aristocrats/military officers who aided America during its revolution

The aviator at once presented his heart to the only American girl who looked—and behaved—as if she had been brought up on the Grands Boulevards; otherwise a gulf yawned between the nations. It was interesting to watch the French faces as they passed the busy corners of the deck where the forty-five Y. M. C. A. secretaries were established, acquiring "French in Two Hundred Words," where the seventeen lady cantineers with Red Crosses on their hats were discussing recipes for the poilu's soup; where the fifty Quakers were going through gymnastics so as to be ready to build portable houses and drive ploughs through mud and barbed wire; where the nurses' aides and the ambulance boys, the teachers of the blind and the tuberculosis and child specialists foregathered, with the salvation or the amelioration of the French race in view. The professor, who had been profoundly moved by the personal experience of the American sentiment for France, confessed to me one day that he nevertheless feared for his country's reputation the exaltation of these three hundred and fifty strenuous idealists. Would they not expect to see on the shores of France some romantic symbol of change and glory—something like the flags of Fifth Avenue, for instance.

"You still imagine war to be a noble adventure," he said, "and for you it is still abnormal. We went into it at the beginning with clenched teeth, and we have endured it increasingly as a family endures a terrible illness; and now it has become so normal that it will deceive you."

Undoubtedly the first shock of France at war does come to our enthusiasm as a cold douche, and it takes the average American perhaps a week to react from his sacrificial state of mind. By way of "reception committee" he is met by the French petty official who greets him much as the American immigration official greets the arriving Serbian, or Italian; the French women of the trains and stations, thoroughly weary of doing "man's work"; the canny French tradesman who—having seen the first American soldiers throw gold out of their car windows in return for Camembert cheeses, seeing the present ones ready to pay double for everything, provided they get "the best"—tries to cheat him out of his eye-teeth. Then Paris, which he had expected to find empty, forlorn, swathed in heavy crape and haunted by ghosts and mutilated men—Paris seems to be accepting war like the rain, going soberly, philosophically, realistically about its business and its pleasures. The widow wears her veil with a most becoming grace, and the *mutilé* conceals his deformity under a smart uniform. There are still flowers on the quais and in the gardens, and couples of the special Parisian variety too, whom separation and "horizon-blue"[5] have made more publicly and more profoundly tender than of old, so that a breath of tenacious life and poignant happiness rises into the cloudy autumnal sunsets and moon-rises. There is still food, delicious food, in the best restaurants of which he may freely partake, provided he has a long purse and a short memory for Hoover principles;[6] are not French officers freely partaking? There is steam heat in his hotel—does not America provide the coal? There are still taxis—nothing in this "crisis" in gasolene. So he reasons, consciously or unconsciously, and if he has a civilian job, almost settles down in the midst of his fellow-Americans to believing war is not.

It was a shock to me, when I moved from a hotel where we had sweet desserts, and meat twice a day, even twice a meal, to find that a pound of sugar and 120 pounds of coal a month were all that I was allowed as a member of a French household. This means that we sweeten nothing but our tea, and choose between a fire for our feet and a fire for our roast. We have one small piece of meat for lunch and none for dinner, and the concierge wakes her little boy at 5:30 to stand in line for the morning milk. The cook's husband has been sent to Italy, and she occasionally asks me what all these Americans in uniform are doing in Paris. Do they never go to the front? The housemaid is a war widow and her mother in Burgundy writes her that the arrival of the American soldiers has tripled the cost of living. You can't buy an egg at any price....

More and more is it borne in upon me that we have a great deal to live up to, to compensate for the inconvenience of our mere physical presence. What is not expected of the descendants of Washington and Lincoln? Up to the spring of 1917, we had been here in relatively small numbers, and, whether in the army, in the hospitals, or in relief work, we were volunteers and guests who

---

5. The color of the French army uniform
6. A reference to Herbert Hoover, who directed the Commission for Relief in Belgium, an international aid organization that provided food to German-occupied Belgium and northern France.

generally possessed long pocketbooks, European outlooks and fluency in the French tongue. Now, on the contrary, we arrive as those having a right here, and a duty; yet we are generally ignorant of the language and daily habits of our ally and try instinctively and immediately to transform his ancient, hand-made, delicately adjusted civilization—a civilization which, in spite of this long invasion appears to have remained practically intact—into the hyper-modern, 10,000 horse-power, free and easy terms of Kansas, California and New York.

That is, theoretically at least, what the French themselves desire. Not only our democracy, our confident and generous youth, our vitality of mind, our fertility of invention, our vast material prosperity, but our efficiency and our scientific method have been a lyric theme, and it is felt that, especially in the industrial world, we can help to break many ancestral chains. Yet one hopes that some lover of the *come'die humaine*[7] is making notes against a less solemn hour, of the actual encounter between the French manufacturer who points with pride to a factory unchanged since his grandfather's day and the American capitalist who asks when he is going to tear it down; between the New York business man, accustomed in five minutes' telephone conversation to start a train of events which will culminate within a week, and the French administrative official who, though war keeps him at his office from 8 a.m. to 9 p.m., has not abandoned his habit of longhand letters, long polite conversations, and long-deferred decisions; between the French peasant who makes his toilet in the barnyard, keeps his gold in a stocking, and lives frugally on vegetable soup in a house inherited from a revolutionary ancestor, and the sergeant from Ohio brought up in an apartment on enameled bath tubs and beefsteak, and who always pays with a cheque; between the poilu who has been holding two-thirds of the western front and a good share of the Oriental front through these bitter years on his pay of five sous a day, and the American private who finds the accumulation of his $1.25's scarcely sufficient to storm the biggest town near his camp on a Saturday night, and drive French colonels from their accustomed chairs to make way for his champagne supper.

7. An apparent reference to *La Comédie humaine*, a series of novels by the famous French novelist Honoré de Balzac, published in the early nineteenth century and styled as a broad-ranging history of society.

The fact is that France and America are exactly in the position of two people who have become engaged by correspondence and are meeting for the first time in the flesh. The color of our hair, our fashion of blowing our noses, are mutually disconcerting. Yet to state these differences is to overstate them; they are only worth noting—deliberately from the French point of view—because we are committed, for the success of our effort here, to a common liberal understanding such as has seldom united two alien nations. On the cordially cooperative lines already established by the American Clearing House[8] and by the American Ambulance Service, which brought young America into such living contact with the rank and file of the French Army, the American Red Cross—that vast and powerful organization—and the American Army are working out their daily routine; and though France has lost the habit of public demonstration—not a flag, or a cry after the victory of Verdun, not a protest in the trains or streets during the recent gravest hour of the war, when vast numbers of French troops were sent off to Italy—the name of President Wilson cannot be mentioned in a French gathering without long applause. It is impossible to persuade the citizen of the "liberated" part of northern France that we alone did not save him from starvation. The Belgian Relief Commission is known to him as the *Ravitaillement Américain*. As for the French woman of the people, that wrinkled and brown old sibyl from whose lips falls much of the wisdom of the race, she sees our "boys" arriving with a deep astonishment, and a deeper pity:

"I saw them at the movies," said my washer woman, "such fine, big fellows—I couldn't bear to look at them. 'First ours, now yours,' I said to myself. Why did their mothers send them over to be killed? Why?"

"But this is our war too...."

"You believe that? So far away? ... But if you knew how we feel.... My Pierre, when he went back from his September permission—it's not gay going back to a fourth winter in the mud. '*T'en fais pas*,' he told me, '*ils sont la, les petits Américains.*'[9] It's they who are going to save us."

---

8. The American Relief Clearing House coordinated all American aid flowing into France.

9. "Don't worry," he told me, "they're here, little Americans."

Americans will gradually come to realize that they are doing Frenchmen an injustice in romanticizing their cause. They have gone about their job of soldiering as they used to do that of peasant, professor, workman, with absolutely no sense of being superman. Indeed, their daily effort is to minimize their pain, conceal their wounds under a twisted smile. (Said the heir to a great name, directing us to the ruins of his ancestral chateau, which the Germans had blown up with dynamite: *"Vous allez rigoler"*—in Broadway English "It's a scream!") If we can ever realize to what degree they are men and *galantes gens*,[10] who have in blood and territory borne the brunt of the war, and still bear it steadfastly, we shall be doing them all the honor they deserve.

Rheta Childe Dorr (1866–1948)

With that kind of police force and that kind of officers commanding it, you can be sure that your sons haven't very much opportunity to go astray.

A Soldier's Mother in France: "'A.P.M.' Magic Letters that Help Our Boys in Straight Path Abroad"
Rheta Childe Dorr
The Courier-Journal (Louisville, KY), July 24, 1918

"I know that my boy is being well cared for in his regiment, and I'm not afraid of what may happen to him as long as he is on duty. But what about his off hours? What is to prevent him from falling into bad company?"

I know that this thought has troubled the minds of many mothers of soldiers now in France. And no wonder. Ever since the first training camps were set up in this country the most lurid tales have been spread abroad about the alleged immorality of the soldiers' off hours. Some of these tales were spread by pro-Germans, pacifists and cowards who hoped to defeat draft laws. Others were the result of a certain kind of imagination. The vast majority of them were untrue.

But even if any of them were true, if boys of 21, away from the restraining influences of home, found unusual opportunities

10. Gallant people

for immorality right here in the United States, what must it be in France? Many American women have it firmly fixed in their minds that France is a shocking immoral country. It isn't, but I do not hope to be able to unsettle the conviction.

M. P. is Everywhere

I will content myself with saying that even if France were a second Sodom or Gomorrah, our soldiers would be safe there. As safe, or safer, than they would be at home. The reason is that they are under military discipline and military supervision every hour of their lives. In their off hours they are supervised by the most efficient and powerful police force in the world, the military police of the American army.

Military police is what we call them for short. They are really assistant Provost Marshals. They are everywhere in France where there are American soldiers. They police Paris and all other cities, towns and villages in our zone. They are found sitting at a little table in all the railroad stations, and every traveling American soldier, be he officer, non-commissioned or private, has to report the minute he arrives to the station marshal. This applies to all holders of military passes, Red Cross and Y.M.C.A. workers and war correspondents.

Watch Over Our Soldiers

The marshal examines the papers of the traveling officer or soldier, stamps them and enters the name and destination of the traveler in his book. This happens when the soldier leaves his base and when he returns. They keep track of our men on their travels.

They also keep track of our soldiers in their daily walks abroad, where on duty or pleasure bent. There are certain rules in our expeditionary force which apply to all alike, from Gen. Pershing down to Bill Smith, private, just arrived from Camp Funston or Camp Upton. One of these rules is that no member of the expeditionary force may associate with women of the submerged class.

If a military policeman sees an officer or a soldier in such company it is his duty to separate the two, and gather the offending man in. If he fails to do so and the fact is established, the policeman is punished. But he doesn't fail.

Some of our officers, only a few, I was assured, didn't believe at first that a simple private soldier would dare arrest them for the offense of having a "good time." Two of these very new Lieutenants tested it out in Paris once. They annexed a pair of women of the underworld and started out to find whatever might be left of the night life of the French capital.

His Revolver Out

What was their indignation when a slim youth of about 25, wearing the uniform of a private, with the sole addition of a brassard marked A.M.P.,[11] walked up to them, saluted and stepped politely between them and the open door of the taxicab.

"Beg pardon, sirs," he said courteously, "I am obliged to remind you that you are transgressing the provisions of Section ----- of regulation ----- of orders ----- relating to associations with women. I shall have to request you to accompany me to headquarters."

The two *very* new young officers declined the invitation, first with indignation, then with good-natured appeals to the soldier's sporting blood. The soldier remained adamant, and then one of the officers, getting genuinely angry, thrust his fist under the man's nose. "What would you do if I were to push your face in and go on my way?"

The soldier policeman promptly drew his revolver and thrust it in the Lieutenant's nose. "I would do my duty, sir," he replied, still courteously. But he was an American and couldn't hold in any longer. "By God," he exclaimed, "I wish you'd try it, You're the kind of an officer the American army could afford to lose suddenly."

Plenty of Cartridges

That settled it. The two officers went to headquarters, and they were punished. The one that attempted to frighten the young policeman got sent back to the United States. The men at headquarters agreed with the policeman that the United States army could afford to lose a man like that.

The military policeman, who is found all over our zone in France, does not wear blue clothes and a peaked cap. Neither does he carry a baton. He wears his soldier uniform and a white armband

11. The article here gives the incorrect initials. They should be A.P.M., Assistant Provost Marshall.

on which the letters A. P. M, assistant provost marshal, appear in letters of red. He wears a belt and a revolver and he carries plenty of ammunition with him.

He is part of a service which has at its head Gen. Allaire, Chief Provost Marshal of the army, one of Gen. Pershing's staff. He lives at the sequestered little town which houses the rest of the staff. Under him are many officers who command the regiments of Assistant Provost Marshals, and they are held responsible for the order and good conduct of the army.

Are a Picked Lot

In Paris the military police had their headquarters in an old-fashioned building in the Rue Ste. Anne, close to the heart of old Paris. The place was a hotel in pre-war days, and it looks very much like a hotel now, with all the boarders in uniform. The big dining room has less style about it than formerly. At present it is furnished with long pine tables, scrubbed clean, and the dishes are mostly white enamelware.

A one-armed French soldier, with a most engaging smile and a pretty good knowledge of English, acts as elevator boy, and he told me once that when the war was over he was going to America. "I want to know how it feels," he said, "to belong, even for part of my life, to a country that can produce such boys as these."

They are a picked lot. It is an honor to be in the service, and only those in whose honor as well as valor the authorities have the greatest confidence, ever make the service.

A Single-minded Man

In Paris the Lieutenant under whose direct command the force works is the most single-minded man I think I have ever met. His whole existence seems bound up in his men. He even spends his off hours with them. One Monday when I went to the house in the Rue Ste. Anne to have a military pass stamped by the proper Provost Marshal, this Lieutenant of Police told me that the day before, Sunday, he had taken the half of his men who were off duty to Versailles. They had a wonderful day, he said. The authorities even opened the palace museum for the Americans.

"Next Sunday," he said, "I am going to take the other half of the force down the Seine to a beautiful place where we can have dinner

out of doors and have a look at French life of the old regime, I mean
that my men shall get all there is in a foreign sojourn."

I told him that I thought he was pretty fine to give all his leisure
to his soldiers. He blushed like a boy and said: "They deserve it
and I enjoy it. Besides, it is a part of my job to make these men
as intelligent individuals as possible. They need to be intelligent.
They have eight hours of particularly responsbile work.

Out For Deserters

"Here in Paris they have to keep their eyes out for deserters. It is
their business to know that every American soldier who walks
through a street here had a right to do it. They have to be keen to
look for spies in American uniforms. Oh, yes, they have picked
up more than a few of those gentry. They might have slipped past
the French soldiers, because they don't know Americans, but they
couldn't fool an American A. P. M. Every suspicious character gets
nabbed sooner or later. If there is any doubt about his status our
men bring him in here. If he can satisfy us, all right. But there is
never an apology due him from the policeman.

"One of our men may be transferred from patrol work to riding
on railroad trains and keeping track of our soldiers on their travels.
He may be transferred to the front, where he becomes a traffic cop
and also one of the men who take captured Germans in charge.

"We have a school for our motorcycle cops. These men become
inspectors of police. They speed directly to the scene of any great
or small disaster, and they assist the French gendarmes and military police. When the long-distance gun[12] hit that church on Good
Friday, killing seventy-six people, our men were the first on the
spot. They helped rescue the wounded and they brought out the
dead. They did excellent service in that great fire near Paris when
the powder works blew up.

A Fine Bunch

"As quickly as an air raid is over men are out on their cycles looking up the damage inflicted by the bombs. They report back here
where every bomb fell. Often they are able to put out small fires
caused by the bombs.

---

12. The Germans bombarded Paris with a long-range artillery piece, known as the Paris
Gun, from March to August 1918. It could fire a shell eighty-one miles.

"They are a fine bunch," ended the Lieutenant. "Not one of my men has ever been in trouble, and the fact that our cooler here in Paris often has as many as 150 people in it shows not only that their work is essential, but that it is performed to the king's taste."

With that kind of police force and that kind of officers commanding it, you can be sure that your sons haven't very much opportunity to go astray. Once in a while a man may evade the military police. Occasionally I have seen it done. But it happens rarely, and the chances are a hundred to one against it happening twice to any one man.

Clara Savage (1891–1956)

*All France is pinning her faith to the dauntless courage
of these square-jawed young Americans.*

"The First Word from France"
Clara Savage
Good Housekeeping, October 1918

The gang-plank was up. We had reached land after a voyage that was expected to last ten days but took twelve. For the past three nights we had slept in our clothes—hair pins, shoes, and all—a life-preserver by our side, and always there had been an underlying sense of danger. Even the merriest of us admitted it was there, and if we forgot for a minute, there were the boat drills and the fire drills and our life-preservers to remind us. The windy, sunny days, when the sea was a green blue flecked with eddies of foam, had been happy. There is nothing quite like the exhilaration of the sea. To be on shipboard is like being in a different world, one where the chief business of life is to let the sun warm your bones and burn your nose, and the wind blow new life into you until you feel as happy and care-free as a small child again, just glad to be alive. The days were like that. The nights were different. For then Fear came and walked the decks with us. No one was allowed to strike a match. No one, might sing, not even the ship's favorite:

> Pack up your troubles in your old kit bag,
> And smile, smile, smile!

The port-holes were closed at sundown to remain closed till five the next morning, and all the lights inside were heavily shaded. The white-whiskered captain of the ship was taking no chances. His boat had been attacked more than once by the Germans and had fought bravely. He showed you the medal she had won and told you of the powerful guns she carried. Several times during the voyage we saw sailors man those guns and knew that danger was near. One morning a great cargo of oranges went bobbing by our stern, and another day we saw a cargo of cotton afloat. Somewhere ships had gone down. Then over the wireless came the news of the sinking of the Canadian hospital ship and the murder of men and women. And so whether we sat in our steamer chairs in the morning, or played games in the afternoon, or walked the decks at night, we knew we were in danger.

My cabin-mate was a girl of my own age, half French and half Italian. For a year and a half in New York we had lived just around the corner from each other, but we met first on shipboard. We had grown to be great friends. Coming off the boat together, we looked around for someone to carry our bags. As we waited for what I expected would be a porter, there came toward us a boy with a cart to which a dog was attached by a chain. Marga immediately hailed this odd pair, heaped our luggage in the cart, and gave the address of a hotel where we hoped to find a room. The boy and the dog and the cart started off at a brisk trot. I ran after and rescued my typewriter. I had no faith at all in this arrangement.

"Doesn't he give you any receipt for your luggage?" I asked.

"Oh, no," said Marga. "I don't believe we'll ever see any of it again," I said.

"Oh, yes, we will," said Marga. I insisted on carrying my typewriter as the most precious of my possessions, and wondered, as the boy and the dog and the cart rattled away out of sight, if I would ever again see my hand-bag. my hat-box, my umbrella, and my new blue cape with polka-dots. It was my first experience in the casual French way of doing things. You must have faith in France. Even when the French seem most easy-going, they are most painstaking. Our baggage was waiting for us when we arrived at the hotel.

It was a small, quiet hotel, and a woman was in charge. In order to get a room for the night, I had to show my passport and make out a slip telling my name, where I was born, my age, and my profession. After these formalities, I was tucked into a tiny elevator that crawled up to the third floor. You ride upstairs in elevators in France, but not down. There is no use in trying to explain to the elevator boy that since he is going down he might as well take you with him. He merely points to the stairs. My room was small, but spotlessly clean and airy. There are seldom closets in French bedrooms, but wardrobes instead. In one corner were running water and towels, but no soap. In another corner stood a bed piled so high with mattresses and puffs that I had to take a running jump in order to land on top of it, but when I did get up there, I found it most comfortable.

At dinner time we went down to the street to hunt a café, since the hotel did not serve luncheon or dinner. We hadn't gone very far when a tall boy in a uniform I didn't recognize accosted me.

"Air yer Scootch?" he asked. I explained that I hadn't been for at least two generations.

"Oh, and I thought by the color of yer hair and yer talk that ye might be," he said. "I am Scootch myself."

There was no mistaking the homesickness in that boy's face.

Marga and I walked on and found places in one of the many cafes. The menu told us it was a meatless day. There was no sugar, and when we asked for bread, we were requested to show the bread tickets that had been given us just before we landed. These tickets entitled us to a hard stick of war bread, brown in color and rather sour in taste.

Three young American soldiers came in and sat down at the next table. They looked at us intently. "Do you think they are French?" asked a tall, brown-eyed boy of his companions.

"They sure are," said one with an unmistakably Southern inflection. Then he turned to us. "*Parlez-vous français?*" he asked with painstaking precision.

We nodded.

"*Je suis Américain,*" he continued unnecessarily. "*Je demeurait en* Tennessee near—I mean *près* Nashville. Ever heard of Nashville?"

"What the dickens do they care where you *demeurait?*" interrupted the brown-eyed one.

They lapsed into silence, distrustful of their French. We were too tired to tell them that we spoke English, and yet no one could do a kinder thing than to talk their own language to some of these boys so far away from home. Convention vanishes when two Americans are strangers together in a strange country. "What part of the States do you come from?" "Where are you going?" "Goodby and good luck!" Over and over you meet and greet fellow countrymen in this way and pass on again, both happier for the meeting.

A woman came into the café. There was no mistaking her. She wore a clinging silk dress that set off the curves of her figure. Her face under a broad-brimmed, black velvet hat was pretty in a hard, pink-and-white way. Her red lips curved, but there was no merriment in them, and her eyes, very much darkened about the lashes, were ferret-like. She came slowly down the middle of the café—hunting.[13] She glanced at every man, and stopped to curve her lips at the three American boys. They made no sign, and she walked on with the undulating movement that is a part of the French street-woman's technique. I looked at the three Americans to see what they thought. It was easy to tell. Disgust was written all over their faces. She was repulsive to them. They were just three typical American boys, young and clean and decent, and instinctively they loathed the horrible, commercial vulgarity of this street-woman of France.

Marga was taking a night train. And after seeing her to the tramway, I was on my way back to the hotel when I met a young American aviator who had been on the boat. We sat down at one of the little tables on the sidewalk outside a café and watched the crowd. Suddenly we heard a great shouting, and along came a motor lorry filled with boys in khaki. They were shouting and waving their hats. It grew dark, and the café closed, as all the cafes in France do now at nine o'clock, and still the motor lorries went by, and through the night I heard young American voices:

"Hello, France! Hurrah for France!"

And the answering shout never failed to come: "*Viva l'Amérique! Vivent les Américains!*"

"They like us. Don't they?" asked the aviator a little huskily. And I couldn't trust myself to speak, because all of a sudden

---

13. During WWI, the U.S. Army estimated that, in Paris alone, there existed forty major brothels, five thousand professionally licensed streetwalkers, and seventy thousand unlicensed prostitutes. The U.S. army had an extensive publicity campaign against prostitution and closely monitored off-duty troops, resulting in a lower rate of venereal disease than in the British or French armies.

there crept over me a poignant realization of the love and close kinship between France and America. They like us? They love us! All France is pinning her faith to the dauntless courage of these square-jawed young Americans.

Next day I went to Paris. "First Class," my ticket read. It meant that I traveled in a small compartment upholstered in pearl gray, with a crocheted tidy for my head, rather than in a smaller compartment upholstered in blue, which would have been second class and rather more becoming in color.

The train rumbled on, and I got vivid impressions of France. Mile after mile we rode through a gently undulating country, chalk white roads dividing the intense greenness of fields or leading to clustering villages of white stone houses topped with red roofs. There were vineyards on many hills and fields of wheat gay with scarlet poppies and blue cornflowers. Women, old men, and children worked here. Here and there a brook ran through the meadows guarded by Lombardy poplars, slim, green sentinels against a blue sky. It was hard to believe that war was only a few miles away from this sunny, peaceful country.

My brother, who is really my brother-in-law but has long taken the place of the brother I wish I had, met me in Paris. After taking a carriage to my hotel and handing over the troublesome matters of baggage delivery to the porter, we went for a walk. We strolled across the Place de la Concorde, looking up the Champs Elysées, and then toward the Seine and the towers of Notre Dame. Slowly it grew dark, and with the coming of night Paris became mysterious. Cafés and restaurants were closed. Here and there a greenish-blue street lamp gave a ghoulish light, taxis rushed by in the darkness, you distinguished carriages as they came within range of the green-blue lights. Here and there green signs spelled "Refuge." They showed the way to subterranean places where a hundred or more persons could stand, packed close, during an air raid.

Paris by day is quite different from Paris by night. The streets are crowded, and every one is apparently going about his business as usual and in the best of spirits. It is true that carriages and taxis filled with women and children, old people, and sick pass frequently. They are being sent to a safer place than Paris. Already thousands have left. Now and then you see French soldiers in metal helmets on their way to the front. And everywhere there are uniforms. Sitting in a café with a man who had been wounded at the front, I received a liberal education in the art of distinguishing soldiers from all corners of the world. There were Italians, trim and *distingués* in their green-gray with black, and Portuguese whose uniforms most nearly resemble the Italian. There were Belgians with bobbing tassels on the front of their caps, Australians with hats pinned up on one side, great, black Senegalese wearing a mixture of khaki-colored uniform, horizon-blue leggings, and red fezes, their cheeks marked with great scars from slashes inflicted after the Senegalese custom, for the sake of beauty. There were other Colonials of all descriptions and many colors, Englishmen with swagger sticks, the horizon blue of Frenchmen, and the navy blue of the "French devils," the plaid kilts and bare knees of Scotchmen, and men with U. S. on their collars, who are just boys from home—all bits of the world war, mingled as in a kaleidoscope.

But you can not saunter the streets of Paris or sit in the cafés with a free conscience until you have obeyed orders and received from the Minister of Agriculture your "*carte d'alimentation*" and your bread tickets. The former entitles you to bread and sugar by the month. At the beginning of each month you must show your card of alimentation in order to secure a new set of bread tickets. One hundred grams of bread at each meal you are allowed, and no butter.

A few days after my arrival I invited an American woman who has lived in France for six years to have tea with me. I spoke of a once famous tea room and asked if we might go there.

"Oh, no," she said in shocked tones. "It's been raided."

My curiosity got the best of me. We Americans have all heard rumors that Paris is a naughty place, and this seemed a chance to find out how naughty.

"Why was it raided?" I asked boldly.

She put her lips against my ear. "They served bread and butter at tea," she whispered.

Finding that there were laws even against having butter served with bread in public places nowadays, it was with some fear and trembling that I made my way to the ancient, barn-like structure where the *préfet de police* has his office. All persons coming to

Paris must make this visit. I told my family history, gave innumerable facts concerning myself, furnished references, handed over six photographs, showed my card of alimentation, and a reference from my hotel. I then received a temporary *carte d'identité* permitting me to remain in Paris. I went over practically the same ground with another official, was given another official document, and told I was "entirely finished." In other words, I am now a resident of Paris.

It was about noon when I left the office of the Chief of Police and, remembering a few things I needed to buy, tried to stop at some of the little shops along the way. They were all shut. Not only were some of them closed, but the door-knobs had actually been taken out. An American officer came along and saw me trying one door after another.

"No. you don't," he said pleasantly. "*Déjeuner*." And seeing my blank expression. he went on to explain: "They're having lunch. It begins at twelve o'clock and lasts 'till two, and you might as well get used to it. It's the most important meal of the day in France. It's the time to meet friends and talk, and they never allow anything to interfere with it."

Later, that afternoon, I wandered about in the old part of Paris, first crossing the Seine and strolling through the Flower Market. All Paris is passionately fond of children, of flowers, and of dogs. Many of the children have been taken away from the city now, but the flowers and the dogs are everywhere. The market was a mass of bloom tended by garrulous old women who pressed upon you bouquets of deep, purple violets and red rambler roses and would have liked to have you purchase great plants of blue hydrangea. Soon I was in crooked, cobbled streets where low houses had their windows filled with flowers and a linnet in a cage swung outside the door. In a court opening out of a narrow alley I came upon a church. It had been built before America was discovered. Outside it was a great iron cage once used as a place of punishment for the wrong-doers of the community but now overgrown with vines and flowers.

I turned back to Notre Dame. The great doors that Victor Hugo described as "each one a page of history" are covered now by false ones built to withstand air attacks. Sandbags are being replaced by these more durable forms of protection. But inside the great cathedral there was the same dim, religious light that has dwelt there through the ages, the same loftiness and vastness. and another generation of human beings kneeling in the shadows. I passed many altars, and then I came to one where a single candle was burning. A woman knelt before it. Over it were the words:

Pro Deo Et Patria[14]

And the flags of all the Allies hung there.

The woman with her head bowed against the railing, her slight, black-clad figure almost hidden by her sweeping veil, might have been France herself mourning her sons dead "for God and Country," even while she lit a candle and prayed for those whom she had sent to take their places. As she prayed, a breath of air stirred the flags above her head. But I saw only the Stars and Stripes, symbol of the manhood that America is pouring out before a scarlet altar Somewhere in France.

And so I think there must come to every American who goes to France, to each in his own way, a moment of overwhelming realization.

14. For God and country

Chapter 9

❖

❖

❖

❖

❖

Americans in the Fight

W hen American troops finally entered combat in Spring
1918, the journalists credentialled with the AEF (all of
them men) enjoyed privileged access to news and the
front-lines. Women journalists were forced to be more resource-
ful. Many of them employed the strategy of connecting themselves
with an aid organization in order to gain greater freedom to travel,
to glimpse a piece of the great war effort, and to get close to the
action at the front.

In support of U.S. troops, the Red Cross, YMCA, YWCA, Salvation Army, and other charitable organizations began to appear
all over the war zone. Volunteers got their baptism under fire
during these months, and women correspondents working with
these groups had opportunities for dramatic war reporting. Clara
Savage traveled with a YMCA entertainment unit, visiting some
of the forward military camps. Maude Radford Warren's canteen
work of delivering food and hot drinks to soldiers took her close
to the fighting.

In the articles included here, both Savage and Warren get
caught in military traffic jams behind a battle. Troops, artillery,
and supply trucks headed to meet the latest threat, while wounded
soldiers flowed in the opposite direction, along with refugees transporting their worldly possessions in wheel-barrows, baby carriages,

and farm carts. Clara Savage explains to her readers that correspondents often tried to see the war and found it too colossal and
confusing to fathom. Traveling in the wake of the American victory
at the Battle of St. Mihiel, Savage gets stalled in traffic. She human-
izes the experience with cameos of her interactions with French
soldiers and civilians and by visiting wounded American soldiers
in a hospital.

Trapped in her own jam of military vehicles that spring, Maude
Radford Warren finds herself amidst units rushing to join battle at
Château-Thierry. She confesses that she doesn't have the sort of
mind that can think of the men as part of military units. "I always see
them as individuals," she reported. To show us the individual men
behind this great military maneuver, Warren steps from her traffic-
stalled truck and goes vehicle to vehicle talking to the soldiers.

The Red Cross and YMCA offered these women correspondent
volunteers telling snapshots of the tragedy: the poignant, heart-
breaking, inspiring storylines of individuals caught in the catastrophe. Military traffic jams proved to be one of the many fascinating,
narrow-focus tableaus of the war.

In her article "When Mothers Ask News of Their Boys in
France," Mary Brush Williams gives us a look behind the scenes
at the Home Communication Service. A unit of the Red Cross, the
Service responded to the worried queries from mothers and wives
seeking news about their loved ones. Williams assures her readers that whether it was to reassure a mother that her boy was safe
or to deliver the tragic news of his loss, the Service tracked every
single soldier and gathered information about them to comfort or
console those at home. As with the Savage and Warren articles,
Brush too draws out the individual soldier from the vast American
military effort.

Clara Savage (1891–1956)

*If you are an American in France these days, you try
not to be too blatantly proud of the fact.*

"Behind the Scenes in France"
Clara Savage
Good Housekeeping, January 1919

One-night stands in the war zone! I had joined a band of roving players, and we were creeping up night by night nearer and nearer the Front, when our passage was blocked.

Trucks blocked it, great, dusty, lurching, powerful camions driven by boys with faces weather-beaten and grimy, boys who are seldom mentioned in the dispatches and yet who are among the bravest of them all. With their hands on the wheels of those great trucks, their arms almost yanked from the sockets by the pulling of the pounding motors, they carry by night and day their loads of supplies—the very bone and sinew of war. It doesn't matter if roads are being shelled, it doesn't matter if the night is pitch black and the winding roads of France are strange to a boy from Missouri or Idaho or Pennsylvania, on they go at command, their gas masks within reach, disguised by steel helmets, on up. The trucks took the middle of the road; wagons and ambulances, cannons and caissons, now and then an automobile eating the dust, followed; and the reserves marched on. A great khaki colored, swaying,

American troops push their way to the front on September 29, 1918, during the Battle of the Argonne Forest. Such traffic jams became newsgathering opportunities for some of the women journalists. *Source:* National Archives and Records Administration, NAID: 530759, via Wikimedia Commons.

dusty cue [*sic*: queue] of men and ammunition and supplies, it choked the road and presaged what was to come.

We looked at each other with wide eyes and said nothing, but to ourselves we were whispering, "The American offensive!"

Ever since that day, in April of 1917, when America declared war on Germany, we had known there would come a time when American troops, under American command, would show the stuff that was in them. This dusty, sweating, dogged cue, one among others that were winding on through the valley of the Vosges, told us the time had come.

If you are an American in France these days, you try not to be too blatantly proud of the fact. You look into the faces of those who have been bearing the brunt of this war for four and a half long years, and read there a record of suffering and sorrow deep written beneath the fire of their devotion and dauntless courage, which fills you with a sudden humility. On the eve of America's first great offensive, even the most optimistic among us had moments when we were afraid. Our boys, with all their joyous confidence and fresh strength, look so young and untried beside the war-scarred veterans of France! Could they, with their short experience in this war, work the miracle of victory by the sheer force of their grit and overwhelming determination to make good for the sake of America?

The town crier brought us the news. It would have taken the most subtle knowledge of the French language to have translated his announcement word for word, but by the triumphant crescendo he reached through a series of musical intonations of the words *"Les Américains! les Américains"* we knew.

The tiny town went wild with joy. French soldiers embraced American soldiers, women kissed their hands, and children covered them with flowers. America had proved herself. Americans had set St. Mihiel[1] free.

Dropping into a small café, I was received as a guest of honor. It was a *rendezvous* of those who wear horizon blue, and at my entrance they jumped to their feet and saluted. Then they pressed forward to shake hands.

---

1. The Battle of Saint-Mihiel, fought September 12–15, 1918, was the first offensive led principally by the U.S. army. It met with surprising success and established the reputation of American troops among their British and French allies.

"*Vive l'Amerique. Vivent les Américain!*" they shouted, and *dejeuner* was turned into a festival of victory.

"The end is now in sight," said a white-haired officer. "It will take some time, but the end is in sight."

Hump-backed Andre, proprietor, headwaiter, and master of ceremonies, echoed in his thin treble, "In sight, in sight!" And there followed a moment of wordless silence very near to tears.

It was during those days, while our Y.M.C.A. "company" was halted by the onward sweep of the offensive, that I met Jesse James Callahan. Two miles out of the town was an evacuation hospital, and here I found him lying on his back in a corner of one of those great, gaunt hospital wards smelling of antiseptics—such a beneficent place, but oh! So bare and unhomelike! It was a gray fall day. Autumn comes early across the fields of France, and already it had crept to the foot of the Vosges, bringing dampness and grayness with it. Little Callahan's face was gray like the day, until he saw he was to have a visitor. Then he propped up his aching elbow, shattered by shrapnel, and smiled.

"We're getting away with it all right, aren't we?" were his first words. And then, with a little encouragement, he began to tell of his part in this war. He had gone over with the first wave of the great offensive and been among those to be brought back wounded.

"Just my luck to get knocked out the first thing," he grinned. "I've been on three fronts and been wounded on each one. First I saw some hot work near Verdun. That's where I got this bayonet wound." He pulled down his shirt to show a great red scar encircling one shoulder. "But I soon got over that, and when the boys went through Château-Thierry I was with them. Most of the men there were new to the game and wild to get a shot at the Huns.[2] We were in holes in the side of a hill and could watch the Boches[3] coming nearer and nearer. When we did let go at them, they got it good and proper. That time, I got hit in the other arm. When I'd got over that, I was just in time to be in on this offensive. Believe me, I wouldn't have missed this first big American one. It was great to see the boys going in. Nothing could stop them; they just ploughed ahead. I got plugged with shrapnel, but what stopped me going was five machine-gun bullets in my hip."

2. Disparaging nickname for German soldiers
3. Another nickname for German soldiers

He was pitifully white, this Jesse James Callahan who had fought on three fronts. His mouth was drawn with suffering, and his voice was the tired, husky voice of a person who is very sick, but he was every inch a brave man, every inch a hero without knowing it. He had been a machinist before he volunteered, but the fact that he had laid down his tools when America needed men and had come over here "to stop a few bullets," as he put it, seemed to him all in the day's work. He would have been surprised and a great deal embarrassed if anyone had told him that he was a hero. He would probably have insisted that he much preferred to be considered a machinist. The letter which he asked me to write to his brother is the best index of the kind of man he is. This was the letter:

> Dear Brother,
>
> Am in a hospital, but don't worry, for I am getting along fine. I expect I can go back to my division pretty soon. I hope so, because there never was a finer bunch of fellows, only there aren't many of them left. It took a hundred and twenty trucks to take us up, but we came back in twenty-nine.
>
> I saw Bill Curtis at one time. We were doing some pretty stiff fighting when I was with Bill, but when things slowed up a little, he asked me if I wanted to see a letter he had just got from his sister. It sure was good to hear from home. I thought I'd die laughing when she wrote you folks had heard I was killed. Say, that is some joke! How is Dan coming along with his farming? Why don't Sis never write to me? Love to Sis and all.
>
> > Your brother,
> > J. J. Callahan.

Not a word about those days when he had risked his life on three fronts, not a word of his suffering in this great hospital so far away from home! But I have been wondering ever since why Sis doesn't write. Doesn't she realize that she ought to be proud and glad to write long letters to a brother like Jesse James Callahan?

A boy in a bed on the other side of the room wanted to know if I would come over and see him. He was badly wounded and pitifully homesick. It comforted him to talk about home and especially about his mother.

"I haven't got a girl," he explained frankly, "but you ought to see my mother. Straight as a whip she is and dresses real nice. To see us together, you'd take us for sweethearts. The fellows at camp did, when she come way to Ohio to see me. I wrote her I would be going soon, I thought, and out she come. I told her, 'Now, for heaven's sake, don't cry when you go. And make an awful fuss the way some fellows' folks do.' And she said, 'All right, I won't, but it's awful hard for me.' She didn't cry either, but kep' a-smiling out the car window till I couldn't see her any more. Some little sport she is, and I sure do love her."

I only wish she might have heard the tribute, that mother who dresses "so nice" and keeps young for her son's sake. For anyone with a heart must know that when the train was out of sight she could no longer keep up her smiling, that brave little sport of a mother!

Another boy in the opposite corner of the room wanted a letter written. "To my girl," he explained in a low voice. "Bring your chair up close so the other fellows won't hear everything I say."

I obeyed, and the letter began. It was the simplest and most straightforward of love-letters. The writer did not search for polished phrases; the words came tumbling out faster than I could write them, straight from the heart, beautiful in their sincerity. It was not a long letter and yet it said all that any woman wants the man she loves to say—that he thought of her always, that she meant so much to him that he wanted to be brave and good for her sake, that he loved her with all his heart and longed to come home and take her in his arms. Then he said something about their having a little house of their own sometime, and there he paused.

"Would you tell her?" he asked me.

"What?" I asked, taken by surprise.

His head was done up in bandages so that only one eye showed; his right arm was in a sling. He dismissed the arm wound as nothing. "It'll be all right," he said. "I can work for her, but—I've lost my right eye, and my face is badly disfigured."

I couldn't say anything for a minute. I felt the other eye watching me. Such courage and pluck and straightforwardness as were in that look!

"It must be pretty hard for a girl to have a man come home mutilated the way I am," he said. "Do you think it will make a difference to her? Do you think a girl can love a man with a face that has been all smashed to pieces and a glass eye?"

There was only one thing to say, and I believe it is the truth. I said: "If she loves you, she won't care what your face looks like. She loves you because she found you fine and good and worth loving, and she will love you more now because you are so brave."

"Then I'll tell her," he said. And tell her he did, gently but as truthfully as he had told me.

As I wrote those words that some girl in America will read, I pitied her from the bottom of my heart, and yet I knew that if she is the kind of a girl that boy thinks she is, she will be brave and will love him even more now, because he so much needs her love.

We played, that night, in a town twenty miles farther up. It was a cold night and very dark, and I wondered by what sixth sense the boy who drove our car found his way along the twisting,

An American Red Cross entertainment tent that followed the soldiers as they went to the front. Clara Savage, *Good Housekeeping*, traveled with such a unit to gather news during the final campaigns of the war. *Source:* American National Red Cross photograph collection, Prints and Photographs Division, Library of Congress, LC-A6196-7291.

narrow roads. We wound through a small village and out to a camp on the edge of it.

The men had built a rough, board stage in a clearing. Deep woods were the only scenery, candles on either side of the piano and a lantern on a rough table the only light. But the open space in front of this improvised stage was packed with men sitting on benches and camp stools. An audience of two thousand welcomed us. There were hundreds of "casuals" among the number—men on their way to the Front, men who knew that before them lay the war! Already they had seen their comrades coming back in ambulances to the hospitals. But it was not of that side of war they were thinking. Not one of them but was wild with pride and joy at the success of the first great American offensive, not one but wanted to have a part in it.

While they waited for the program to begin, they sang. "They go wild, simply wild over me," they sang. "Meaning the Boches," whispered my neighbor, a great, powerful young Viking with a clear tenor voice.

A boy on my other side was reading a history of France by the light of a pocket electric light. "I'm mighty glad to get hold of this," he announced. "I certainly was one fool when I went to school. Thought I was smart because I could get through without studying. But now I'd give a good deal to know some history. This France makes you feel that way. It's so old. Makes America look pretty young in comparison, but pretty fine all the same."

And then the entertainment began. There were three players— a man who looked in every-day life like a quiet, middle-aged American citizen; a girl from New York, who had been accustomed to playing on the best of pianos before large audiences, and an American girl who had lived for several years in England. The latter was a violinist—a slight, frail-looking girl with amber eyes and a mass of glowing, copper-colored hair. The man came on, and in a moment he was not a quiet, middle-aged citizen at all, but Tony Welter,[4] straight out of the Pickwick Papers. Then he changed to a hobbling, droll, old darky, and after that to a hayseed farmer. Without a dab of greasepaint or the shred of an accessory he made his characters so real that he kept the whole

---

4. A warm but bumbling character in Charles Dickens's novel *The Pickwick Papers*

great audience rocking with laughter. Out there in the darkness, somewhere in France, he made those men forget what was ahead of them.

"I was up in your front lines not so very long ago," he said.

"I saw you there," shouted a boy with his arm in a sling. "Remember the day when they sent over a barrage and you went right on with your pieces?"

The middle-aged man laughed down the burst of applause. "I was up in one of your camps, one day," he went on, "and a private asked me to taste something he had in his tin cup. I did, and he asked me what I thought of it.

"'I think it's pretty good soup,' I told him.

"'Yes, but our mess sergeant wants to call it coffee.'"

After the laugh died away, the girl from New York tried the piano. Several keys were missing, and it was in tune only as far as an amateur plumber with a monkey-wrench had been able to make it. But this pianist didn't mind. She ran her fingers over the keys, and the red-haired girl tucked her violin under her chin and began to play. From the first moment when her bow swept the strings, the great audience of men, some with ears trained to music, others with no musical education but loving music instinctively, sat hushed and listening. Brahms and Grieg and Chopin, Dvorak, Beethoven, Liszt, Chaminade—on and on she played, standing there where the candle flame found the lights in her burnished hair, and the music stole into the hearts of her listeners.

Why is music so sad now? Even the gayest lilting melody has hidden beneath its tripping gladness a sound of sobbing. Perhaps because it dares to speak of reality, dares to make those who listen realize the gamut of it all. As she played, life became a mighty pageant marching on to the sound of music, a tremendous thing of color and movement, of harmony and dissonance. Sometimes it marched to the cadence of joy and hope, of love and laughter, and then would come crashing chords that accompanied fierce struggle. Millions marched in the great procession, carried onward by the sweep of it, they hardly knew whither, blinded by the immensity of it, yet catching, sometimes, a glimpse, of its glory. A mighty pageant rolling on from birth toward death.

The music died away in one clear, sweet note that echoed through the darkness of the woods behind the camp. There was utter silence when the red-haired girl paused with drawn bow. Those men, sitting there in the darkness, so far from home, with God knows what of suffering before them, had put away, while they listened, the masks of laughing, brusque stoicism that they assume nowadays. The music had found their hearts.

It was the next day, just before I said good-by to the little company of players, that I got to know the red-haired girl. We were walking along the country road that led to the hospital. She was going to gladden that place of pain. I tried to tell her how beautiful her music was, how much comfort and happiness it brought to these boys for whose sake she was sacrificing a whole season's professional engagements.

"I'm glad, she said. "It's my war job to bring them my music, and my whole heart is in it. I thought I hadn't any heart left, until I took my violin and came over here. You see, I was going to be married. Then the war came. My man was among the first to go. I never saw him again. He was killed at Salonica."

We walked along through the late fall sun light in silence.

Coming back alone, I thought of a sentence in a letter from my own sister, whose husband is somewhere in France. "I hope," she wrote, "you will help us women, away over here, to realize better the war. Tell us how French women find faith to bear its sacrifices and rise above its devastating horrors."

To realize the war! It is hard to do that even when you are as near it as we are here in France, even when you have experienced the bombing of a city by aeroplanes at night, or the destruction wrought by long-range guns, even when you have been under shell-fire and have seen our reserves going in. Correspondents are always trying to see this war and finding it too colossal to see. Even the men in the thick of it see only their small corner. And it is not by seeing the actual mechanism of it that realization comes. It is by watching the unfaltering courage with which a dusty, khaki-colored cue [sic: queue] goes marching on through the valley, by coming face to face with a boy like Jesse James Callahan, whose strong, young body is forever crippled because of war, by talking to the boy who is thinking about his mother, or the boy with the disfigured face, that you realize this war as an expression of forces that are stronger than a man's love of life, than the love of a boy for his mother, or the love of a man for a woman.

And the faith by which French women and millions of other women bear their part in war? It sings in the music of the girl whose lover died at Salonica. You can read it in the faces of French women grown old during these last four years—an unconquerable faith in beauty and love and a Something outside themselves—and yet within themselves—that is stronger than agony, and that will never forsake them.

Mary Isabel Brush Williams (1888–1944)

Mrs. Collins, of Wyoming, writes to ask how her son died; was he comfortable? Had he ever "gone to work," or did he die on the very threshold of France? Did he speak of her on his deathbed?

"When Mothers Ask News of Their Boys in France"
Mary Brush Williams
New York Tribune, June 2, 1918

General Pershing received a very important letter in his mail the other morning. He receives many important letters, and whether you regard this one as of greater or less consequence depends on your basis of comparison and your point of view.

This one came from some place in Iowa and read:

> "Dear General Pershing: I am writing to you to see if I can find out anything about my dear son, Corporal Albert Dawes. He was captured on December fourth, and if you have found anything about him I want you to let me know. We are so anxious about the dear boy. I am writing a few lines to him for you to send him if you can possibly find out where he is. It is something awful to give those dear boys up and then not hear from them. I have put in many a dreary hour since he left. I am going to ask one favor of you. If he gets out all right and they get peace, I want you to send him home among the first. You know he was only a boy. I will close. Won't you write and tell me all about him and if you think he is still alive and in the hands of the Germans? Please answer these few lines right away, from his heart-broken mother."

General Pershing did not answer them. If you think this letter is amusing or queer, at least your government and the head of your expeditionary forces in France do not.

Not This Letter, Was too Trivial

General Pershing disregarded that mother's request for him to write not because it was too trivial, but too important for such superficial attention as he could give. A whole bureau, with floor space, files, typewriters, telephones and field auxiliary forces, is necessary for an adequate reply to a letter like that. Such a bureau has been established in Paris. It is known as the Home Communication Service and is part of the Red Cross.

This bureau occupies [a] restricted area on the fourth floor (without elevator service) of the vast Red Cross building at No. 4, Place de la Concorde. Major Henry Allen, of Kansas, is its head. He has a small office, with double doors across two sides of it, and a single door on his lefthand wall. You have to pass through two of these to get to any part of the floor where your activities may lead you. The doors slide open easily and everybody about the place, from the office boy to the major, opens them whenever he takes a fancy. Thus inaccessible is Major Allen. His is not the kind of job one can conduct from behind barred doors.

He is in contact, not only with these intimate surroundings, but with the mysterious, remoter regions of the front. He communicates on a few hours' notice with any of the American military hospitals in France and he even pierces the curtain of silence which isolates Germany. That is to say, through the American Central Red Cross Committee for American Prisoners at Berne he gets accounts of our men who are prisoners of war. To Major Allen and his organization General Pershing therefore turned over the letter from the mother in Iowa for reply.

Long Before the Letter Arrived

Long before the letter arrived Major Allen's department had begun a search for Corporal Dawes. The day he vanished his name was given in to the bureau as among the missing. The department immediately sent his name to all of the hospitals in France where Americans are received. In every one of these there is a woman called a searcher.

Her duty is to know the men and to seek out information. If there was not anybody in her territory by the name of Corporal Dawes, she was supposed to know whether she had any one present from his company. If she had, she asked him where he had seen his missing comrade last. He might say, "Corporal Dawes was beside me when we went into action. I never saw him after that." He might report that he saw him killed, or that he saw him taken prisoner. That he saw Dawes taken prisoner is what a soldier at a hospital down in the south of France did say regarding Corporal Dawes. The searcher reported the information and almost at the same time information came from the Central Red Cross Committee at Berne that this young American was in the hands of the Germans. All of this information was in the possession of the Home Communication Service before the letter from Iowa came. It was therefore able to send the mother this reassuring answer by return post:

> "Your letter of January 21, addressed to General Pershing, has been referred to me as chief of the information service of the American Red Cross. I am glad to know that by this time your anxiety will be relieved, as you will have received official notice from Washington that your son, Corporal Dawes, is a prisoner of war in Germany, having been captured about December 2. As soon as we learn the name of his prisoners' camp we shall send him regular prisoner's food parcels through our committee, the American Red Cross Central Committee for American Prisoners. We are allowed to send him through this committee six packages a month, containing a varied assortment of necessary food, and a sufficient provision of clothing, tobacco and so forth will be sent by our committee.
>
> "You may rest assured that we shall look after your son as far as possible. With the sympathy of the Red Cross for you in your great anxiety, we are, sincerely yours, _____. For Chief of Bureau."

They Were Like Blue Flowers at Home

Sometimes the letters are necessarily sadder than this one. Mrs. Collins, of Wyoming, writes to ask how her son died; was he comfortable? Had he ever "gone to work," or did he die on the very threshold of France? Did he speak of her on his deathbed? Was it pneumonia?

Major Allen sends to the searcher who was with the boy at his death and asks her. He receives these notes in reply: "Henry Collins died peacefully. He had pneumonia. Was conscious until a few hours before his death. Spoke of his mother, and wanted some blue flowers in a vase to be set near him because they were like the flowers at home. Were other flowers in the room, but he would not have them. Blue flowers have been forwarded to mother. Received three letters from home the day before he died. Is buried in a beautiful cemetery overlooking a lovely river. Have visited his grave twice. Somebody has placed a bunch of violets on it. The Stars and Stripes wave over his head."

A Dearer One Yet Than the Others

Sometimes inquiries come from people other than mothers, as in the case of Private Collins. A letter came in bearing the postmark of Sigourney, Iowa. It asked all of the tender questions of the mother's letter, and more. It bore the signature "From his lonely, faraway sweet heart."

Not all the questions come from America, however. Sometimes the boys need to have trifling errands attended to here in France. A boy wrote in that he had bought some lace for his sisters. Would this department of the Red Cross send it back to them? It would, and did. A boy had left word with the American Express Company for them to forward his mail to him at the front. None had reached him, although he felt sure that his family had written. Major Allen's department investigated and found that the American Express Company had not understood. Two letters were there for him, and they were promptly forwarded.

The boys over here get desperately eager sometimes for news of home. Has the last payment been made on the town lot which the soldier and his brother were buying together for their parents? Is his sweetheart lonely for him? Is mother well? Every boy in the American army is at liberty to stop any Red Cross man he sees and ask him about any situation at home that troubles him. The Red Cross man entrusted with a question carries it to the office of Major Allen and someone there immediately cables America for information regarding the point. The matter is referred to the local

Red Cross, and they, after an investigation, return a reply to the headquarters in Washington, whereupon full particulars of the case are cabled here.

Thus are our men and their families, although separated by miles of land and ocean, kept in close touch with one another.

Maude Lavinia Radford Warren (1875–1934)

And we were just a stone's throw from men about to enter upon the last stretch of their lives.

"We Took the Hill"
Maude Radford Warren
The Saturday Evening Post, November 2, 1918

When we set out upon that moonlight drive I had no shadow of a thought that we were going to see the rear of a battle. Still less did I realize that it was the decisive battle for the big hill, the taking of which was perhaps the chief urge the Germans had in the beginning of their panic-stricken and disheveled flight toward the north. There we were in La Ferté, which had been shelled only two or three days before by the Germans, and from La Ferté our troops were going up toward Vaux and toward Château-Thierry, that night still in the hands of the Germans.

Over here, especially when a new action begins, it is pretty hard to find out what is going on. You at home, in a way, know more about the conduct of the war, as a whole than we do, because you can stand away from it a bit and see it in full proportions. Over here we are too close, even in Paris; while if we are practically in the midst of a part of the action our sense of values is quite distorted. All I knew of the offensive before I went to La Ferté was that various whispers had circulated throughout Paris to the effect that our men had begun suddenly to push the Germans northward. A very few minutes after my arrival in La Ferté, before I had time to ask questions, I had set out upon this moonlight drive. Even if I had asked questions, I doubt if I should have received any coherent reply.

On this night we were taking the moonlight drive for the purpose of carrying a field secretary to his next position with the artillery, of finding out where certain other secretaries were who had gone ahead with the troops they were assigned to, and of estimating what supplies they would need. As usual we had the car loaded with chocolate and cigarettes in case we came upon troops who needed them; for we never knew from hour to hour what we should meet or what was required of us.

Twilight had not yet come when our car swung out upon the Château-Thierry road, edged with wonderful tall trees. At the top of the long hill just outside La Ferté there was an entrancing view of the Marne, flowing in its sea-green tranquility between varicolored harvests, checkered like a piece quilt. From that view we looked up the road. It should have afforded a wonderful vista, but all its long spaciousness was blotted out by traffic, above which the dust rose in swirling clouds. Yet somehow the peace of the evening and the strong promise of the twilight neutralized the effect of that warlike traffic.

The time was to come when, seeing it at high noon or early afternoon in terrible heat and blinding dust, I was to feel to the hilt what it all meant. But just at the moment I was merely passing the gray ammunition trucks, each marked, "Load not to exceed three tons," and camions crowded with soldier boys, sitting or standing, stooped over, peering out to look at us, laughing and waving. It was as if the meaning of it all was suspended. These boys were merely rehearsing for war. We were all just taking a drive in the moonlight, the true meaning of which was not yet revealed to us.

No Yellow Streak

We swept on while twilight drew down and the moon struggled to rise. Suddenly we stopped at the château owned by the Baroness Huard, at that moment occupied by some officers; at the present moment used as a field hospital. What it will be used for next week no one knows, so fluid are circumstances in this war.

Here one of our secretaries dismounted with supplies for the artillery batteries he cared for. They were camping in the ground outside the château, were to move at midnight, and would bring up they knew not where. It was quite uncertain when we would see our fellow worker again. When we did he looked ten years older. He had saved the courage of a boy and had sent him into the fight a real soldier. He had made hot drinks for the men;

he had slept on the damp ground without a blanket; he had walked miles carrying burdens and comforting the soldiers; and he made no remark about his experiences, except to ask for more supplies.

It was just here that I became aware of Pep, the driver, who leaned back and whispered to me that there was nothing yellow about our fellow-worker. Pep's name is Peppin, but no one has ever called him anything but Pep. He shows his Gallic origin in his dark, vivacious face and his genial but critical eye. He is an ex-aviator and he had an obsession against yellowness. If you have even a touch of yellow, though you possess the best virtues of Napoleon, Saint Francis of Assisi and Abraham Lincoln, yet you cannot convince Pep. Conversely, if you are not yellow he will forgive you any other sin.

Pep refuses to wear a helmet and he courts danger. He likes to tell of the time he got careless and fell seventy-five feet out of his aëroplane and nothing happened to him. The conclusion seems to be that nothing can; and, indeed, he impresses one as being a spontaneous favorite of Fortune.

We swung on. The moon had still not quite overcome the clouds and a mysterious half darkness shrouded the road in front of us, which was no longer the main road. Whatever traffic it carried had for the moment quite ceased. One side of it was lined with camions of sorts, drawn up to camp for the night. Dimly I could make out kitchens and mechanics' trucks and trench supplies.

Letters From the Field

Of a sudden out of the darkness stood up the rectangular bulk of a farm. Our car swept into the courtyard and I became aware of subdued movements in the gloom. Figures rose about us, and the chief secretary asked a quick question: Was our Mr. Smith there or had he and his troops moved on?

Our Mr. Smith presently loomed up tall and weary, and from his talk I gathered that we were in the support line, that the troops for which he cared were just about to move up to the front, and that he wanted a truckload of supplies to be at a certain point to-morrow.

I got out and talked to the soldier boys. As always they were glad to see an American woman; and as always we plunged at once into friendship, for this prompt war makes shortcuts inevitable. Either you get at once down to realities or you part.

A boy detached himself from the group and handed me a letter.

"Will you post this for me," he asked. "I've been writing the folks at home that I am safe so far. We were just having a discussion before you came. Some of these birds here are always volunteering for dangerous jobs. Well, I don't see it that way. You go out and get killed, and your family gets the Croix de Guerre. And what good does that do them for you? If I am chosen for it I'll go willingly; but I'm not going to volunteer."

There came a tangled volley of argument from the other side: "It's as much a fellow's duty to volunteer as it is to enlist. We're over here to give every bit of ourselves to hurry up the end of this war. Some fellows have got to volunteer and one man isn't any better than anyone else."

It rushed over me that these lads were about to march toward death. They had been in action before, but never, as it afterward turned out, had they faced such danger as this. There they stood, some of them ready to march, some just shouldering their packs, some stooping over to lift their packs—dark figures, stirring a little against the dim white walls of the farm buildings. There they were, about to move toward the supreme hour of their lives, and they were discussing a point of ethics just as if they had been in camp or at home. It is a safeguard and a mercy that they can care about any kind of discussion. Such talk is perhaps the main continuity, the main kind of permanence they have in the hand-to-mouth sort of living that warfare necessitates—that and their loyalty to their particular companies. These interests will help them back to normal living, once the war is over.

When we left the farm the platoons were beginning to form in line for the march. In something over an hour they would be the battalions that were going into action at dawn. Boy after boy gave us letters to post and we assured them and our Mr. Smith that a truck with sweets and cigarettes would be at their heels tomorrow when they should be resting from having gone over the top. Though in this offensive the fighting was in the open, the soldiers still liked to use the expression "Over the top."

We parted cheerfully. They told us, in that way they sometimes have of playing with death, that we need not worry about

"our Mr. Smith." He never got killed; but the people on each side
of him always did. They waved and shouted that they would see us
again to-morrow night; and I felt, as I was so often to feel during
the next three weeks, such a passion of humility before the bravery
of these boys. If we are a very great nation it is not now because
we are a nation of quick business instinct, great enterprise, great
commercialism; it is because our plain common young men have
strong moral fiber, have the spirit and the will to do their duty with
bravery and cheer and patience and uncomplainingness. They
have given much and relinquished much, and no talk of "It has to
be done!" can minimize the sacrifice that every individual private
has made, and that their parents and wives and sweethearts behind
them have made.

Our car drew away from the marching men. We drove along
another bare stretch of road to another rectangular farm, which
was another support line, where we were told where we were to
carry supplies for the next day. The one farm in the darkness
looked like the other. Soldiers clustered about us, asking for news
and telling what they knew; the one experience was much like the
other, yet a thousand repetitions of boys going out to war could
never dull such a scene for me.

Because I haven't the kind of mind that can think of a company
of soldiers as "part of our forces" or "a small percentage of those who
fight," I always see them as individuals. And behind them I see the
little home in Scarborough, or East Aurora, or Decatur, or Davenport,
or North Yakima, or the little apartment in New York or Chicago that
sent them forth, where anxious relatives are waiting for letters.

Hot Food for the Boys

Every boy is infinitely more precious than he would seem at home,
because he is concentrating in a few days all the strain and suspense
and danger he could ever know in a long civilian life, and because
he stands ready to die for his country, and because it is such
strange luck that just he should be in this hazard instead of the
men of the last generation or the generation yet to come.

Among these boys about to march to the front there was excited
talk of the hill. Had we taken it? Or had we not? If not, then their
arrival would mean that it would be taken. As we left the farm and
drove along a little side road full of fresh shell holes made that

morning, it dawned on me that, though every group of soldiers we met talked about "the hill," they were not talking about the same hill or going to the same place, or aiming at the same objective. Though there was more than one hill, each group of soldiers realized but one between him and the Germans; saw the taking of it as the symbol of ultimate victory. We swung out of the side road into a wide one lined with great trees that flung out their branches in broad camouflage. On the east of this road moved a procession of shadowy figures. Peering hard at them, we made out that they were a detail of men carrying food up to the front. Each two bore between them, suspended from a thick stick, a huge bottle full of hot food. They resembled a Bible picture of my infant days which represented young Israelites carrying, in just that fashion, provender from the promised Land of Canaan.

In spite of the darkness they made out our Red Triangle,[5] and hailed us joyfully. "Say," one called softly, "can you give some of us a lift? We are going up to a wheat field to take a hot meal to some fellows that are going over the top at two o'clock. It's their last hot meal for Lord knows when, and I bet you they're longing for it and cursing us. We are an hour late already, and we should like to get there before they have to pull out."

We stopped. We are used to being thus informally commandeered by the army and are proud to be of use. The soldiers sorted themselves out, the beefsteak-and-potatoes boys coming with us, the coffee and bread and sirup and pie boys staying behind. This, as the lad in charge informed us, was an especially bang-up feast; the fellows were going after Fritz[6] lined with the best of Uncle Sam's rations. Loaded to the guards inside and out with cookies and boys, we proceeded slowly, listening to snatches of talk.

Cookies and Chocolates

"The fellows we're feeding have to go out and finish taking the hill. This steak will make them just eat up that hill!" "Say, the fellows that have come through in the ambulances tell us that the Germans are running like cooties in a delouser!" "But they're leaving behind them machine gunners that just rained down the lead on our fellows."

5. The logo of the YMCA includes a red triangle.
6. Nickname for German soldiers

"Gee, you ought to see the souvenirs the fellows have! A man could afford to supply about five best girls if he is allowed to keep all he picks up." "Say, it's no Sunday-school picnic to take that hill; open wheat fields to climb, with the Germans shelling and grinding out machine-gun fire from the edge of the wood!"

Most of us have had the experience of being in real danger that, nevertheless, does not seem real; of being on the verge of a vital experience that persists in seeming dreamlike. We were in danger; we were going along a road that had been shelled a few hours before and that at any moment might be shelled again. Our voices were lowered, because any ditch, any shell hole or any sheltering clump of trees might conceal a German spy able to pick up from our chance words information valuable to his fleeing countrymen. We were in territory that was unknown to all of us; not one of us had trodden it before, while only a few hours since it had been in the possession of the enemy, who knew it as thoroughly as we knew our streets at home. And we were just a stone's throw from men about to enter upon the last stretch of their lives.

It did not seem as if our car was moving. Seemed as if the road began slowly to unroll columns of figures and objects—horses and men, camions and limbers. We were suddenly in the midst of young clamorous soldiers who said they had had no chocolates or cigarettes for two days.

"Here you are, buddie," said Pep, dumping out for distribution all we had. "Break the bars of chocolate and boxes of cookies in two and there will be enough for everybody."

As the marching soldiers passed us a feeling of reality sank in on our hearts. On they went, these young creatures who are our shield and buckler. The sound of their marching feet rose above the noise of the car. The moon went behind the clouds and a light drizzling rain started. Behind the men camions loomed in the darkness, chiefly wagons full of ammunition, their drivers hunched forward, staring anxiously ahead into the blackness. Machine-gun wagons passed, too, and small supply wagons, their roofed heads making them look like gypsy carts. Sometimes a number of men on horseback jingled by, speaking softly each to each or to their mounts.

It was all real enough now, and yet it was in a sort of dream fashion we drifted away from that main road, unwinding its silent freight of battle. The sound of it lessened by the way and nothing was left except the droning of our car and the whispered remarks of the soldiers we carried. We drove along the stretch of heavily darkened road and then came into a lightened area where a little broken village stood up our progress.

"I'm sorry," he said, "but you can't go any farther. A car makes too much noise just here. You can walk on a little way if you like; not too far, though, unless you are anxious to step on Fritzie."

"Gee, we've been in luck!" said our soldier passengers as they clambered down. "Our outfit is over there where that wheat field and wood meet. So long! We'll have the chow to them in ten minutes."

They dismounted, took up their Land of Canaan burdens, and melted into the pale wheat field. By now the moon was showing again and we could see clearly the crumbled gables of the little village.

"Follow that path," said the M.P., "and cross in front of that farm, where the engineers are. Then you'll be on the main road. You can see Vaux and Château Thierry, where the Germans are. You can see the hill that our fellows are taking. Some say they have taken it. You can see No Man's Land if you have good eyes. They say there's another hill to the left that our men are fighting for. We never know anything for sure. Mind the barbed wire."

We walked with our eyes on the ground minding the barbed wire, threaded our way through the wheat fields, and stood suddenly among the gaunt farm buildings. Here a group of men rose about us, armed with rifles and picks and shovels—the engineers.

As usual at first they were amazed and pleased to see an American woman, and then accepted it as naturally as we accept any fact in this war. We were just about to move on when an engineer said:

"Won't you wait a moment? The sergeant wants to meet the lady."

The Suspicious Sergeant

The sergeant bore down on me, a great creature, grave, even grim. I suppose he was tired and I was glad to see him relax after a minute or two and smile. As we were talking a group of mud-spattered men materialized out of the darkness and addressed him:

"Say, we're the -----, sent to police up a bit of road here. Anywhere we can sleep?"

"Cowshed would do if the floor was cleaned up a bit," replied the sergeant.

"It will do without being cleaned up," muttered a boy; and a dozen weary men led a self-appointed guide to the cow shed.

Meantime a young engineer whispered:

"We had to hold you back to meet the Sergeant because he had heard that a lady spy was on the road, and he had to see for himself that you weren't a spy."

"A spy!"

"Well, if you could see the way these foxy boche ladies can pretend to belong to the different organizations! But it's funny they always give themselves away pretty soon—that is, any of them that pretend to be helpful women. The parasite sort of spy puts it over a little longer sometimes."

He offered to be our guide, and as we left the farm and followed a twisting path through a wheat field he spoke to me of the thing nearest him.

"I have a brother out there," he said, "fighting for a hill; not the hill you'll see in a minute; not the hill everyone will be talking about to-morrow. There're two hills, and maybe more. I suppose they'll make all the fuss about the big one; but how about the men who will die taking the little one?"

I tried to give him some comfort.

"Well," he said, "I've always laughed at superstitions; but my great-grandfather and his younger brother were scouts in the Mexican War, and the younger was killed. My grandfather and his brother fought in the Civil War, and the younger was killed. My father and his brother were in the Spanish-American War, and the younger was killed too. My mother has just us two left. She worries."

There's so much I used to believe in history that I now began to doubt. There is that story, which I took as gospel truth, about the Spartan matrons who commanded their sons to come back with their shields or upon them. I don't believe that even Spartan matrons ever went in for concerted heroic action like that.

The soldier guide had been trying his best to follow the brother's movements, but he could speak only in piecemeal. It is so that one hears of a battle. Of course, since the beginning of time, it has been hard to get at the absolute facts of history. In this offensive I have found events clouded within two days of their happening, and people whom I have considered perfectly reliable contradicting each other as to what really had happened. Each company knows what it has to do and generally what the rest of the battalion in action are doing; but it is not sure as to the objective of any other battalion, still less of the regiment.

A Moonlit Battlefield

As the soldier guide and I walked along the winding path in the wheat field, that memorable Saturday had not yet fully passed and the hill was still being taken. He pointed out to us a row of trees and went back. We stumbled into a dark road where figures rose and bent over shell holes, which they were rapidly filling. Nauseating charnel odors floated to us; but of a sudden we forgot them, for before us a battle sprang into being.

Directly in front of us and on the left the sky was shot with a flashing curtain of pink and crimson, and cannon mouthed in multitudinous sounds. It seemed as if a full half of the horizon was alight and was pounding and roaring with menacing, sweeping sound. It is strange how cannonading always gives the effect of motion.

The moon shone clearly, and we saw ahead the broken village of Vaux and the great hill for which there had been such bitter struggles. A wide, dark mound it was, fifteen kilometers round, as the soldiers who had flanked it afterward told me; innocent-looking enough by day, with its stretches of green and blue woods, its open meadows and harvests; innocent and quiet enough now in the darkness, except for the barrage that burst across it.

We were looking straight into No Man's Land; almost it seemed as if a few moments' walk would take us into it. Very lights,[7] as we gazed, soared aloft, remained suspended a moment, and then gently slipped again to earth.

There is something singularly soft and beautiful about these lights. They are like electric globes, turned mellow and irregular in shape, gone, as if spontaneously, upon some high adventure in the skies. It is hard to associate them with daring and spying and death. One after another they flew high, lighting up No Man's Land—wheat fields and dark woods. Ever the high

---

7. "Very lights" are flares fired into the air to give temporary illumination.

A wounded soldier is removed from the destroyed village of Vaux during fighting in July 1918. *Source:* National Archives and Records Administration, NAID: 530731, via Wikimedia Commons.

color flashed behind them and above them; and the sound of the cannon never ceased.

There were thousands of men fighting on that hill and in No Man's Land. By now, for it was long past midnight, the boys whose supper we had helped carry were advancing through those wheat fields on our left. Others of our men were sweeping, steadily up the long slope. Almost we thought we could see the brave figures steadily pushing on.

A battle, a decisive battle, was progressing there in the half darkness, and we civilians were helpless. All we could do was run back quickly, and get more supplies, and be ready to take them to-morrow to the soldiers. All we could do was to stand aside, ready for the deeds of peace, while these young lads gave their courage and faith and pain for their country.

We watched the battle for a long time. After we had made our way again over the winding path in the wheat field, and Pep was once more driving us southward, we kept looking back, watching the crimson interleaping fires of the barrage, listening to the deep mouthing of the cannon. The moon was bright now, but the Very lights still rose and soared; and behind us, as we went closer and closer to safety, the young soldiers passed through anguish and suspense and fire.

We drove a few miles down the Château Thierry road slowly, for the upward-moving traffic never ceased, of men in camions, of ammunition and guns and supplies. About us was a mysterious world of moonlight and shadows, crimson disks of cigars, the sudden flashes of pocket lights, whispering voices, creaking wheels, the heavy breathing of horses and mules, the drone of a distant aëroplane and everywhere the sense of eager anticipation, of excited zest.

We left the main thoroughfare, drove a side road, and presently turned into the little irregular main street of the little deserted town of Bezu. In a triangle of ground stood a row of ambulances, large and small; behind them a church and one or two lesser buildings. Into one of the latter were carried wounded men, where their wounds were examined and perhaps redressed. The seriously hurt were taken on at once to the hospital at La Ferté.

The slightly wounded were taken into the church. Some boys were lying on the floor with eyes closed, too weary to speak, but not too weary to carry the ghosts of smiles. One young lieutenant wore a wide lambent grin, and as I bent over him to lift his head to a cup of tea his litter jingled like a wreath of sleigh bells. He motioned me to throw back his blanket. I did, and saw a German officer's helmet, a pair of splendid field glasses, a belt and buckle, a canteen, a knife and its sheath, and a dispatch case.

In the Passing of Arthur, Tennyson has a line to the effect that in that last conflict, where Arthur died, there was many a noble deed and many a base. I believe that in every battle for the hills there was no base deed on our side. In the soft gloom of that church I came upon dozens of wounded men who were where they were not only because they were brave but because they were more than that.

Chained to Their Guns

There was the gassed boy covered with his eyes swollen shut, because during a gas attack he had not used his own mask until he had put on that of his buddie, who had been shot through the hands. There was the second lieutenant and his five men, all shell-shocked; they had been overlooked in a certain part of the wood, and, having had no orders to leave, had stayed where they were under shell fire and without food for sixty hours. There was the boy with broken arms who had been protecting a wounded friend against three Germans. There was the "gas-sniffer" who had gone out in the wheat fields for his wounded lieutenant and had carried him back under machine-gun fire with a bullet in his leg. There was the little lad of sixteen who turned a machine gun against a squad of Germans as they crossed a road, sprayed half of them down, and when they ran for cover he ran for another position, so as to reach with his deadly rain those still able to try to get away from him. These were but a few instances. And, on the other side, man after man told me stories of Germans chained, for fear of cowardice, to their machine guns. Our soldiers were able to describe minutely enough how it was done. The machine guns were in shelled trenches; behind them sat the gunners. Each was fastened by two chains, which went from his ankles to two trees, giving him just enough freedom to load and to fire his gun. Later on, in a wood toward the Vesle,[8] I saw two such chains still fastened to the trees. The gunners are told that they must fight to the end, because the Americans will kill them with all the cruelties of red Indians.

Story after story, too, I heard of the treacherous Red Cross bearers. On the famous hill several groups of our soldiers passed men, in the uniforms of French poilus, carrying a covered litter. One of our men lifted the blanket to look at what he supposed was a dead Ally, and found a German machine gun; and he saw then that the thwarted faces above it were German faces. After dark, when the stretcher bearers went out on their errands of mercy, some of the German Red Cross men were found to be carrying machine guns on litters. Several of the prisoners taken had in their pockets Red Cross brassards.

Boche Treachery

Such were some of the stories I heard as we helped feed the wounded men. And I heard snatches of half a hundred others that would have been rich material if I had had time to listen; but I wanted

---

8. Vesle River

to relieve parched throats. From the soft brown gloom of the floor, heads were constantly lifting, and voices were calling:

"Where did you get yours? Mine's through the knee." "Do you know whether the major is safe? He went right over the top with us; we could not hold him back." "Big Hun had been firing the machine gun as hard as he could on us when we came across the wheat field; and when I ran down on him he yelled 'Kamerad!' After he had fired every last belt he hollered: 'Kamerad.' I said: 'Kamerad hell!'" "Say, weren't those big boche shells sweet? I tell you one of those big shells will convert more boys than the finest sermon Billy Sunday ever preached." "General Pershing says: 'Hell, Heaven or Hoboken by Christmas!' And I sure did think to-night that I never would see Hoboken again." "Don't you ever think a signalman's work is a cinch! I tell you, this afternoon when I got mine I was out stringing a line pretty near up to the Kaiser's ear." "Well, it wasn't any tea party, but still I wouldn't have missed it; and I'm darned lucky to be alive and to have my eyes and arms. What's a little hole in the shoulder?" "I got mine before I saw a single Fritz—three wounds. I'm going back and get a Heinie for every wound." "I didn't think I'd get nicked at all— we chased them clear away from the hill and had taken it, lock, stock and barrel; and then I had to get my right arm smashed! But, anyhow, I was in it till we took the hill."

That phrase was like a triumphant chorus: "We took the hill!" The ambulances had almost ceased to come and there was little work to do. We drove away slowly along the road that, only two or three days before, had been shelled, and which was now safe—safe forever surely. Signs of war were there in broken walls and gables standing blank in the moonlight, but already refugees were coming back to them.

A few hours of rest, and for other soldiers, unwearied soldiers, there would be other hills to take. But this hour belonged to the lads who were dead, wounded and asleep in the woods; who had taken that objective set before them which each called The Hill.

It had been ordered; it had been done. And by whatever name the American soldier calls his objective he obtains it; and he obtains it quickly. This is the magnificent and simple process by which the Germans are being conquered. The American soldier recognizes no impossibilities. He takes the hill!

Chapter 10

✦
✦
✦
✦
✦

After the Fighting

The signing of the armistice on November 11, 1918, did not end the dramatic news stories coming from Europe. It did not even end the fighting. In Western Europe, America began sending home its two-million-man army, while commencing a mammoth support effort to help the war-devastated nations rebuild. Allied troops took up the occupation of Germany, while the countries and would-be countries of Eastern Europe sorted out grievances and national aspirations. Russia convulsed in three years of brutal civil war.

Several of the women journalists who had covered the war remained to report on its aftermath, including: Mabel Potter Daggett (*The Delineator*), Elizabeth Frazer (*The Saturday Evening Post*), Eleanor Franklin Egan (*The Saturday Evening Post*), Maude Radford Warren (*Good Housekeeping, The Saturday Evening Post*), and Peggy Hull (Newspaper Enterprise Association).

In late October 1918, Peggy Hull became the first woman to be officially credentialed as a war correspondent by the U.S. army. Rather than hurry to Europe, which was already being well covered by an army of correspondents, she opted to follow the American Expeditionary Force, Siberia into Russia. Ostensibly sent to Siberia during the Russian civil war to guard the war materials stockpiled in Vladivostok, U.S. troops found themselves on an ill-defined and thankless mission of monitoring the numerous warring factions and Japan's territorial ambitions amid the dire conditions of a Siberian winter, famine, disease, and rapacious warlords.

Ironically, the army's first credentialled female correspondent arrived in Vladivostok three days after the war had ended. What her reporting clearly established for her American readership, however, was that the Russian civil war was still a hot conflict. Two of her brief articles included in this chapter reveal the horrendous conditions in Siberia and the challenge facing American troops.

Following the armistice, Maude Warren carried out her YMCA canteen duties with some of the most advanced U.S. army units as they entered liberated French towns and moved into Germany. Along the way, she became one of the first war correspondents to capture snapshots of the stunned moments immediately after the fighting ended.

Her article "The First Invasion," excerpted here, reveals the tensions between the victors and the vanquished in occupied Germany, by highlighting her relationship with a German family in whose house she was being quartered. Through this tableau of military occupation in one German town, Warren puts a human face on the enemy and reveals how the war has impacted everyone.

When all of the leaders of the warring nations met with German representatives in Versailles on June 28, 1919, to sign the formal peace treaty ending the war, Elizabeth Frazer was there for *The Saturday Evening Post*. During her three years of reporting from warring Europe, Frazer had experienced many dramatic moments. For her, the treaty ceremony seemed decidedly anti-climactic. In this excerpt from her article "The Signature," Frazer gives an impressionistic account of the signing ceremony and reflects on more impactful moments from the war.

Peggy Hull (Henrietta Eleanor Goodnough Deuell, 1889–1967)

Siberia is on the threshold of its blackest period. Twice a victim—first to monarchy and then to anarchy—its people this winter will die by the thousands.

"Allied Troops Unpopular Now in Vladivostok"
Peggy Hull
The Tampa Times, January 17, 1919

Vladivostok, Siberia, Jan. 17—The lot of the peacekeeper is a hard one.

And that is the role of the American forces in Russia, and the other allied troops.

Our program, as far as I can learn, is to sit tight until it is determined which is the proper party to support in the regeneration of Russia.

Meantime our forces must keep the Bolsheviki from coming out of their hiding places and the various Russian factions from starting new revolutions.

The result of this interference is to make allied troops unpopular on all sides.

Gen. Graves[1] faces a problem which is harder to handle than an active campaign. A commander has then but one course to pursue. He pits his armies against the enemy and wins or loses.

These people are on the borderland of a new existence and each party believes that it alone is strong enough to rear the ideal government in Siberia. Gen. Graves, with the other allied commands, wish to give their entire support to the proper party but how to determine which is the right one is a question which is putting more than one wrinkle in their foreheads.

In the meantime, American headquarters is swamped with alleged representatives of the government.

"I am representing the Omsk government" announces the Russian.

"But so-and-so was here yesterday and said he represented the Omsk government," replies the general.

"Never heard of him," says the envoy indignantly. "I'll go right up to Omsk and find out about this."

And in Omsk, 3,000 miles away, the seat of all temporary governments, there are as many changes of control as in Mexico in the days of Madero and Huerta.

Our part, apparently, is a bloodless campaign among friendly enemies. A situation piled high with tricks and as uncertain as

---

1. Major General William Sidney Graves commanded U.S. forces in Siberia, the Siberian Expedition, as part of the Allied post-war intervention in Russia.

an April day. Already I have sensed many undercurrents and my interest increases with the days.

Siberia is on the threshold of its blackest period. Twice a victim— first to monarchy and then to anarchy—its people this winter will die by the thousands. They are freezing to death now and the coldest weather is still to come. Farther inland where the disorganization of the railroads has made it impossible to carry supplies they are starving to death, while roving bands of Bolsheviki and bandits terrorize the unprotected communities. Murder, pillage, starvation and bitter cold—what a desperate outlook!

Peggy Hull (Henrietta Eleanor Goodnough Deuell, 1889–1967)

The "death train" episode, more than any other tragedy which has occurred since the allies came, showed how insensible the people have become to the cause of humanity.

"Peggy Hull Tells 'Death Train' of Russian Bolshevik"
Battle Creek Enquirer, March 2, 1919
Peggy Hull

Vladivostok, Siberia, March 1.

New horrors pounce upon me from every direction. Atrocities fade the plunder and rape of Belgium into insignificance. The Bolshevik reign is surpassing all history in premeditated viciousness.

Siberia is face to face with a power that has reverted beyond even a state of savagery—for savagery knows only brute strength, but the perpetrators of the present-day crimes over here have perverted their civilization to make their deeds more appalling.

Bishop Buried Alive Officer's Body Carved

The night the news came through of the fall of Perm there were tense, low spoken groups everywhere. Solemn faces and white cheeks and eyes that glowed with apprehension, for we knew that a few thousand miles to the west madness had taken full sway, and we shuddered in anticipation.

Bulletins brought the details.

Peggy Hull became a credentialed correspondent with the U.S. army when she reported on the activities of the American Expeditionary Force, Siberia in 1918–1919. She is wearing the uniform of a credentialed war correspondent, an officer's uniform without designation of rank and an armband with the letter "C," designating Correspondent. *Source:* Newspaper Enterprise Association photo, author's collection.

A bishop had been buried alive and his priests had been killed by driving nails into their backs.

Then we received the details on the capture of a young Czech officer. His comrades found his body with epaulets carved out of his skin on his shoulders. Facsimiles of the buttons on his uniform were crudely cut into his torso, and there were other mutilations too horrible to write about. No one knows how long he lived under these tortures.

In a battle that followed a few hours after the body was found 600 Bolsheviks were made prisoners. General Galda, the youthful commander of the Czecho-Slovaks, made them pay the price, and they faced the machine guns in squads of 10.

Raiding Bolsheviks along the Trans-Siberian line whip many of their captives to death. Some of the railway employees who have stuck to their posts through the various changes of government often meet a sad and pitiful end at their hands. Their favorite procedure now is to occupy territory off the railway line and to make sudden visits to stations when troop trains are not going through. Many valuable supplies are obtained in this way, and the Bolsheviks suffer no losses, as there are no armed forces to oppose them.

"Death Train" Filled with Freezing People

The "death train" episode, more than any other tragedy which has occurred since the allies came, showed how insensible the people have become to the cause of humanity.

The inmates of the train were Bolshevik prisoners rounded up in Samara last October. There were 2,100, including men and women found in the provincial jail who claimed they had been arrested by the Bolsheviks because they wouldn't espouse their cause. Sixty people were packed into box cars which could legitimately hold 40. There were no provisions for heating, and the sanitary arrangements consisted of small openings in the floor of the cars.

This train was started for Siberia, and when it reached a small station on the western side of Harbin early in December, American railway engineers reported to the American Red Cross that 775 had died en route. Some were shot by the guards when they tried to get food and water at the stations. Typhus, typhoid, dysentery, scurvy and pneumonia took the largest toll. One boy of 17 was found dead across the doorway of a car when Red Cross workers entered. He was naked with the exception of a piece of gunny sack tied around his loins. It was then five degrees below zero. Half his face had been eaten away by scurvy.

None of the prisoners had been permitted to leave the cars since their arrest, and they all wore what was left of the clothing they had on when taken into custody.

In spite of the rapid work of the Red Cross the prisoners were dying 15 a day. And no one knows who was responsible for the train—no one knows who sent it to Siberia and no one knows who ordered it out of Nikolak the evening after the worst cases had been taken off and the remainder bathed and issued pajamas. It went, and all the generals in Vladivostok stormed, but to no purpose.

It went east toward Samara with 800 sick and dying men and women clothed only in pajamas, and the thermometer clinging around 50 below in that direction. It was last heard of in the vicinity of Chita, where Semenoff, the Cossack ataman, presides. That was a month ago, and it is hard to believe that any of the victims still survive.

Maude Radford Warren (1875–1934)

I wondered if the millions of grieving mothers ever meet in the land of dreams where there is no war and where the children are always young, always care-free.

"The First Invasion"
Maude Radford Warren
Good Housekeeping, June 1919

It was late afternoon when our car stopped before the largest building on the main street of the little German village. We could see blinds drawn aside, could hear whisperings, for we were the first conquering Americans these villagers had seen. We were the first of the invaders. The long, white house before us belonged to the Burgomaster. Over the door was a sign that showed that it had lately been used by the German army as a telegraph and telephone headquarters.

The Burgomaster stood in the doorway, wearing a picturesque green Alpine sort of hat and a becoming green coat. He was also smoking a becoming long German pipe. A handsome, portly, impressive looking person he was. He should have been expecting us, a small party of Y. M. C. A. people, for the day before our splendid divisional director, Theodore Smith, had requisitioned rooms for us. But his face was not welcoming, and he did not step out of the doorway.

"What's the matter?" asked Mr. Smith of me. "Your German is better than mine. Ask him if the rooms are ready."

In imperfect German I remarked that we had come to occupy the rooms we had engaged.

"An American officer arrived this morning," replied the Burgomaster, "and requisitioned the rooms."

"Did you not tell him that we had already bespoken them?"

"No."

"But why not?"

"I did not wish to."

Did not wish to! His tone was impenetrable. Was he defying us, or was he afraid to refuse anything an American officer asked?

While we hesitated, the American officer appeared.

"Not a bit of it!" he said, when we proposed to fare farther. "They've got an extra room, and we'll double up, and you can double up. Come along."

He entered the hall. To the right was a more or less formal parlor, to the left a living-room, and behind that a kitchen. "We were going to have a sitting-room and dining-room up-stairs," the officer said, "but we'll just use that as a bedroom and take the parlor for you and us as a combined sitting-and-dining-room."

He turned to the Burgomaster and spoke in German. The Burgomaster's face changed; he took out the pipe and strode to the door on the right, threw it open, and at the same moment a little grayish woman crept out of the living-room on the left and stood timidly behind him.

"Impossible," the Burgomaster said. "It would not be seemly for you to have this room. You can see for yourself it is a family room."

It was a little square place crowded with things. Directly opposite the door was the piano, loaded with music sheets and with standing photographs. The most striking object on it was an iron cross in a case. Above the piano hung three pictures, one a black and white study of the Burgomaster, the highest of all; to the left was a large photograph in colors of the Kaiser; to the right a photograph of the same size of the father of the Kaiser. On another wall hung various family pictures, the most striking a black-edged photograph of a young man in officer's uniform. It was clear that he was the Burgomaster's son, that he was dead, and that the iron cross had belonged to him. At one side of the piano was a table loaded with books and portfolios of photographs. On the other side was a stove. The rest of the wall space was taken up with landscape pictures, and the floor space was littered with chairs.

"You see it is a family room," repeated the Burgomaster, as excited now as he had been unmoved before.

"We'll use this room as I directed," said the officer crisply. "You will please put in a dining-table."

"But, Herr Officer, we need this room for ourselves."

My eyes had scarcely left the German woman's face. In the beginning of the conversation she had watched her husband anxiously; then she had watched the American officer. Now at his words she crept silently away. Her husband made a gesture to detain her, but she pretended not to see him. She was entering the sitting-room as the officer said sternly,

"You have a sitting room for yourselves."

"But if the Herr Officer will listen —"

The Herr Officer might have reminded the Burgomaster of the brutal fashion in which the Germans, when they entered France and Belgium, took rooms and everything else they wanted. He might have alluded to the bloody way in which all objections were silenced. He merely said, in a tone, however, of which the authority was unmistakable, "You have heard the order."

At that moment the little German woman crept in with a shovelful of coals. She moved as if she wished to be inconspicuous, but I observed that she passed directly in front of the officer. She had known when it was time to yield. And in the few conflicts we had with the Germans it was always the women who were the first to see that defiance was impossible.

The Burgomaster bowed, put the pipe in his mouth, again the imperturbable official, and watched his wife making the fire. She refused help from the officer, poked away with her red coals, and then stepped out with a flicker of her eyelids in the direction of the photograph of the young German officer.

Such was the end of our first day in Germany, a day full of emotion. It had begun that morning, as our car swept down a cobbled street leading to a river and a bridge. Just a river, just a bridge, but on one side lay Luxembourg, on the other Germany. Over the bridge poured a battalion of men in khaki: their feet gave back a throbbing sound; their faces were composed, even inscrutable. They "registered" nothing of the traditional picturesque entrance of a victorious army: no glory of high color, of waving plume, of high-stepping steeds and high-sounding bands. The advancing heroes took their entrance into Germany in the same quiet way in which they had taken the news that peace had come. They were just tired boys not yet recovered from the fierce fighting of the Argonne, and for the most part wearing the same clothes in which they had slept in the mud during those bitter, dragging autumn days.

Yet it was a dramatic entrance; the inscrutable faces of the soldiers alone showed that. For two peoples who had been at war were to come into a much closer relationship than they had known when they were killing each other. We were to live side by side, we, the conquerors, and the Germans fresh from the shock of defeat, knowing now the long list of their human losses, knowing, too, their commercial and financial disaster. No longer were we separated from our enemies by the reach of a shell, the range of a machine-gun. We knew what their hatred of us had grown to be in a year and a half, and now we and they were to share the little common places of daily living.

When we first crossed the bridge and halted on the other side, there was not a German to be seen. To the left was a house or two with lines of well-washed clothes, and on both sides, as we advanced, were rich fields. In France I had seen many fields uncultivated for lack of laborers; not so here—freshly plowed ground, fields of wheat, all in admirable shape, all precise and trim; here and there a stretch of excellent orchard; here and there a stretch of carefully tended forest. And then the villages, sometimes clean and modern and sometimes with the manure piles in the front yards like those we had seen in France.

But what was it that teased my mind with a sense of unaccustomedness, almost of unseemliness? Of course; not a hint of the ravages of war, no broken villages, no shell-torn trees, no pockmarked earth! Prosperity! Had these people given up easily then? How would they have behaved if their country had, like France for four years, been fought over, ravaged?

Maude Radford Warren stands with Lt. Col. Ruby D. Garrett and Major R.T. Smith of the
117th Field Signal Battalion, 42nd Division, in Bachem, Germany, on January 1, 1919,
during the period of American occupation. *Source:* George Grantham Bain Collection,
Prints and Photographs Division, Library of Congress, LC-B2- 4932-5.

Our car soon left behind the soldiers marching steadily to whatever their job in Germany proved to be. After we passed through
the first village, we heard behind us running feet, subdued voices;
people were coming out of their houses to look at us. There-
after, as if warned by some underground telepathy, whenever

we entered a village, the inhabitants were standing against their houses or on their doorsteps to look at us. I remember especially the rows of little children on banks or walls, on any elevation, and all of them as still as if they had been posed. Many little boys and old men; not many of soldier age. From what we heard later, we believed that the young men at first kept themselves in the background, not quite knowing how our soldiers would treat them.

What I noticed at once was the expression of the faces—the children frankly curious, interested; the elders showing either carefully masked expressions or else sullenness, frank resentment, hatred. What I noticed next was the extraordinary number of children, the large majority of whom were boys. Germany has suffered fearful human losses, but a generation or so ought to recoup her as far as numbers go. As far as the deeper losses go, hearts must break as miserably in Germany as elsewhere.

Finally, what I saw was the appearance of these villagers; well-dressed they were, and well-fed they looked to be. Plenty of plump, pink cheeks among the little square-headed boys and fair-haired girls, warm clothes, good boots. I had heard of a shortage of leather in Germany. There was no lack of it in the Rhineland. I can't look at the black, stocky, military boots without shuddering; they have the same baleful connotations for me as the round German soldier-caps. But my constant thought was, how different these people are from the brave, suffering, underfed, insufficiently-clothed inhabitants I saw in devastated France!

For the most part, all these Rhinelanders stared at us immobile, but now and then there was a flutter, a whispering among the women. For with me in the car were two other Y. M. C. A. women, and we were the first of our sex these people had seen.

And thus we came in the late afternoon to the Burgomaster's house. The question of the rooms being settled, I was requested to ask the Frau Burgomaster if we could have dinner at seven, as it had been arranged previously that we were to buy our meals from the family. I found her in the kitchen—the largest room in the house, I think—lined with cupboards, the stove burnished and glowing, a big table piled with cabbages and potatoes.

"Yes, at seven." she agreed.

"Fourteen are a good many to cook for. Will you let me help you?" I asked.

"It is not necessary, Madame. I have two daughters."

The two daughters had so far not appeared.

"Two daughters?"

"They are up-stairs. I didn't know—soldiers coming —"

"Nobody will harm you or yours, Frau Burgomaster. Our soldiers are humane; they are not revengeful."

Her little gray figure seemed to cast a gray shadow over the room. She looked down at the cabbages, fingering a leaf nervously as she said, "It is terrible, the war. I sometimes dream of the days when the children were little and my boy played with a tin sword. It is all so peaceful, and I see them all there in the sunlight with their hats thrown on the grass. The little boy who grew up to be my eldest daughter's fiancé is there; he is dead now, too. I begin to call out to them to put their hats on. Then I wake up and remember—the war!"

An Englishwoman who had lost a son in the war had told me of some such dream. I wondered if the millions of grieving mothers ever meet in the land of dreams where there is no war and where the children are always young, always care-free.

"I used to be angry." she said, "at the Russians and English and French for making this war, for forcing us to defend ourselves. But now I am past all that. I say to myself only, 'I do not think God intended this war.'"

I forgot that she was German and my late enemy—indeed my enemy still, until the peace terms should finally be delivered to Germany. I remembered only that men, women, and children all over the world are suffering because of the war, and that we should never have another.

Outside I heard the measured tread of marching feet. I went to the front door. There was a battalion of soldiers of the 89th coming up the street, those men of the middle-western states who did such magnificent work in the St. Mihiel drive and in the Argonne. On they marched, wearily, steadily, in the heavy mud. All of them were hungry, and some of them were miserably shod. Yet they came up smiling, just as they had come up after their bitter fighting in the Argonne.

From the houses all up and down the street the inhabitants looked out. Little flocks of children hopped nearer and nearer like birds. And presently this child and that child was smiling in the arms of this big Missourian or that big Kansan. These little enemies came to our soldiers as unerringly as had come the children of France, of Belgium, of Luxembourg.

"Your soldiers, they are fond of the little ones," sighed the Burgomaster's wife behind me. "Our German soldiers—I have seen them knock the children aside. But I suppose they were tired. They are very good men, our soldiers."

Twilight drew down. One by one the groups of soldiers dispersed. As I turned back from the doorway, I heard the Burgomaster say, "You shall not wait on their table."

He was speaking to a girl whose face I did not see, a short girl who held high a lamp which cast a burnished light on her ruddy hair. I passed into the parlor. A girl was setting the table, a tall girl with yellow hair and a pale, pretty, scholarly face. But her eyes, as she gave me a sidelong glance, were hostile.

"Good evening, Fraulein." I said.

"Good evening." she muttered.

The door opened noisily, and the ruddy haired girl shot in with all the effect of a bounce. "He won't let me—" she began, and paused as she saw me.

She had a little, elf-like face; her quick, uneasy eyes had in them the look of the faun. She was evidently the younger of the two. From one glance at the sister I knew that it was the elder who had lost her fiancé; the younger one was untouched by grief, untouched, too, by experience.

The elder girl left the room with a warning look at the younger to follow her, a look that was disregarded.

"Do you speak English, Fraulein?" I asked. "No, but my sister does. She will not let you know it, but she does. She went away to school in England, but I have never been farther than Coblenz or Cologne, never. And since the war began I have been nowhere, just shut up in this little village."

She was speaking slowly that I might understand, but her voice was so passionate that I felt as if her words were racing.

"I'm afraid it's rather dull and sad here," I offered.

"*Ach*, yes; for four years nothing to see but soldiers coming and going and perhaps a few Belgian or Russian prisoners passing through. Dull! Dull! Always the same! No one to talk to. How much does it cost to go to America?"

She spoke half-glancing over her shoulder. Her country was beaten, her brother was dead, but the craving for adventure, for a full life, beat loudly in her veins. I understood why the Burgomaster had decreed that she should not wait upon the table.

Before I could reply, the Burgomaster entered the room, his long pipe in his mouth. He removed the pipe and merely looked at his daughter. Quickly averting her head, she left the room. He evidently still had her under the rough control, but I wondered how long that control would last, for hers was a feverish force to reckon with. No doubt the Burgomaster had lost money; Germany had lost money. How would there be the gaiety, the excitement, this avid girl craved? Would there be a husband for her? And if not, in what particular way would that fierce little river of self over-reach the bounds?

The Burgomaster put back his pipe into its permanent home and looked at me imperturbably. Rather a wonderful person, that Burgomaster, and just because he was such a story-book sort of type, I found him a great refreshment. While we gazed placidly at each other, there came the sudden report of five shots and the quick rushing of feet. The Burgomaster took his pipe out of his mouth again and made a hasty exit in the direction of the kitchen. I ran to the front door.

A big M.P. loomed up out of the darkness and said: "Don't get anxious, lady. That was only a practice alarm. We have to know how quick the fellows can get on the job in case anything ever starts."

There was no doubt that they were on the job. Long files of soldiers, bayonets fixed; ready for action, and not a German in sight. Probably, like the Burgomaster, they had withdrawn to the background. But I felt sure that, wherever he was, his pipe was back in his mouth.

"The crazy bird that shot the pistol," chuckled the M.P., "went and sliced the telegraph wires. He'll get a sweet calling down."

My watch said seven o'clock, but there was no sign of dinner. It did not appear until seven o'clock German time. The Germans were told at the beginning of our occupation that they must change to French time, but I noticed that this was a point on which they were always slow to yield. Indeed, we always found some Germans ready to make various experiments in disobedience.

The dinner was excellent. Good meat, mealy potatoes, cabbage, German bread, which we discarded in favor of our own army bread, butter, salad, cookies, and preserves. The price was reasonable, much less than we would have had to pay for the same food either in the United States or in France. The time was to come when we were unable to get butter, but in these country regions we found no lack of butter, eggs, or milk, the very food that the Germans were said to lack. Doubtless there is difficulty in distributing food, but in some parts of Germany, certainly, it is as plentiful as it is here.

The tall, pale girl with the blonde hair waited on us. As far as possible she treated us as if we were not there, answering, if we spoke, briefly, her eyes down, a strained smile on her face. She pretended that she did not understand English, but I noted that she followed what we said. Outside the door stood the other girl, taking the dishes, the peri outside paradise. I could see her eager, gleaming eyes when her sister passed through.

After supper I went for a walk along the still little street. Lights gleamed here and there in the up-stairs windows of the houses, but no Germans were abroad. Once I heard a child's voice singing. Once I heard the sound of a violin. A voice called for Herman to bring in some wood. Strange—the American soldiers had come in, we were the concrete proof to these people that their fortunes of war had changed, and yet they were going about their common concerns as usual. And out under the stars, in countless graves, were the men who had forever left behind their little earthly concerns, who had died each believing in the moral integrity of his nation. Grass would presently grow over these graves, and the world was rolling on about its big concerns, but surely it could never again be the same world.

I passed various M.P.'s and guards and came at last to the final outposts.

"Halt! Who goes there?" At least I think that was what he said. I know he lifted his bayonet, upon which I was not minded to die, after having escaped death so often in the St. Mihiel and Argonne drives.

"Y. M. C. A.," I said promptly.

"Oh, all right, lady. Why, hello, it's the lady that was at Beney. Gee, didn't they shell the devil out of us—I mean, wasn't the shelling heavy up there?"

We began reminiscing, an occupation dear to the hearts of those who have soldiered together. We can not always talk fully or comprehensively to people who have not lived through those experiences with us, but we can talk to each other.

"And how do you like Germany?" I asked.

"Gee, it was kind of queer marching past those guys today," he replied, "and remembering that about five weeks ago, if we'd been that close to them, we'd have poked our bayonets into them. And here we were going by as if they weren't there, and some of the girls grinning at us. Coming in, one of the fellows dropped his pack, and a German jumped to pick it up for him. I'd not have done it if I'd been him. Don't believe, if I was a girl, that I'd smile on the enemy. Why, those folks must hate us like poison! I'd have some respect for them if they pretended they didn't see us."

"I remember all the things you boys were going to do to the Germans, once we invaded," I remarked.

The soldier laughed indulgently. "Oh, that was while we were still fighting. A doughboy can't take it out on women or children or folks like these that are helpless."

Just one day had that soldier been in Germany, and already he had the feeling at which all our men instinctively arrive. They do not hate a beaten foe. They are even willing, if not prevented, to fraternize to a certain extent with him—especially with her. But if the war began again tomorrow, they would fight the Germans with the same deadly earnestness with which they warred up to November eleventh.

"Not that I trust them," the soldier went on. "To tell the truth, I'm kind of glad to have had this little spiel with you. I was kind of lonely out here. Not scared, you understand, but I kept thinking how easy it would be for a couple of Germans out in the brush to get me. I guess we have 'em scared, but if they wanted to start anything, I'm their safest victim."

"They'd be afraid of reprisals. No matter how much they may believe that the Germans were not guilty of atrocities in Belgium and France, they know the use the Germans made of the white wall and the firing squad."

"Oh. Yeh, just before you come I was sort of smiling to myself, wondering what the folks at home who've been yelling to us to eat 'em alive, would think if they could have seen us this evening feeding chocolate to the German kids."

Next morning, as I walked through the village, I was struck, as often before, with the amazing rapidity of war-time adjustments. Our soldiers strolled about with a settled air, as if their occupation were already an old story. If the Germans did not draw near in the easy way of French civilians, at least they did draw near, looked, sometimes smiled, showed no fear, accepted the invaders. In the Burgomaster's house we had all fitted into our places.

The Burgomaster had pointed out to me on the map places in the United States where his relatives lived. His little gray wife, after her first confidence to me, had shrunk into herself. Her eyes warned me that she would talk only of those practical matters which concerned our lives in the same house. The younger daughter had somehow managed to scrape acquaintance with the officers; the older had so far unbent as to pet our mascot dog and to accept a cake of chocolate from one of our Y. M. C. A. men. We had all got upon a livable basis.

Yet that afternoon I lost for a moment my sense of security, got a vivid realization of the uncertainty there must be from moment to moment, until the terms of peace were finally settled. Two of the Y men and I went for a walk. We passed down a cross street amid groups of staring children with colds in their heads, and struck into a muddy road which led at last into a majestic forest. Decades ago someone had planted fir-trees in even rows, so that as we walked through them, it was like passing along living aisles of eternal green. Under foot the moss was thick. When we stopped to dig it, our fingers went far, far down into the curly, brown, tendril-like roots. The underbrush had been cleared away. The place was wide, fragrant, lofty. It made the spirit expand. We thought of poetry, of all sorts of beauty, wondered how a people with this glorious background could have fallen in nobility, in common honesty.

Then we came across rows of oak-trees which had been planted like the pines, but they had not behaved like the pines; they had leaned in and out and away. The forest paths twisted and turned. Once we came to a gloomy, sinister stretch of woods. The trunks of the trees were a dark, silvery green, the branches were gnarled and dark; shadows behind gathered into a curtain of blackness. As we passed through it, we fell silent.

Of a sudden we were aware that twilight was on us and that we had lost our way. We had no idea of the direction from which we had come, no idea of the name of the village or even the name of the Burgomaster. The men went ahead, smiling, searching for the main road. As I followed them, I looked over my shoulder. There, behind the barrier of brush, were three German faces under the round caps of soldiers, three enemy faces, glaring after us. One mouth was lifted in a snarl.

I acted as if I had seen nothing. I did not call to my friends. But I remembered what the guard on outpost duty had said to me the night before. How easy it would be for these three men to kill us, to bury us, to leave no trace, for no one knew we had gone for a walk! The village could be punished, of course, if we were not found, yet how easily might these soldiers, drunk with hate, forget the helplessness of the village.

Just a rush of unnecessary foreboding, for when I looked around again, the heads had disappeared behind the brush. But the little incident made me feel how insecure the world still was. The Germans were helpless indeed, but war was not yet over. I thought of all the little German boys I had seen, good material for warriors, and I wondered if it would not be an appallingly heavy task to train the German nation until at last it accepted for itself the traditions of peace.

We found the road, a black canyon now, and on it we found a soldier, pack-laden, weary, who had lost his "outfit." All he knew was that they were "away ahead somewhere."

"Where are you going to sleep?" I asked.

"Search me; there, maybe," he replied, pointing to the forest aisles.

Here he was, his first day in Germany, without any knowledge of the language, marching alone, fearlessly, along strange roads. Are there any soldiers in the world as brave, as happy-go-lucky, as our own men?

During the short time we stayed in this, our first village, we and the inhabitants more and more got the habit of each other. The children learned to cry aloud with guttural joy when they saw a new unit of men in khaki advancing, for that meant new gifts of chocolate or biscuits.

The looks of hate had turned to amiability, fraternization had grown. The German speaking soldiers reported that the Germans said we and they were really more alike than any other two nations, that they never had wanted to fight with us. The Burgomaster had said that he hoped the day would come when he could travel to America. The elder daughter had accepted more chocolate and now sometimes lifted her eyes when she spoke to us. The younger had been seen talking, with coquettish smiles, to a corporal who spoke her own tongue, talking in a spot well remote from the Burgomaster's vision. Yet all this was but surface adjustment. On the last day of our stay occurred an incident which showed beyond doubt that these people tolerated us only. The officers and two or three other people were in the parlor, looking over the books of photographs.

"Just see here," called the Captain. "Here's something interesting, a book of views made by the Germans of places they took from France. Sort of cold-blooded thing to make all of these pictures of ruins. Ghoulish sort of exulting, I call it. Why take pictures of the ruins? Must have been some buildings left standing. All the same, I'd like to have some of these. I wonder where they bought them."

At that moment the door of the living-room opened, and the blond girl entered to lay the table. In the hall behind her was the Burgomaster, his green coat darkened in the shadows, his pipe in its usual haven.

"Will you tell me," said the Captain to the girl, "where I can get a copy of these views?"

Like a flash her face flamed with the wild, red blood surging into it. She threw down the table-cloth. She fairly sprang at the Captain and tore the views from him.

"American pig!" she cried. "How dare you!"

I glanced at the Burgomaster. He had taken his pipe out of his mouth; he looked bitter, resentful. In a moment, however, his face turned suave, as he entered the room.

The girl had snatched up the other books of pictures and her brother's iron cross. "American pig!" she repeated, half sobbingly.

"That is no way to talk, my child." The Burgomaster said. "You should not behave in this way."

She threw him a rebellious look. "They shan't have them; they shan't!" she cried, and flashed through the doorway.

The Burgomaster put back his pipe. He had made a sort of apology; that was enough—for Americans. But I had seen his face. I knew that he resented us as much as did the girl.

"Well, after all," said the Captain tolerantly, "it must be rotten luck to know you've lost, and to suffer the irony of invasion when your temperament calls for haughty victory."

Next day we drove away. The Burgomaster's family shook hands with us and wished us *"Auf Wiedersehen"*—all except the older daughter, who was not visible. They stood smiling and bowing in the doorway as if we were honored guests.

We had gone a mile when I discovered that had left my watch behind. We drove back for it. Every door and window of the Burgomaster's house was open wide, as if to get rid of every last trace of us. The younger daughter was turning the parlor back into the family room; the elder was viciously scrubbing the stairs. They let me enter and leave again as if I were an unsubstantial shadow.

The scars are there, on our side and on theirs. For all that, people can quickly adapt themselves to whatever circumstances arise, and for all that the Germans and we have already, in a measure, shaken down together—neither side forgets—and the Americans should not forget. Those on both sides who have suffered personal losses, especially, recognize a chasm that can not be crossed. So it was in our Civil War. People can get upon any practical basis that necessity demands, but the heart makes its own barriers that no national requirements can affect. When the lonely graves under the stars are level, when all war debts have been paid, when the girls for whom there can be no mates have long since stifled their dreams, when war as a means of settling disputes is obsolete, then that chasm will be bridged, and the last flames of bitterness will have died.

Elizabeth Frazer (1877–1967)

After them came the American delegates, headed by Wilson,
marching firmly, head erect, a smile playing about his lips.
By my watch he signed at thirteen minutes after three.

"The Signature"
Elizabeth Frazer
The Saturday Evening Post, August 30, 1919

Fighting Through the Throng

In Versailles, having anchored our ship and the skipper in a quiet backwater, we made our way to the big grilled gates which in ancient days protected royalty from the mob. And here was a turbulent tide. Conceive a stream composed of ten thousand excited jabbering units trying to force its way through an entrance less than two feet wide. With yellow tickets, blue tickets, red tickets, no tickets, but making good the lack with foot and shoulder and elbow and tongue. And after we had passed that first gate there was yet a second in the court.

"Red tickets! Red tickets!" bawled the brawny guards barring the way. "Red tickets only at this door." With our red tickets held on high we were picked up and borne on the tide of exasperated ticketless, pushing, shoving spectators, and flung like bits of cork into the inner court. Alas for my sash! Alas for Friant's sartorial pride!

"Staircase on the right!" chanted our guides. Spent and breathless, we mounted a side staircase and were passed from hand to hand, from lofty state chamber to lofty state chamber, by gorgeous Republican Guards, spectacular demigods in grand tenue of whitebuckskin breeches, black varnished top boots, crimson tunics, silver and brass helmets with flowing horsehair manes. Handsome and impassive as the statues of Apollo in the Louvre, they glanced at our tickets and came to life for a second as they haughtily waved us on. Thus we won past all the patrols and outposts, and entered the Promised Land. At least I thought it was that until I entered. Later I discovered my error.

In order to visualize clearly what follows conceive a long, narrow, lofty room, whose proportions, roughly, are twenty by a hundred feet. Along the entire length of the inner wall mirrors cloudy and yellow with age, set in frames of chiseled gilt, brass, reflected back the assembled crowd; while on the opposite side seventeen long French windows gave upon the superb formal garden outside. At the far end of the hall leading into the adjacent salon was a noble sculptured archway, through which the German delegates would pass. At the far end also—too far by half—were arranged tables in the form of an open rectangle, the openside next to the windows, with a small table set in the center. This table held the Treaty of Peace.

A German Asks a Favor

Farther toward the rear, rows of benches covered with red tapestry filled up the body of the hall. And these benches bore seat numbers that tallied with the numbers on the red entrance cards. All these details I did not at first take in. For immediately on entry there struck on my eardrums a mighty gabble and drone. It was like the loud drone that rises from a crowded afternoon reception in a small drawing-room—the kind of a gabble you can hear a block away. Entering that long narrow room I beheld the guests, packed to suffocation, desperate, unable to see, climbing upon the benches, standing on each other's feet, hanging on their neighbors' shoulders, climbing rashly up on the windows and walls or milling aimlessly back and forth through the narrow aisle or sitting with moody rebellious despair in their seats. The day was warm. The air was heavy, turgid, overcharged. Every one of the seventeen windows was hermetically sealed. With difficulty I found my seat and sat down therein.

"Where are the plenipotentiaries?" I demanded in perplexity of my neighbor. "I don't speak English," he replied in halting French. I glanced at him more closely. He was fair, with a black and white ribbon in his buttonhole. I decided he was a Norwegian, and repeated my question in French.

"Away down there," he nodded carelessly toward the far end of the hall, so distant it might as well have been in China.

"Have the Germans entered yet?"

He did not reply, but rose and asked "Will you guard my seat? I'm going up forward."

"But I don't have to guard it. Your number is on your red card."

Without responding he moved away. Later I discovered he was a German correspondent, and his ribbon denoted the Iron Cross.

And now in order to see I boldly climbed up on my bench with the rest. Halfway down the hall my vision was blocked by solid wall of red. It was those big Republican Guards again. With their silver-and-brass helmets and flowing horsehair manes, orange cockades and shining cuirasses they stood shoulder to shoulder, their great gleaming sabers at the slope—and I could see just nothing at all.

"Are they going to remain there during the entire ceremony?" I demanded of a passing photographer, who with his apparatus under his arm was wildly scanning the ceiling, the walls, the cornices for some lofty foothold.

"Lord, I hope not!" he groaned savagely. "This thing is a scream." Perspiration streamed down his crimson face. He passed on, still searching on high. I looked at my watch. It lacked several minutes of three. At three the Germans were due, and the ceremony would begin. The turbulence, the excited impatient conversation became more intense. And now the French master of ceremonies for the correspondents—a pale, anxious but polite French officer, with triple rows of decorations—began shooing the guests to their seats.

"Messieurs! Mesdames!" he cried in a clear penetrating whisper behind his hand, "I beg you, I implore you—sit down! The séance is about to begin. Madame, I beg you. Sit down. Monsieur, will you have the goodness to sit down?" He begged, implored, he entreated them to stay in their seats. Up and down the aisle he passed, like the leader of an orchestra, waving, gesticulating, signaling, patting the guests to their places, whispering behind his hand: "Messieurs! Mesdames! Sit down!"

And as he passed, the guests, who were in fact the world's correspondents, cowered down in their places like mischievous, guilty children under the severe urgency of his stern official eye; but when he moved on they popped up again on top of their benches like puppets in a Punch-and-Judy show. For though they desired to please the amiable official gentleman they desired still more to see. Some of them had waited weeks in Paris to report this very event. His pleadings grew more frantic. They were augmented by the rude cries of sundry invited ones in the rear, who, not being able to see in any circumstances, sat comfortably in their seats and bawled cheerfully in three languages, "Down in front!" To be more exact, the British and the English shouted, "Down in front!" The French hissed "*Assis! Assis!*" and the Italians roared what sounded to my ears like "*Seduto*"—but perhaps it was "Spaghetti!"

But overall, everywhere, up and down the aisle, came the persuasive official whisper "Messieurs! Mesdames! I beg—I entreat—sit down! The Germans are about to arrive." Upon which, straightway all the guests scrambled excitedly up on top of their benches or fell in between them, to see the Huns[2] arrive! The confusion redoubled. Photographers, unable to see aught but the sea of wildly bobbing hats, held up their cameras at arm's length overhead and shot anything in sight. Never have I seen such savage agonized countenances.

My own conduct at this juncture I confess was neither better nor worse than that of the rest of the invited guests. I cowered and crouched under the firm official eye of that Frenchman; as he appeared I slid as low as possible and lowered my head in shame— grieved not only for myself but for every guest in the room; but as soon as he passed I sprang up eagerly upon the bench, and when as he returned I caught his melancholy reproachful eye I pretended that I had not been standing up at all but was, so to speak, in the first or initial part of the movement of sitting down—if you get me.

But such conduct is very lowering to the self-respect. I do not recommend it in the least. Moreover, I desired earnestly to please that Frenchman. He was laboring so sincerely on his job. So I cast about to discover if I might not win his approbation and see at the same time. Across the hall, standing on a bench placed close against the wall, was a group of guests, able to see right over into heaven and still preserve the peace. From afar I measured that bench with my eye, as the hunter measures the stag for a vulnerable spot, and I counted the persons thereon—one, two, three, four, five, six. It would just hold another in the rear, and seven is the perfect number. Threading my way across the room with careful haste I arrived at the coveted bench and spoke to the French woman who occupied the extreme rear position.

---

2. Germans were often referred to derisively as Huns, a reference to the nomadic people who devastated Europe in the fifth century.

The Germans a Little Tardy

"Madame," I whispered in my best insinuating French, "would it inconvenience you too greatly if I mounted behind you? I can't see down here."

She regarded me, I fancied, with a cold eye before she said: "If you mount I fear we both shall fall."

"No, no, I assure you. If I fall I fall alone."

"Very well. Try, try." She shrugged impatient shoulders and turned to the front again.

I mounted—and what a scene lay before my eye. I felt like Moses on Mount Pisgah, for here, spread out beneath me, was the Promised Land. One corner of it, to be sure, was blotted out by a brandishing plume on a novelist's hat, but the rest I saw to perfection. Those serried guards had removed themselves to the side lines, and the table, the notables and the plenipotentiaries were laid bare to my eye. Directing my gaze to the table I discovered Clémenceau, flanked by Lloyd George and Wilson, the three profiles standing out as clearly against the dark mirrors as if sketched by an artist on a slate. At the near corner of the rectangle of tables sat Paderewski, with his great mane of yellowish white hair, deep in his papers. And scanning the various faces I discovered General Smuts of Africa, Hughes of Australia, the high-bred face of Balfour, Venizelos, fat little Tardieu, and the finely chiseled features of the Maharaja of Bikanir.

And what were they doing, these stalwarts? Laughing, joking, shaking hands, reaching over each other's arms to sign souvenir programs or addressing post cards!

And still the Germans had not come. But even as I marked their empty seats the director of the protocol announced them, and they advanced and took their seats. And now for a space comparative silence reigned. Comparative, not absolute. For behind my back I was constantly aware of a suppressed but angry commotion; of persons climbing up and falling down, of muttered imprecations of disgust or despair. Clémenceau rose and spoke a few brief phrases, in which the words "irrevocable," "loyalty," "faith" rang forth clear as a bell. Then the Germans advanced to the small table, signed, and resumed their seats. After them came the American delegates, headed by Wilson, marching firmly, head erect, a smile playing about his lips. By my watch he signed at thirteen minutes after three. The first place of signature after the Germans belonged by right to the French, as the chief sufferers in the war; but this right was courteously waived by Clémenceau in favor of Wilson as the founder of the League of Nations. America was followed by Great Britain, then her colonies, after which came the French, Clémenceau stepping out with the agility of a boy. In due order came Italy, followed not by Belgium, as everyone expected, but by Japan.

Not a Single Big Moment

With the signature of Belgium the chief interest in the affair waned. Conversation, which had died down at the opening of meeting, was resumed. It began to be whispered about that the Chinese had refused to sign; that General Smuts had signed only to preserve harmony, but protested on the three main principles of punishment, colonies and indemnities. Typewritten copies of his protest were handed round. It is not to be supposed that all this [happened] while the French official whose duty it was to preserve silence had forgotten his task. He still passed and repassed, waving, gesticulating, begging messieurs and mesdames to sit down. But by now his naughty children openly jeered at him.

"*Mon cher Leroux*," called in a loud stage whisper a rotund Frenchman standing on his bench to a neighbor in the same position, "give a good example to others. Sit down."

"No, I shall not give a good example. I shall give a bad example!" cried the worthy citizen; then seeing the official advance upon him he hurriedly placed the seat of his trousers in the space where his feet had been. Whereat his friend giggled like a schoolboy.

Presently the final signatures were affixed, Clémenceau pronounced the séance at an end, the Germans slipped out quietly, and the other delegates with laughter and congratulations filed out into the garden. The meeting had lasted forty-five minutes, during which there had not been one noble or impressive second. I pondered on this strange phenomenon as I stood at a window of the Galerie, looking down at the crowds on the terraces. Here indeed, out in the open, was color, animation, life. The exquisite Old-World beauty of gardens, the playing fountains, the whirring aëroplanes overhead, the blue cloud of poilus dark against the encircling wood, the glittering splendor of the Republican Guards and the mounted dragoons—and above all the cheers and acclamations of the eager crowd as some famous figure in the world drama appeared—all these things gave the heart a thrill.

But what had been the matter inside?

That night, tired by the exertions and excitements of the day, I decided to dine in my room. Entering at seven I found Friant,[3] not yet departed, swearing softly as she sewed a button on my boot.

"This rotten thread!" she exclaimed in disgust. "What is France coming to?"

"Use dental floss," I suggested.

Two minutes later, trying to break the same with her hands, Friant burst into laughter. For all her fifty years and her sorrows she has a laugh sweet as a mocking bird's.

"Mon Dieu," she cried, "this thread is strong enough to hang the Kaiser!"

"Friant," I objected, "you mustn't talk like that—any more. To-night we're at peace with the Kaiser."

The little French woman was on her feet, her dilated eyes blazing like those of a cat. "Me!" she shrilled, "me at peace with the dirty pig that killed my little son, *mon petit bonhomme*!" She broke off suddenly and said in low altered tones, "Mademoiselle"—I knew what was coming—"Mademoiselle, you know that society I told you of—the last one I went to for information concerning my son? Well, I went again this afternoon, for I thought perhaps upon this day of days—this day of peace for all the world—that perhaps they could tell me some little word—but—" She pressed her finger to her trembling lips, and the gray old head with its thatch of ragged curls sank slightly—but only slightly.

Before I could speak someone knocked at the door. It was François, chef of floor, with his menu, ostensibly to ask if mademoiselle dined to-night in her room—but actually to learn the news of the afternoon. Friant had turned her back and was putting on her hat. I had a sudden inspiration.

"Friant," I said, "will you give me the pleasure of dining with me to-night in honor of peace? François, tell the waiters on the floor to slip in when they have a moment, and I'll tell them all about the ceremony to-day at Versailles before it is out in the

3. The maid in Frazer's hotel

papers. This was your war. Every one of you fought in it. Most of you were wounded. And now this is your peace. You have a right to know what happened, before the civilians, and I am going to tell you. So ask the men to come in."

François, distinguished as a duke, looked extremely pleased but he only said politely, "Mademoiselle, then, dines in her room with Madame?"

"Yes. And I want you to choose the dinner. Use all your taste and intelligence. Give us a ravishing masterpiece—for to-night we are at peace!"

François bent his head and studied his card thoughtfully. "Mademoiselle desires soup?" he murmured.

"No."

"A nice little filet of sole, sauce Dieppoise?"

"Good. And then?"

"How about pigeonneau en cocotte? 'Tis very tender, with French peas, little mushrooms and bacon. I recommend it, mademoiselle."

I knew about those succulent little pigeons, steamed in a casserole, and Friant and I voted viva voce without a dissenting voice for the dove of peace. "And after?"

"Mademoiselle doubtless would like some tender salad. Chicory?"

"No, no. It's too much like eating the family mattress."

"Endive?"

"Good. And after that the sweet, which I leave to you. That's all."

Friant Evidences Thrift

"Mademoiselle will drink something," he suggested delicately, "to celebrate peace?"

"Very well. You choose it, François."

"Mademoiselle liked the *chambertin* I sent in the other day?"

"Wasn't it *chambertin* that gave me such a headache the next morning?"

Friant burst into a laugh, while François looked pained reproach. He comes from Bordeaux, where they live to eat, and he considers jesting on such sacred matters deuced bad form.

"Mademoiselle had only one little half bottle," he protested gravely, "and of that she did not drink enough to give a headache to a fly."

"Very well, then. A bottle of *chambertin*."

"*Une demie-bouteille*," softly emended the thrifty Friant.

"Good. A half bottle for us. And then, François, another bottle of the same, with my compliments, for the waiters on the floor. Tell them to drink to Peace—and to me. For this week I leave your France for my country—a bone-dry, stone-dry country[4] where flows no *chambertin*."

"Why should mademoiselle exile herself in such a bizarre place? Stay here in France."

I shook my head, and François went off to command the dove of peace and collect the clan.

Inside half an hour they were all in my room. There was François, tall, suave, distinguished, chef of the floor. There was Jean, the grouch, my valet de chambre, a peasant poilu who had fought at Verdun, on the Aisne and the Somme, and declared bitterly that peace was tougher than war. There was Henri, the best educated of all, a lieutenant in the army, who, wounded, had gone to America with the French Mission and had been military instructor in one of our large Eastern universities. In Boston, in Washington, Henri had been fêted, dined and wined, and had sat down at table with men whom he now served behind their chairs. There was Jacques, young, shy, countrified, just learning to stammer English, whom I had caught one morning reading my Shelley. All of these men were decorated. All had been wounded in the war. And it was as warriors, not as waiters, that they had collected to hear and discuss the news.

Ex-Poilus Give Their Version

If I ever ate a better dinner or was served by more perfect minions or heard better talk, I cannot remember the fact. For these Frenchmen talked! They discussed the war, the battles they fought, the British and the American élan in fighting. They discussed France, the future, their fears. For they were all afraid. They were afraid of the power of Germany, her determination to wipe them out. This League of Nations—how, literally, would it protect them?

---

4. The Eighteenth Amendment to the U.S. Constitution, prohibiting production, importation, transportation, and sale of alcoholic beverages, was ratified on January 16, 1919. The country would not go dry until one year later.

The triple alliance just signed—would America ratify it? That would be protection indeed! Most of them were liberals. They thought Clémenceau[5] should go. His task was done. But they spoke with tenderness of this live and vibrant old fighter, as a single-hearted lover of France.

Bells rang, rang urgently up and down the corridor, and when the voice of an irate client was heard upraised in a bellow of wrath some one of them glided softly out and appeased him and returned, velvet-footed again.

At length, when the story of the afternoon had been laid before them in fullest detail, and for Friant's benefit I had described the bed of Marie Antoinette in the Queen's suite, I put to them the question which had been troubling me all the afternoon: "Why was that ceremony so dead?"

"Because," opined Friant delicately sipping her wine, "there was no romance. Bald-headed elderly civilians in black coats and hats for the chief actors. My faith, what can you expect?"

"Because," growled Jean, the socialist, "the real people were not there. They were—" He puffed out his big cheeks for a fiery speech, when Friant interposed slyly, "___ sweeping out mademoiselle's room and smoking a secret cigarette on the stair."

"Because," said François quietly, "mere signatures mean nothing at all. You have to possess a reputation for honesty to make good that signature. And the Huns —"

"Because," said Henri, "the value of a document lies in its application, and this document has not yet been applied."

"Why, Henri," I cried, "that is exactly what the great Jules Cambon[6] said."

"*Vraiment?*" retorted Henri mockingly. "Well, I say so too."

Bells began to peal again. One by one these demobilized soldiers, having come back not to the jobs they preferred but to the jobs they could find, thanked me and said goodnight. Then Friant too trudged her lonely way toward home to write a peace letter to her little morsel of veal, as she calls her son over in Germany.

Worn out by the events of this big day, which still had not turned out so big as it ought to have been, I went to bed and almost

---

5. Georges Clémenceau, the prime minister of France
6. Jules-Martin Cambon, the French ambassador to Germany prior to WWI

immediately fell asleep. And after that I dreamed. I dreamed that Friant stood beside me, radiant, transfigured with joy. She clutched my hands in her toil-hardened little claws, and with tears streaming down her face she sobbed: "Oh, mademoiselle, they have found my son! My little boy! *Mon petit bonhomme!*"

But of course it was only a dream. Peace cannot do that. I suppose it was the *chambertin*.

Appendix

Journalists mentioned in *American Women Report World War I*

Ellen Adair (May Christie) (1890–1946): Philadelphia *Evening Public Ledger*. English-born Adair was editing a newspaper Women's Page in Philadelphia in 1914, when war broke out. She began to include war news in her columns, aimed at female readers. She traveled to Europe in 1915, 1916, and 1917 to report on the home fronts in England and France.

Bessie Beatty (1886–1947): *San Francisco Bulletin*. The *Bulletin* sent her on a round-the-world news-gathering trip in 1917, but she abandoned that assignment to cover revolutionary Russia. Her association with socialist reporter John Reed gave her access to key events surrounding the Bolshevik Revolution. Following the war, she became editor of *McCall's Magazine* from 1918 to 1921. From 1940 until her death, she hosted a popular radio show on WOR in New York.

Nellie Bly (Elizabeth Jane Cochran Seaman) (1864–1922): *New York Evening Journal*. Bly rose to fame for her "stunt" and exposé journalism at the *New York World* in the 1880s and 1890s. She had been retired from journalism for nearly two decades when a chance visit to Vienna, Austria, in August 1914 coincided with the start of the Great War. She used the opportunity to become one of the first American journalists to report on fighting on the Eastern Front.

Louise Bryant (1885–1936): Bell Syndicate. Along with her husband, John Reed, Bryant covered Russia's Bolshevik Revolution in 1917. Their socialist backgrounds gave them access to revolutionary leaders and events. A collection of her articles about Russia was published in 1918, *Six Months in Red Russia*. In 1918 and 1919, Bryant defended the Bolshevik revolution before Congressional committees and on a nationwide lecture tour. After Reed died in 1920, Bryant continued to write about European affairs. The 1981 movie *Reds* was about her time with Reed.

Mary Chamberlain: *The Survey*. Chamberlain, on the editorial staff of the magazine, *The Survey*, reported on the Women's Peace Congress at The Hague in April 1915.

Rheta Childe Dorr (1866–1948): *New York Evening Mail*. Dorr was a popular muckraking journalist and political activist, supporting the causes of women and the working class. She became the first editor of the influential newspaper *The Suffragist*. Dorr had several journalistic assignments in Europe prior to the war, including one to Russia after its 1905 revolution. She returned there to report on Russia between its two 1917 revolutions. She visited France in 1918 to write a series of syndicated articles titled "A Soldier's Mother in France."

Madeleine Zabriskie Doty (1877–1963): *New York Tribune, Chicago Tribune, New York Evening Post, Good Housekeeping*. A lawyer, peace activist, and social reformer, Doty made three trips to report on the war. She reported on the Women's Peace Congress in The Hague in 1915. During her 1916 travels in Germany, she reported on the severe food shortage and the wartime culture. Her final war excursion came as part of a round-the-world trip to assess the uneven social and economic development in different countries, particularly as they concerned women. She reported on revolutionary Russia in 1917.

Eleanor Franklin Egan (1879–1925): *The Saturday Evening Post*. Few journalists had a better résumé as a reporter and war correspondent than Egan. She covered the Russo-Japanese War and the 1905 Russian Revolution for *Leslie's Weekly*. Her reporting during WWI is notable for the number of locations from which she reported, including difficult and dangerous locales, such as Serbia, Turkey, and Mesopotamia. She remained in Europe after the Armistice to write about the turmoil in the immediate post-war period. For nearly a decade after the war, Egan continued to travel widely and write for *The Saturday Evening Post*.

Mildred Farwell (1880–1941): *Chicago Tribune*. She reported from France, Belgium, Italy, Russia, and the Balkans. In 1915 she grabbed headlines for being held captive by Bulgarian troops in Serbia.

Dorothy Canfield Fisher (1879–1958): *Everybody's Magazine*. A writer, educational reformer, and social activist, Fisher lived in France during the war and wrote stories and semi-biographical sketches of life there. They were collected in the book *Home Fires in France* in 1918.

Elizabeth Frazer (1877–1967): *The Saturday Evening Post*. Frazer volunteered as a nurse in France in 1916. After the entry of the United States into the war in April 1917, Frazer became a regular contributor to *The Saturday Evening Post*. She wrote several articles about the extensive wartime role of the Red Cross and through her Red Cross connections, gained access to frontline hospitals and proximity to American battles.

Alice Hamilton (1869–1970): *The Survey*. A physician by profession, and an expert in public health and workplace safety, Hamilton was a delegate to the Women's Peace Congress in The Hague in 1915. She traveled with Jane Addams to the warring and neutral capitals to present the resolutions from the congress, calling for immediate peace. She reported on the congress and life in the warring capitals.

Peggy Hull (Henrietta Eleanor Goodnough Deuell) (1890–1967): *El Paso Morning Times*, *Chicago Tribune* Paris Edition, Newspaper Enterprise Association. Hull got her first war correspondent experience covering the U.S. army's "Punitive Expedition" along the Texas-Mexico border in 1916. The connections she made there, including with General John J. Pershing, helped her to gain privileged access to an American training camp in France in 1917. In the closing days of the war, she became the first woman to be officially credentialed as a war correspondent with the U.S. army. She covered the army's expedition into Siberia, during the Russian Civil War. She lived abroad for some of the inter-war years and took on freelance assignments, including reporting on the 1932 Japanese attack on Shanghai. In 1943, she took on her second world war, reporting from the Pacific theater for the *Cleveland Plain Dealer*.

Ruth Wright Kauffman (1885–1952): *The Outlook*. Kauffman traveled to Europe with her journalist husband, Reginald Wright Kauffman. Much of her wartime reporting focused on women.

Mary Boyle O'Reilly (1873–1939): Newspaper Enterprise Association (NEA). At the outbreak of war, O'Reilly was serving as the London bureau chief for the NEA, a news syndication service. She hurried to Belgium to report on the German invasion and occupation of that country. She remained in Europe, visiting many of the warring countries, until early 1917, when she returned to the United States and lectured about her war experience.

Jessica Lozier Payne (1870–1951): *Brooklyn Daily Eagle*. Payne visited England and France in 1916. Her popular articles on conditions in these countries were reprinted in the booklet, *What I Saw in England and France*.

Mary Roberts Rinehart (1876–1958): *The Saturday Evening Post*. Rinehart was America's most popular mystery novelist when she traveled to Europe in 1915 to be a war correspondent. By winning the endorsement of the Belgian Red Cross, Rinehart gained unprecedented access to the front. Through that endorsement, she also arranged to interview Belgian and British royalty and the commanders of British and French forces.

Helen Ring Robinson (1878–1923): *The Independent*. Robinson wrote for the *Rocky Mountain News* and the *Denver Times* before entering politics in Colorado in 1913, becoming the first (or second) woman to serve as a state senator. In office, she championed causes affecting women and lectured widely on women's rights. She traveled on the Henry Ford peace mission to Europe in 1915, but became disillusioned with that effort.

Alice Rohe (1876–1957): United Press. A veteran newspaper woman, she worked for ten years for the New York *Evening World* before becoming the Rome bureau chief for the United Press in 1914. She reported on developments in Italy during the war and remained in that country post-war. She wrote a 1922 article for the *New York Times* introducing Italy's new premier, Benito Mussolini.

Clara Savage (1891–1956): *Good Housekeeping*. After U.S. entry into the war, *Good Housekeeping* sent its associate editor, Clara Savage, to France. By traveling with the YMCA, she got access to the war zone not typically given to reporters. Following the war, she became editor of *Parents' Magazine*.

Elizabeth Shepley Sergeant (1881–1965): *The New Republic*. Sergeant reported during the period of American involvement and published two books about her war experiences. On October 19, 1918, she was severely wounded by the accidental discharge of a hand grenade while on an official French army press tour. In the book *Shadow-Shapes: The Journal of a Wounded Woman*, she told about the long period of her recovery in a French hospital.

Sophie Treadwell (1885–1970): *San Francisco Bulletin, Harper's Weekly*. Treadwell reported from France in 1915. She would later work for the *New York American* and *New York Tribune*. She wrote the popular 1928 feminist play *Machinal*, based on the life of a woman who murdered her husband.

Mary Heaton Vorse (1874–1966): *The Century Magazine*. A noted pacifist, suffragist, and labor journalist, Vorse attended the Women's

Peace Congress in The Hague in 1915. Following the conference, the day after a German submarine sank the British liner *Lusitania*, Vorse traveled into Germany to gauge reaction. After the war, Vorse continued to report on and advocate for labor reform.

Maude Lavinia Radford Warren (1875–1934): *Woman's Home Companion*, *The Delineator*, *The Saturday Evening Post*. Born in Canada, Warren graduated from the University of Chicago and then worked in Chicago as a journalist. In 1914, she reported on Canada's mobilization for war, and in 1918 reported from France. By traveling with a YMCA canteen unit, she gained access to the front lines. She accompanied the U.S. army when it assumed occupation duties in Germany.

Edith Wharton (1862–1937): *Scribner's Magazine*, *The Saturday Evening Post*. A renowned novelist, Wharton had been living in France before the war and continued to do so during the war. Through numerous charities and fund-raising projects, she supported the French war effort. In 1915, the French army took her on extensive tours of the Western Front to raise awareness in the United States about the French war effort and its need for charitable support. She described those tours in a series of articles for *Scribner's Magazine*.

Mary Isabel Brush Williams (1888–1944): *The Saturday Evening Post*. Brush was in England for the *Chicago Tribune*, working on the story, "How I Paid My Way into English High Society," when war intervened. *The Saturday Evening Post* sent her to Russia in the fall of 1914 to write about its adoption of prohibition upon entering the war.

Bibliography

Adair, Ellen. "Women and the War." *Evening Public Ledger* (Philadelphia, PA), December 18, 1914, 10.

Beatty, Bessie. "The Rise of the Proletariat." *Asia: Journal of the American Asiatic Association*, 1918, 542–548.

Bly, Nellie. "Paints Horrors of War's Work." *Tensas Gazette*, February 26, 1915, 2.

Bryant, Louise. *Six Red Months in Russia*. New York: George H. Doran, 1918, 27–34.

Chamberlain, Mary. "The Women at The Hague." *The Survey*, June 5, 1915, 219–222.

Dorr, Rheta Childe. "'A.P.M.' Magic Letters that Help Our Boys in Straight Path Abroad." *The Courier-Journal* (Louisville, KY), July 24, 1918, 6.

———. "Women Soldiers of Russia May Rescue the Republic." *The Sunday Star* (Philadelphia, PA), October 21, 1917, 20.

Doty, Madeleine Zabriskie. "At the Hague," *Short Rations: Experiences of an American Woman in Germany*. New York: A.L. Burt, 1917, 14–25.

———. "War's Burden Thrown on Poor of Germany as Food Supply Dwindles." *New York Tribune*, November 19, 1916, 1, 8.

———. "War Cripples." *The New Republic*, November 13, 1915, 38–39.

Egan, Eleanor. "Behind the Smoke of Battle." *The Saturday Evening Post*, February 5, 1916, 12+.

Egan, Eleanor. "In the Danger Zone." *The Saturday Evening Post*, April 28, 1917, 14+.

Farwell, Mildred. "Americans Try a Big Bluff to Save Serb Food." *Chicago Tribune*, May 7, 1916, 14.

———. "Bulgars Seize Serb Food Left with Americans." *Chicago Tribune*, May 8, 1916, 10.

Fisher, Dorothy Canfield. "The Sammies in Paris." *Everybody's Magazine*, September 1917, 286–288.

Frazer, Elizabeth. "The Signature." *The Saturday Evening Post*, August 30, 1919, 16+.

Hamilton, Alice. "At the War Capitals." *The Survey*, August 7, 1915, 417–436.

Hull, Peggy. "Allied Troops Unpopular Now in Vladivostok." *The Tampa Times*, January 17, 1919, 2.

———. "Peggy Hull Tells 'Death Train' of Russian Bolshevik." *Battle Creek Enquirer*, March 2, 1919, 5.

Kauffman, Ruth Wright. "The Woman Ambulance-Driver in France." *The Outlook*, October 3, 1917, 170–172.

O'Reilly, Mary Boyle. "Baby's Value in Europe." *Bismarck Daily Tribune*, July 26, 1916, 5.

———. "Star Woman Runs Blockade." *Seattle Star*, February 17, 1917, 1, 8.

———. "Woman Writer Sees Horrors of Battle." *Seattle Star*, September 23, 1914, 1.

Payne, Jessica Lozier. "Soldiers' Graves Dot Farms on Marne Battlefield." *Brooklyn Daily Eagle*, November 14, 1916, 2.

———. "Women Work Tirelessly Making Shells for the Front," *What I Saw in England and France*, New York: *Brooklyn Eagle*, 1916, 5.

Rinehart, Mary Roberts. "For King and Country, No Man's Land." *The Saturday Evening Post*, May 8, 1915, 57+.

Robinson, Helen Ring. "Confessions of a Peace Pilgrim." *The Independent*, February 14, 1916, 225–226.

Rohe, Alice. "Once Gay Vienna Now City of Gloom." *The Washington Times*, October 23, 1914, 12.

Savage, Clara. "Behind the Scenes in France." *Good Housekeeping*, January 1919, 35+.

———. "The First Word from France." *Good Housekeeping*, October 1918, 38+.

Sergeant, Elizabeth Shepley. "America Meets France." *The New Republic*, December 29, 1917, 240–243.

———. *Shadow-Shapes: The Journal of a Wounded Woman, October 1918-May 1919*. Boston: Houghton Mifflin, 1920, 15–23.

Simonton, Ann. "Four American Women Who Have Been to the War." *New York Tribune*, August 21, 1915, 13.

Treadwell, Sophie. "Women in Black." *Harper's Weekly*, July 31, 1915, 111–112.

Vorse, Mary Heaton. "The Sinistrées of France." *The Century Magazine*, January 1917, 445–450.

Warren, Maude Radford. "The First Invasion." *Good Housekeeping*, June 1919, 56+.

———. "Madame, C'est la Guerre!" *The Outlook*, June 27, 1917, 328–330.

———. "We Took the Hill." *The Saturday Evening Post*, November 2, 1918, 49, 53.

Williams, Mary Brush. "When Mothers Ask News of Their Boys in France." *New York Tribune*, June 2, 1918, IV, 1.

Wharton, Edith. "In Lorraine and the Vosges." *Scribner's Magazine*, October 1915, 430–442.

Index

Page numbers in *italics* refer to photographs.

A

Abdul-Hamid, 93n12, 96

Adair, Ellen, 57–60, *58*, 287

Addams, Jane, 113, 114, 129, 134–135

aid organizations

American Relief Clearing House, 210n8

arrive in France to support US troops, 199–200

Quakers, 38n11, 200, 207

Red Cross, 83, 87, 183, 237, 260–261

Salvation Army, 225

YMCA (Young Men's Christian Association), 225, 256

air raids, 220

Allen, Henry (US Major), 237

"Allied Troops Unpopular Now in Vladivostok" (Hull), 256–258

ambulance drivers, British women, *75*

Ambulant Artisans, 22–23

"America Meets France" (Sergeant), 205–211

American Ambulance Service, 210

American Central Red Cross Committee for American Prisoners, 237

American delegation to Women's Peace Congress, *116*

American Expeditionary Force, 255–256

American lines in the Argonne, traffic jam behind, *227*

American occupation of Germany

American troops occupy German home, 261–270

in Bachem, *265*

creates anger, 274–275

danger from German soldiers during, 273

and emotional scars of war, 275

fraternization with German
soldiers during, 274
American Red Cross entertainment tent, *232*
American Relief Clearing
House, 210n8
American soldiers in destroyed
town of Vaux, *250*
American soldiers in Paris, *203*
Americans, attitudes toward
after Battle of St. Mihiel,
228–229
as American troops parade
through Paris, 201–205
anger toward, 109
blame for ammunition used by
Allies, 134
from Germans, 274–275
reception of Americans at
International Congress of
Women, 115
in Vosges Mountains, 22n19
"Americans Try a Big Bluff to Save
Serb Food" (Farwell), 145–150
Arabic (British ocean liner),
163n10
Armenian Genocide
Armenian woman with dead
child, *98*
Armenians join Russian Army
in opposition to Ottoman
Empire, 93
Armenians not permitted
necessities during
relocation, 102
attempted launch of Holy War
as justification for Armenian
treatment, 94–95
concentration camp in, 98
exposed, 89–102
initiated by Mehmed Talat,
100n14

massacre of Armenians during,
93n12, 96
only escape by changing
faith, 93
Ottoman Empire issues
propaganda against
Armenians, 91–92
resettlement orders given to
Armenians in, 92
status of Armenians in Ottoman
Empire, 80–81
armistice, signing of, 255
artillery
British women inspecting
shells, *75*
brutality of Russian artillery, 84
at Corbeek-Loo (Belgium), 6
new type of warfare, 15
obus-holes, 20n18
Paris Gun, 215n12
Asquith, Herbert Henry, 131n2
Association of Agricultural Woman
Laborers, 125
"At the Hague," (Doty), 114–120
"At the War Capitals" (Hamilton),
130–137
Augspurg, Anita, 125
Aurora (Russian cruiser), 194
Austria, censorship in, 83–84
Austria-Hungary, 79
Austrian Women's Union, 125

B
"Baby's Value in Europe"
(O'Reilly), 67–68
Bandersea (Belgium), 6
Battalion of Death
emergence of, 172
journalist travels with, 178–179
Maria Botchkareva, founder of,
180–182
Marie Skridlova of, 182–183

in Petrograd hotel, 188
photo of Maria Botchkareva, 180
traitor found in, 184
women enlist in, 183–184
Battle Creek Enquirer, 258
Battle of St. Mihiel, 226
Battle of the Argonne Forest, *227*
Battle of the Marne, 28
Beatty, Bessie, 186–197, 287
"Behind the Scenes in France"
(Savage), 226–236
"Behind the Smoke of Battle"
(Egan), 89–102
Belgium
on atrocities in, 5–6, 8, 272
Commission for Relief in
Belgium, 208n6
German invasion of Louvain, 1–9
invasion viewed as military
necessity by Germans, 134
Treaty of Peace signing by, 281
war on civilians, 1, 134n6
Bismarck Daily Tribune, 67
Bismarck Denkmal (monument),
104–106, *105*, 107
Bly, Nellie, 80, 86–89, *87*, 287
Blythe, Samuel, xv
Boches, 229n3
Bolshevik Revolution
atrocities of, 258–261
capture of State Bank in, 191
civil war erupts in Petrograd, 189
Congress of Soviets
(Convention) during, 193–197
defended to Congress, 288
encourages soldiers to desert
Russian Army, 172
eyewitness reports of, 173–178,
186–197
Politburo founded to manage,
195n10
promises of, 189

Botchkareva, Maria, 180–182
British Volunteer Ambulance
Drivers (VAD), 56–57
Brooklyn Daily Eagle, 35
Bruce, Peebles & Co., 69
Bryant, Louise, 173–178, *174*, 288
"Bulgars Seize Serb Food Left with
Americans" (Farwell), 145–150
Bureau de Renseignements pour les
Familles Dispersees (Office
of Information for Dispersed
Families), 28, 44n15, 46

C

Callahan, Jesse James, 229–230
camions, 227, 246, 251
censorship, 81, 83–84
Century Magazine, 37
Chamberlain, Mary, 120–130, 288
Châuteau-Thierry, battle at, 226,
229, 240–241
Chicago Tribune, 27, 143
children, value of during war,
67–68
churches and cathedrals
attacked or destroyed, 4, 17, 28,
36, 215
Kazan Cathedral, 183–184
Notre Dame, 222–223
people drawn toward in sorrow,
62–63, 85
propaganda pasted on church
walls, 5
protection by, 184
Reims Cathedral, 38
as shelter for wounded, 251
and wounded of Vienna, 79, 83
Clémenceau, Georges, 114,
280–281, 285n5
Cobb, Irvin, xv
Commission for Relief in Belgium,
208n6

"Confessions of a Peace Pilgrim"
(Robinson), 137–142
Congress of Soviets (Convention),
193–197
Conseil National des Femmes
Françaises, 126
Corbeek-Loo (Belgium), 6–7
Cossacks, 177–178
Courier-Journal, 211
Courtney, Kathleen, 123
Croix de Guerre, 168n15
Cross of St. George, 181–182

D
Das Bund Neues Vaterland, 133
Daugaard, Thora, 125
Delbrueck, Hans, 135
diseases, 114, 219n13, 256,
260–261
dog of Flanders, 4
Dorr, Rheta Childe, 178–185, *179*,
211–216, 288
Doty, Madeleine Zabriskie, 29–34,
31, 102–112, 114–120, 288
doughboys, *203*
Dutch National Committee for
International Interests, 122

E
Egan, Eleanor Franklin, 89–102,
143–144, 150–162, *152*, 288
entertainment, xvi, 225, *232*,
233–234
Evening Public Ledger, 57
Everybody's Magazine, 200

F
Farwell, Mildred, 145–150, 288
"First Invasion, The" (Warren),
261–275
"First Word from France, The"
(Savage), 216–223

"Firsts" in World War I
first access by journalist to No
Man's Land, 3
first American troops parade
through Paris, 200
first editor to embrace concept
of woman's side of war, xv
first exposure of Armenian
Genocide, 89–102
first eyewitness account
of German invasion at
Louvain, 1–9
first five *Post* writers, xv
first front-line tour for
reporters, 2
first gathering of women from
belligerent and neutral
nations, 115–116
first peace advertising expendi-
tion in history, 141
first use of trench warfare, 9–19
first woman war correspondent
officially credentialed, 289
Fisher, Dorothy Canfield, 200–205,
202, 289
"For King and Country, No Man's
Land" (Rinehart), 9–19
Forbes, Harry, 145–148
Ford, Henry, 136, 140, 141
France
American troops parade through
Paris, 199, 201–205, *203*
Croix de Guerre, 168n15
French make light of wartime
shortages, 49–53
les sinistrées, 38–49
philosophical differences
regarding war, Americans vs.
French, 207–211
police force of Paris, 215–216
signs Treaty of Peace, 281
Zone des Armées, 206n3

Franco-Prussian War, 134n6
Frazer, Elizabeth, 276–286, 289
Fritz, 245n6
Frölich, Bertha, 125
"From the Frontier to Petrograd," (Bryant), 172–178

G

Garrett, Ruby (US Lieutenant Colonel), *265*
gas masks, 165–166, 183, 227
Genoni, Rosa, 125
George, Lloyd, 280
Germany
  American troops occupy German home, 261–270
  and *Arabic* (British ocean liner), 163n10
  and belief of citizens that Germans fight in self-defense, 133–134
  engages in unrestricted submarine warfare, 144
  International Alliance for Women Suffrage plans conference in, 122
  International Women's Congress delegation to, 114
  and invasion of Belgium, 134
  and invasion of Louvain, 1–9
  and *Lusitania* (British ocean liner), 114, 133–134, 135
  occupation by American troops begins, 255
  and Paris Gun, 214n12
  and raiders, 163n9
  response to sale of munitions by, 134
  US severs diplomatic ties with, 144
  wartime impressions of, 132–133
Golinska, Darynska, 125

Good Housekeeping, 200, 216, 226, 261
Graves, William (US Major General), 257n1
Great Britain
  calls for increase in munitions production, 69
  signs Treaty of Peace, 281
  suspends traffic between England and Holland, 124
Grey, Edward, 131n3
Gücklich, Vilma, 125

H

Hamer, Eugene, 126
Hamilton, Alice, 130–137, *132*, 289
Harden, Maximilian, 136
Harper's Weekly, 60
Harris, Corra, xv
Henry Ford Peace Expedition
  initial reception in Norwegian press, 141
  mission of, 139, 141
  reception in Scandinavia, 141–142
  role of Rosika Schwimmer in, 137–138
  support in Holland, 142
heroism
  of ambulance drivers, 75–78
  of Capuchin monk in church tower, 17–18
  of Maria Botchkareva, 181–182
  of Maria Skridlova, 182–183
  of nurses, 57–60
  of soldiers, 251–252
Heymann, Lida, 125
Hindenburg Denkmal, 110
Holland
  British government suspends traffic between England and Holland, 124

clothing in, 120
Dutch National Committee for
International Interests, 122
fear of crossing German border
into, 125
International Congress of
Women meets at The Hague,
113, *116*, 136
Maastricht, 9n9
mobilizes for war, 116
Women's Peace Congress
representatives received by
court of, 129
Home Communication Service, 237
Home Fires in France (Fisher),
202, 289
home front reporting, xvi
hospitals and care stations
American hospital in Paris,
144, 169
American Red Cross hospital in
Budapest, 86
businesses converted into, 74
château as field hospital, 241
at La Ferté, 251
Oxfordshire (hospital ship),
57–60
at Place de Secours, 31n3
sinking of Canadian hospital
ship, 217
in Vienna, 79, 83
House of the Barrier, 11–13
Hughes, Laura, 124
Hull, Peggy, 257–258,
258–261, 289
Hungarian Feminist Alliance, 125
Hungarian Peace Association, 125
Hungary, 80, 86–89
hunger and food shortages
Armenians, 92, 99, 102
bread tickets in Paris, 221
Galicia, 85

Germany, 80, 102–104,
106–108, 111–112
Serbia, 146–147
train to Siberia, 260
Huns, 229n2, 279n2

I

Imperial War Press Bureau, 97
"In Lorraine and the Vosges"
(Wharton), 19–26
"In the Danger Zone" (Egan),
150–162
Independent, 137
influenza, 114
International Alliance for Women
Suffrage, 122
International Committee on
Resolutions, 123
International Congress of Women
(Women's Peace Congress)
and American delegation to, *116*
and attempts to halt, 123–125
on controlling international
traffic in munitions, 128
delegations to Holland and
Great Britain, 130–131
goals of, 118–119
influenced by sinking of
Lusitania, 114
meets at The Hague, 113,
116, 136
reactions of various countries
to, 121
and representative organizations,
125–126
resolutions of, 127–129
International Council of
Women, 136

J

Jacobs, Aletta, 130, 134
Jones, Jenkin Lloyd, 141n9

K

Kauffman, Ruth Wright, 71–78, 289
Kazan Cathedral, 183–184
Kerensky, Alexandr
    discussions to replace, 189
    orders troops to defend Petro-
        grad, 175–176
    rumors about murder of, 173
    search for, 191
Korniloff, Lavr (Russian General),
    173n1, 176, 189
Kriegspressequartier (KPQ), 79–80
Kulka, Leopoldine, 125
Kultur, 157n8

L

L'Alliance Belge des Femmes pour
    la Paix par l'Education, 126
League for the Care of
    Prisoners, 125
League for the Protection of
    Mothers, 125
Lenin, Nikolai (aka Vladimir Ilyich
    Ulyanov), 195–196
les sinistrées, 28. *see also* orphans;
    refugees
Lexington and Concord act, 8n8
Lindhagen, Anna, 125
Lorimer, George, xv
Louvain (Belgium), German
    invasion of, 1–9
Louvendane (Belgium), 6
Lusitania (British ocean liner)
    German opinions about sinking
        of, 133–134, 135
    International Congress of Women
        influenced by sinking of, 114
    President Wilson and,
        133–134n4, 134n5
    Women's Peace Congress dele-
        gation arrives in Germany
        after sinking of, 114

M

Maastricht (Holland), 8, 9n9
machine guns, 36, 252
Macmillan, Chrystal, 123
"Madame, C'est la Guerre!"
    (Warren), 49–53
Manila Times, 156n7
Maria Theresa and Prince Schwar-
    zenberg, monument of,
    102–103n4, 103n5
Markin, John, 5
Marne battlefield, 28, 34, 35–37
Mayor of Soissons, 41–42
McKenna, Reginald, 123
Menshevik Internationalists,
    196–197
Mensheviks, 195n11, 197
military police, 212–216
Misar, Olga, 125
Mohammed V, 96–97
munitions
    anger over US sale of,
        127–129, 131
    controlling international traffic
        in, 128
    female munition workers,
        69–71
    munition workers in Britain, 75
    sales to warring nations by
        Germany, 134

N

New Republic, vii, 205
New York Tribune, 102, 236
Newspaper Enterprise Association,
    1, 144
No Man's Land, 3, 9–19
nurses
    heroism of, 57–60
    hierarchy of, 170n20
    serving in Battalion of Death,
        182–183

women war correspondents
serving as, xviii, 29–31

O

obus-holes, 20n18
"Once Gay Vienna Now City of
Gloom" (Rohe), 81–85
O'Reilly, Mary Boyle, 3–9, *4*,
67–68, 162–165, 289
orphans, 46–47
Ottoman Empire
Armenian Genocide, 80–81,
89–102
Armenians join Russian Army
in opposition to, 93
attempted launch of Holy War
as justification for Armenian
treatment, 94–95
censorship in, 81
issues propaganda against
Armenians, 91–92
massacre of Armenians in,
93n12, 96
resettlement orders given to
Armenians, 92
Outlook, 49, 71
Oxfordshire (hospital ship),
57–60

P

"Paints Horrors of War's Work"
(Bly), 86–89
Paris
American soldiers in, *203*
churches and cathedrals,
222–223
civilian police, 215–216
different by day than night,
220–221
flower market, 222
military police, 212–216
Paris Gun, 215n12

Payne. Jessica Lozier, 35–37,
69–71, 290
Peace Pilgrims, 138
"Peggy Hull Tells 'Death Train' of
Russian Bolshevik" (Hull),
258–261
Pershing (American General),
236–238
Peshkoff, Zeni, 30–32
pneumonia, 260
Pogány, Paula, 125
poilu, 204n2
Popoff, (Russian Colonel), 146
priests
Capuchin monk in church
tower, 17–18
conscript priests, 23
soldier-priests of Belgium, 18
torture and murder of, 8, 260
in Vienna, 85
prisoners of war, 237–239,
260–261
prostitution, 212–213, 219n13
protests against wealthy, 85
Provisional Government (Russia)
Council of the Republic meets,
191–192
ends, 191–192
Kerensky as Prime Minister of,
173n2, 189, 191
Korniloff attempts to
strengthen, 173n1, 176, 189
President Avksentieff, 192
Savinkoff as Deputy War
Minister of, 189n7
troops ordered to defend
Petrograd, 175–176
Winter Palace fired upon, 194
Prussian army, 4–5, 8, 42–43

Q

Quakers, 38n11, 200, 207

R

raiders, 163n9

Red Cross
American Red Cross hospital in Budapest, 87
attends prisoners on death train, 260–261
Home Communication Service, 237
information on American prisoners of war, 237
nurses serving in Women's Battalion of Death, 183
in Vienna, 83

Red Triangle, 245n5

Reed, John, 172, 174

Refuge family, 46

refugees
among classes of war victims, 38
Belgian, 5–6, 115, 118
Bureau de Renseignements pour les Familles Dispersees (Office of Information for Dispersed Families), 28, 44n15, 46
family in France, 46
with lost family members, 47
with no protection, 81
schools as housing for, 44

Reims Cathedral, 28

restrictions, military, xviii, 28

Rinehart, Mary Roberts, 9–19, 10, 290

"Rise of the Proletariat, The" (Beatty), 186–197

Robinson, Helen Ring, 137–142, 139, 290

Rohe, Alice, 81–85, 82, 290

Roosevelt, Theodore, 142n10

Rotten, Fraülein, 125

Russia. see also Bolshevik Revolution; Provisional Government (Russia); Russian Revolution; Siberia
Armenians join Russian Army in opposition to Ottoman Empire, 93
brutality of artillery, 8
civil war erupts in Petrograd, 189
female soldiers of, 172, 178–185
US mission to Vladivostok, 255–256

Russian Revolution
Aurora (Russian cruiser), 194
civil war erupts in Petrograd, 189
Cross of St. George, 181–182
deposes czar, 171
discrepancy in dates of Russian Revolution, 172
female soldiers of, 172, 178–185
wins favor of West, 178–185
Winter Palace, 191, 194, 197

S

Saloman, Alice, 133

Salvation Army, 225

"Sammies in Paris, The" (Fisher), 200–205

Sarton, Mademoiselle, 126

Saturday Evening Post, The, 9, 89, 150, 240, 276

Savage, Clara, 216–223, 226–236, 290

Schwimmer, Rosika, 125, 128–129, 137–139

Scribner's Magazine, 19

scurvy, 260–261

searcher, 237–238

Seattle Star, 3, 162

Section du Travail du Conseil National, 126

sentries, 5, 6, 11, 16, 19

Serbia
Austria-Hungary declares war on, 79
Bulgarians seize food stores belonging to, 145–150

Eleanor Franklin Eagan in, 143–144

hospital established in, 148n4

invasion by Bulgaria, 145n1

Mildred Farwell detained by Bulgarians in, 143

Sergeant, Elizabeth Shepley, 165–170, *169*, 200, 205–211, 290

Shadow Shapes: The Journal of a Wounded Woman (Sergeant), 165–170

Siberia
death train to, 260–261

disease in, 256, 260–261

Major General William Graves commands US troops in, 257n1

origins of Maria Botchkareva in, 181

on threshold of dark period, 257–258

Trans-Siberian line and treatment by Bolsheviks, 260

US troops mission in, 255–256

Siegfried, Jules, 126

"Signature, The" (Frazer), 276–286

"Sinistrées of France, The" (Vorse), 38–49

Six Months in Red Russia (Bryant), 288

Skridloff, (Russian Admiral), 182–183

Skridlova, Marie, 183–184

Smith, R.T. (US Major), *265*

Socialist Revolutionists, 195, 197

Society of Friends. *see* Quakers

Society of Temperance, 125

soldiers
American soldiers in Paris, *203*

heroism of, 251–252

nicknames for Germans, 229n2, 229n3, 245n6, 279n2

parade through Paris, 199, 201–205

at Red Cross Hospital in Budapest, 86–89

sending letters home, xviii, 230–232

traffic jams of, *227*

in Vaux, *250*

wounded, 31, 34, 40, 253

"Soldiers' Graves Dot Farms on Marne Battlefield" (Payne), 35–37

Soldier's Mother in France: "'A.P.M.' Magic Letters that Help Our Boys in Straight Path Abroad" (Dorr), 211–216

spies, 83, 97, 123, 215, 246

St. Trond (Belgium), 8

"Star Woman Runs Blockade" (O'Reilly), 162–165

Stöcker, Helene, 125

Sudekum (Socialist member of Reichstag), 131

Suffragist, 179

Sunday Star, 178

Survey, 120, 130

T

"take the hill," 244–245, 253

Talat, Mehmed (Talat Bey), 100n14

Tampa Times, 256

Tensas Gazette, 86

torture
by beating soles of feet, 94

of bishop and priests, 260

of Czech officer, 260

of prisoners on death train, 260–261

tours for journalists
    battlefield of Mont-Bligny,
        162–165
    Edith Wharton on Western
        front, 291
    France offers packaged-war
        tours, 28
    Marne battlefield war tour, 28
    in war zone, 2
trains, 77, 83, 260–261
treachery, 184, 252
Treadwell, Sophie, 60–66, 61, 290
Treaty of Peace (Versailles),
        signing of, 276–286
trenches and trench warfare,
        12–14
Trotsky, Leon, 194–195
Turkey. see Ottoman Empire

U

U-boats and submarine warfare
    attack by Austrian U-boat,
        155–162
    as one of most dangerous war
        fronts, 144
    President Wilson protests
        German submarine policy,
        133–134n4, 134n5
    sinking of ships, 217
    unrestricted submarine
        warfare, 144
uniforms, soldiers'
    American, 227
    distinguishing between
        uniforms of different
        nations, 221
    of female Russian soldiers, 183
    French, 49
    German, 165–166, 251
    horizon-blue, 208n5
Union of Democratic Control in
    England, 133

United States
    American troops enter
        combat, 200
    American troops parade
        through Paris, 199,
        201–205, 203
    begins occupation of
        Germany, 255
    begins sending army
        home, 255
    declares war on
        Germany, 228
    enters combat, 225
    enters war, 199
    Major General Graves
        commands US troops
        in, 257n1
    Maude Radford Warren
        and officers in Bachem,
        Germany, 265
    and philosophical differences
        about war, Americans vs.
        French, 207–211
    reports prisoner conditions
        on death train to Siberia,
        260–261
    signs Treaty of Peace, 281
    US troops mission in Siberia,
        255–256

V

VAD (British Volunteer Ambulance
        Drivers), 56–57
Vaux, 249, 250
veneral disease, 219n13
Versailles, 256
very lights, 249–250n7
Vladivostok (Russia), 255–256,
        258–261
von Bethmann-Hollweg,
        Theobald, 134n7
von Jagow, Count, 132, 134

Vorse, Mary Heaton, 37–49, *39*, 290–291
Vosges Mountains, 22n19

W

war, philosophy of
differences between Americans and French, 207–211
differences between men and women, 40–41, 48–49
"War Cripples" (Doty), 29–34
war millionnaires, 141
war on civilians, 1, 37–49, 134n6
Warren, Maude Radford, 49–53, 240–253, 261–275, 291
Warren, Maude Radford with American officers, *265*
"War's Burden Thrown on Poor of Germany as Food Supply Dwindles" (Doty), 102–112
Washington Times, 81
"We Took the Hill" (Warren), 240–253
wealthy, protests against, 85
Wharton, Edith, 3, 19–26, *21*, 291
What I Saw in England and France (Payne), 56, 69, 290
"When Mothers Ask News of Their Boys in France" (Williams), 236–240
Williams, Mary Brush, 236–240, 291
Wilson, Woodrow
on America as nation too proud to fight, 164n12
and approval of French, 210
as founder of League of Nations, 281
and *Lusitania*, 133–134n4, 134n5
severs diplomatic relations with Germany, 163n11
signs Treaty of Peace, 280–281
Winter Palace, 194, 196
Wollf ten Palthe, Frau, 130
"Woman Ambulance-Driver in France, The" (Kauffman), 71–78
"Woman Writer Sees Horrors of Battle" (O'Reilly), 3–9
woman's side of war, xv
women, changing role of
British women ambulance drivers, *70*, 74–75
British women inspecting shells at artillery factory, *75*
and experiences of loss, 60–66
munition workers, 69–71
overview of, 55–57
and value of children during war, 67–68
"Women and the War" (Adair), 57–60
"Women at the Hague, The" (Chamberlain), 120–130
"Women in Black" (Treadwell), 60–66
women munition workers, *70*
"Women Soldiers of Russia May Rescue the Republic" (Dorr), 178–185
women war correspondents of WWI
Adair, Ellen, 57–60, 287
Beatty, Bessie, 186–197, 287
Bly, Nellie, 86–89, 287
Bryant, Louise, 172–178, 288
and canteen duties distributing food to troops, 225, 256
Chamberlain, Mary, 120–130, 288
comforting wounded, 229–232

Dorr, Rheta Childe, 178–185,
    211–216, 288
Doty, Madeleine Zabriskie,
    29–34, 102–112,
    114–120, 288
Egan, Eleanor Franklin, 89–102,
    150–162, 288
Farwell, Mildred, 145–150, 288
Fisher, Dorothy Canfield,
    200–205, 289
Frazer, Elizabeth, 276–286, 289
Hamilton, Alice, 130–137, 289
Hull, Peggy, 256–258,
    258–261, 289
Kauffman, Ruth Wright,
    71–78, 289
O'Reilly, Mary Boyle, 3–9,
    67–68, 162–165, 289
overview of service, xvii–xviii
Payne, Jessica Lozier, 35–37,
    68–71, 290
posting letters for soldiers, xviii,
    230–232, 243
reception of by civil authori-
    ties, xvii
reception of by military, xvi
Rinehart, Mary Roberts,
    9–19, 290
Robinson, Helen Ring,
    137–142, 290
Rohe, Alice, 81–85, 290
Savage, Clara, 216–223,
    226–236, 290
Sergeant, Elizabeth Shepley,
    165–170, 205–211, 290
serving as nurses, xviii, 29–31
traveled with entertainment
    units to serve troops, xviii,
    226–236, 232
Treadwell, Sophie, 60–66, 290
Vorse, Mary Heaton, 38–49,
    290–291

Warren, Maude Radford, 49–53,
    240–253, 261–275, 291
Wharton, Edith, 19–26, 291
Williams, Mary Brush,
    236–240, 291
"Women Work Tirelessly Making
    Shells for the Front" (Payne),
    68–71
Women's Battalion of Death, 172,
    179–182, 183
women's magazines, American, xvii
Women's Peace Congress
    (International Congress
    of Women)
    and American delegation
        to, 116
    attempts to halt, 123–125
    on controlling international
        traffic in munitions, 128
    delegations to Holland and
        Great Britain, 130–131
    goals of, 118–119
    influenced by sinking of
        Lusitania, 114
    meets at The Hague, 113,
        116, 136
    reactions of various countries
        to, 121
    and representative organiza-
        tions, 125–126
    resolutions of, 127–129
women's suffrage
    Dutch sign petition for, 118
    International Alliance for
        Women Suffrage, 122
    opposition to meeting at
        The Hague, 126
    organizations, 125–126
    resolution at International
        Congress of Women, 113
    The Saturday Evening Post
        embraces cause of, xv

wounded
    assisted by French military
        police, 215
    assisted by women journalists,
        xviii, 30–31
    but not bitter, 40
    Elizabeth Shepley Sergeant,
        166–170
    at Invalides, 34n7
    Jesse James Callahan, 229–230
    making bandages for, 65
    Maria Botchkareva, 181
    on *Oxfordshire* (hospital ship),
        57–60
    at Place de Secours, 31n3
    at Red Cross Hospital in
        Budapest, 86–89
    soldiers in Bezu, 251
    soldiers in Vaux, 250
    soldiers making light of
        wounds, 253
    in Vienna, 79
    Volunteer Ambulance Drivers
        (VAD) and, 56–57, 77
    Zeni Peshkoff, 30–32

Y

YMCA (Young Men's Christian
    Association), 225, 256

Z

Zenovieff, Grigory, 195n13
Zipemowsky, Anna, 125
Zone des Armées, 206n3